Beyond Homeless

Beyond Homeless

Good Intentions, Bad Outcomes,
Transformative Solutions

by Mary L. G. Theroux, Lawrence J. McQuillan,
Jonathan Hofer, Christopher J. Calton,
Adam B. Summers, Hovannes Abramyan,
and Scott Beyer

Edited by Mary L. G. Theroux
and Adam B. Summers

Copyright © 2025 by Independent Institute

ISBN: 978-1-59813-350-9
eISBN: 978-1-59813-352-3

Cataloging-in-Publication data on file with the Library of Congress

All rights reserved. No part of this book may be reproduced or transmitted in any form by electronic or mechanical means now known or to be invented, including photocopying, recording, or information storage and retrieval systems, without permission in writing from the publisher, except by a reviewer who may quote brief passages in a review. Nothing herein should be construed as necessarily reflecting the views of the Institute or as an attempt to aid or hinder the passage of any bill before Congress.

Independent Institute
100 Swan Way, Oakland, CA 94621-1428
Telephone: 510-632-1366
Fax: 510-568-6040
Email: info@independent.org
Website: www.independent.org

Cover Design: John Caruso
Cover Image: AleksandarGeorgiev / iStock #1194548736
Interior Design: Jason Sunde

10 9 8 7 6 5 4 3 2 1

Contents

	List of Tables and Figures	vii
	Foreword Dr. Drew Pinsky	ix
	Foreword Scott Ackerson	xiii
1	Introduction Adam B. Summers, Mary L. G. Theroux, and Christopher J. Calton	1
2	The Tragedy of Homelessness: By the Numbers Lawrence J. McQuillan	11
3	Factors Contributing to Homelessness Hovannes Abramyan and Adam B. Summers	21
4	Housing First Puts People's Most Critical Needs Last Adam B. Summers	35
5	The Promise and Pitfalls of Harm Reduction for Reducing Homelessness Jonathan Hofer and Mary L. G. Theroux	55
6	The Homelessness-Industrial Complex: Spending More but Falling Further Behind Lawrence J. McQuillan	73

7	Alternative Models: Improving Outcomes with Housing Readiness		
	Scott Beyer and Christopher J. Calton		91
8	Recommendations and Conclusions		
	Mary L. G. Theroux and Adam B. Summers		107
	Acknowledgments		125
	Appendix: Homelessness Terms and Definitions		127
	About the Authors		133
	Notes		137
	Index		171

List of Tables and Figures

Tables

1. Rates of Homelessness and Unsheltered Homelessness in California, Florida, and Texas, 2022 — 18
2. Comparison of Homelessness Assistance Program Approaches — 37
3. California State Spending on Homelessness Programs by State Agency and Fiscal Year — 80
4. Total State Revenue and Transfers to San Francisco from California Mental Health Services Act Taxes, Fiscal Years 2019–23 (in Millions of Dollars) — 84

Figures

1. The Growing Problem of Homelessness in California, 2010–22 — 12
2. The Surge in San Francisco's Population of Those Experiencing Homelessness, 2009–22 — 14
3. Oakland's Soaring Homeless Population, 2017 and 2022 — 15
4. San Jose's Surge in Homelessness, 2009–22 — 16
5. The Wave of Homelessness in San Francisco Bay Area Counties, 2009 and 2022 — 17
6. The Stunning Surge in California Homelessness, 2017–22 — 20
7. Number of US Beds to Assist Individuals Experiencing Homelessness (by Program Type), 2005–22 — 38
8. Number of California Beds to Assist Individuals Experiencing Homelessness (by Program Type), 2005–22 — 39
9. Spending More but Falling Further Behind on San Francisco Homelessness, 2013–23 — 85

Foreword

Dr. Drew Pinsky

I HAVE WATCHED helplessly while well-meaning so-called activists and elected officials have systematically subverted the mental health delivery system. Two prevailing philosophies have seemed to motivate these groups: a resistance to institutionalization and an unwillingness to require treatment of addiction.

More than half a century ago, Ken Kesey's book about a psychiatric hospital became a hit movie, *One Flew over the Cuckoo's Nest*. Americans watching the movie reacted as though they were watching a documentary about psychiatric hospitals, even though modern psychiatric care is nothing like the circumstances chronicled in this book written nearly 80 years ago. This reaction dovetailed with the dismantling of the states' psychiatric hospital systems, which had taken more than 150 years to develop and, despite having fallen into disrepair in some states, served chronic psychiatric patients who needed custodial care. President John F. Kennedy initiated this dismantling and, in fact, endorsed it with his final signature before his fateful trip to Dallas.

The well-intended Community Mental Health Act of 1963 failed. Hospitals were dismantled with no plan for managing chronically ill patients, many of whom were released from these institutions only to become entangled in the criminal justice system and end up in prison. Some went to nursing homes; the others ended up on the streets of our cities, where too many have remained ever since. As their presence there combined with the opiate-prescribing catastrophe and America's saturation with illicit and ever more addictive pharmaceutical agents, addictions exploded. Methamphetamine became one of the most egregious contributors to addictions that lead to life on the streets. The inevitable consequence of methamphetamine's cheap, sustained high is meth psychosis. The disorganization and paranoid distrust, as well as the tendency to aggression and violence that are symptomatic of meth psychosis, make these patients nearly unreachable. On the streets, meth is often combined with opiates, addiction to which is progressive and often fatal.

For some reason, governments have taken the position that homelessness is strictly a housing problem. Of course, housing is part of the problem, but for most of those experiencing homelessness—and by "most," I mean the vast majority of people on the streets—their condition makes them unwilling or even unable to tolerate being indoors. So, even when government corrects the housing problem, we are still going to have a population in need of care. I was recently approached by a young woman who was working hard to help with placement of homeless individuals; she expressed to me her surprise that even once an individual is given a home, "it turns out we're not done." Yes, of course those who have been unhoused need comprehensive medical and psychiatric care. Naturally, time on the streets leads to a variety of serious medical conditions. But the most difficult part of the problem is that the most seriously psychiatrically ill people experiencing homelessness—who have addictions, serious mental illness, or both—deteriorate to the point that they are not just homeless but are actually able to do little more than lie down on a city sidewalk.

Laws have been systematically put in place that make it more difficult to assist addicts and patients struggling with serious mental illness. Some states have even created laws that enable addicts and push them into criminal activities to support their habits. In California, for instance, addicts can steal as much as $950 per day with the only consequence being, essentially, a citation—which, of course, they ignore. California's Lanterman-Petris-Short Act of 1967 set the criteria for permitting short-term holds of patients with life-threatening brain disorders when their brain disease blocks their insight into what is happening as a result of the disorder. Many patients fell into the "gravely disabled" category of the act as their disorders progressed and they became unable to work and eventually to house themselves or attend to their own basic needs. Because gravely disabled individuals, under the act, can be held only for short periods of time—rather than being placed in long-term care—they continue to deteriorate. Many have been sick and using for so long that it has become nearly impossible to sort out those who have addiction and a concomitant primary serious mental illness from those who have addiction that is causing psychiatric symptomatology.

Recovery from addiction and mental illness requires time, structure, multidisciplinary care, and participation on the part of the patient. These are brain diseases, and the fact that we treat them differently from illnesses of any other organ system is truly bizarre. What is even more distressing is that central features of these brain conditions are disturbances in motivation and insight. The goal must be to get patients free of substances and to control their psychiatric symptoms for a long enough time that they can begin to have insight into what has happened to them. With that insight comes motivation to get better.

So much of the discourse about homelessness and the litany of laws making care difficult has completely overlooked the anosognosia associated with addiction and serious mental illness. Anosognosia biologically blocks patients' ability to perceive the consequences of their condition, even when those consequences are profound and life-threatening. It follows that we should be working to enhance motivation to participate in care. Doing so requires asking addicts and patients with serious mental illness to do *something*—something as simple as refraining from sleeping on the sidewalk or defecating in the street, as simple as not engaging in criminal activity to maintain a drug habit, as simple as being willing to take medication to improve their symptoms and hopefully eliminate their suffering.

By now, the situation has deteriorated to the point that these patients, who have complex psychiatric and medical issues, are being cared for by a well-funded homelessness-industrial complex that determines what care is provided. The industry has created a sanitized term, "wraparound services." These are the services that have always been provided in psychiatric hospital settings. But in the streets, the crucial element of psychiatric care is typically left out of wraparound services! Patient care is provided not by physicians or nurses, but primarily by nonmedical providers such as social workers. I have the most profound respect for my social work colleagues, but they are not trained to manage these terrifically complex cases. This is akin to asking a physical therapist to perform orthopedic surgery; social workers are not trained to perform this care.

Our streets are now open-air psychiatric hospitals that forbid physicians and nurses from providing care—and people are dying as a result, in the tens of thousands. An actual hospital that served patients this way would be immediately shut down and would face massive malpractice and criminal liability—because, in fact, what is happening on our streets is negligent homicide.

This book, *Beyond Homeless*, addresses this horrific situation not just by explaining how badly we are serving those experiencing homelessness under the systems now in place, but by pointing to a better future. The book describes approaches being implemented now that have far better outcomes and delineates the obstacles faced by those approaches. Finally, the book, which should be required reading for anyone wanting a comprehensive understanding of the homelessness crisis, offers solutions that could actually lift people to a place beyond homelessness.

Dr. Drew Pinsky
Board-certified physician; addiction medicine specialist; and television, radio, and podcast host

Foreword

SCOTT ACKERSON, LMSW

MY THIRTY-YEAR CAREER as a social worker has spanned enhancing child welfare, enabling young adults to exit the foster care system, developing and operating homeless and behavioral health programs, and promoting affordable housing. I have learned firsthand that homelessness is not a homogeneous phenomenon, even though we often treat it as one; its causes are broad and varied. Because of those variations, there is no one-size-fits-all solution.

There is no linear path into or out of homelessness, and if we expect to find one, we set ourselves up for failure. Because homelessness is not a homogeneous phenomenon, we cannot expect standardized, one-size-fits-all interventions to be effective.

With that said, I am pleased to see the Independent Institute tackle the issue of homelessness in the broad manner of this volume.

The causes of homelessness are many and are often attached to trauma, with a strong correlation to mental health issues. Other progressions into homelessness could involve compounded health issues, hospitalization later in life, losing resources, or becoming financially impoverished. Each of the pathways into homelessness calls for long-term, personalized, and customized care if a solution is to be successful.

A big part of the current homelessness crisis stems from the unintended consequences of the 2009 Homeless Emergency Assistance and Rapid Transition to Housing (HEARTH) Act. Our nation shifted from providing funding for emergency shelters to focusing solely on permanent housing and supportive services. Theoretically, that is not a bad way to approach homelessness, but, as described in more detail herein, the "Housing First" approach is effective only if the housing capacity is available to make sure people have a home and the necessary resources are available to provide wraparound services.

In reality, this funding shift caused many cities to either downsize or eliminate shelters due to a lack of available financial resources and created a ripple effect so that people on the street did not have any safe, secure places to go.

A larger part of the problem is the lack of affordable housing across the nation. The authors describe the factors driving California's housing crisis, many of which are also present in cities across the country, resulting in unobtainable housing for the middle class. When the dual phenomena of a lack of emergency shelters and an inadequate housing supply arise, the eventual alternative is the street.

It is important that the solutions offered herein address both homelessness policies and housing. Homeless intervention does not end or prevent homelessness; it helps only the individuals currently experiencing homelessness. To end homelessness, we must address and solve the upstream issues, which include access to safe, affordable housing.

Beyond Homeless contains profiles of several selected programs across the country that are achieving positive outcomes, and I am proud of my association with one of them: Haven for Hope of Bexar County, located in San Antonio, Texas. Like most cities dealing with homelessness, San Antonio had the police department, emergency medical services, hospital systems, mental health systems, and nonprofit services providers all working in silos instead of collectively to have an impact. In creating Haven for Hope, we were able to bring all these systems together to move collaboratively in the same direction, thus making Haven a community-wide model.

Most cities do not have such a complete integration of police and fire departments, emergency services, hospitals, psychiatric providers, and all other homeless service providers. Communities across the United States could benefit substantially from looking at the homelessness issue through a more systemic lens.

Ultimately, homelessness in itself is not the problem; it is a symptom of larger systems-level problems. We need to enact systems-level solutions to truly address the root causes of homelessness.

As a nation, we can largely overcome homelessness. To do so, we have to stop dealing with the symptoms and start dealing with the real underlying issues. This volume offers a good starting point.

Scott Ackerson, LMSW
Licensed master social worker with WestEast Design Group; Haven for Hope's former vice president of strategic relationships

I

Introduction

Adam B. Summers, Mary L. G. Theroux, and Christopher J. Calton

Jackie Mason was supposed to go on a weekend trip to San Francisco's Pier 39 with her daughter and grandchildren, but her daughter, Venus Mason, had not heard from her in days. That was unusual, as the two usually enjoyed daily phone calls to keep in touch. Jackie would never miss the opportunity to visit her grandchildren, so Venus knew something must be wrong.

Jackie lived in the Winton Hotel in the Tenderloin district of San Francisco, which was leased to the city's Department of Homelessness and Supportive Housing (HSH) to provide permanent supportive housing (PSH) for the homeless. PSH programs ballooned in response to the federal government's adoption of the Housing First strategy for solving homelessness, which reserves grant money for initiatives designed to provide housing for the homeless.

Like many residents, Jackie suffered from long-standing substance abuse issues. She was provided a case manager, but she was not required to seek treatment for her addiction. Housing First guidelines, in fact, prohibit grant recipients from imposing sobriety or rehabilitation requirements. Even if she wanted treatment, though, the shortage of rehabilitation and sober-living facilities is a perennial problem in San Francisco.

Venus called her mother's case manager to conduct a wellness check. The case manager knocked on the door of Jackie's apartment, but nobody answered, so she had the building manager open it. They found Jackie lying on her bed, where she had passed away from an overdose days earlier.

The discovery was tragic but unsurprising. PSH programs often inadvertently reinforce addiction by placing people with substance abuse disorders together in cramped buildings that are plagued by not only drugs but also crime, vermin, and a litany of other problems. "She was on drugs for 32 years," Venus said of her mother. "Why put her here?"[1]

The scale of the homelessness problem, especially in California, means that the human side of tragedies such as Jackie's often get lost in the statistics. Overdose deaths among the homeless occur so frequently in PSH buildings that the Winton Hotel started holding funeral services for multiple residents at a time, sometimes as many as a dozen. But we must always remember that behind every number is an individual human being, suffering and needing help.

Jackie's story is, unfortunately, typical of many who fall victim to well-intentioned but misguided policies that frequently exacerbate the very problems they are designed to address. These outcomes are not inevitable, however. Although many stories end in tragedy, others end in triumph.

Lemanda Del Toro offers an example of triumphant recovery from homelessness and substance abuse. In common with many addicts, she was the victim of violence and sexual abuse as a child. She had been a drug dealer and gang member in California before becoming homeless, but it was not in the state's many PSH facilities that she found redemption.

In 2015, when Lemanda was sleeping under a tarp in the California desert, her sister-in-law called her to recommend a homelessness program in San Antonio, Texas, known as Haven for Hope. Overhearing the conversation, a nearby drug dealer attacked Lemanda, leaving her with two black eyes, a broken nose, and the determination to make the trek to the Lone Star State.

Haven for Hope provided not only housing but other supportive services as well (see Chapter 7 for more information about Haven for Hope). Lemanda joined the organization's recovery program and got clean. Eventually, she was able to move off campus and live independently. She even returned to Haven as an employee, helping others achieve the same transformation she did.

Like Jackie Mason, Lemanda Del Toro also had a daughter, whom she had relinquished custody of many years earlier. But instead of getting a phone call to tell her that her mother had died alone in public housing, Lemanda's daughter received a call informing her that her mother had finally put her life back together. They have since been able to reconnect and start to rebuild their relationship.[2]

The authors of *Beyond Homeless* recognize that people like Jackie Mason and Lemanda Del Toro have agency over their lives and that recovery is impossible until they are willing to take steps to improve their situation. We also recognize, however, that the difference between Jackie's tragedy and Lemanda's triumph is often decided by public policy.

Our hope is that the discussion in the following pages will add to our collective understanding of what we can do to ensure that the loved ones of those suffering from homelessness receive phone calls worth celebrating. Transformation is never inevitable, but neither is it impossible.

That said, it has become self-evident that homelessness is a substantial—and growing—problem in California, even as it declines in many other parts of the country. The problem is growing not only in terms of sheer numbers but also in visibility, with even well-to-do neighborhoods, such as Cupertino[3] and parts of Orange County,[4] experiencing the rise of tent cities—along with the crowded, unsanitary conditions that have fueled outbreaks of diseases otherwise rarely heard of in modern, developed nations.

From Governor Gavin Newsom[5] to the authors of various news reports,[6] more and more people are decrying "Third World" conditions in California and the return of "medieval" diseases in encampments for people experiencing homelessness. In recent years, we have seen encampments ravaged by a typhus outbreak in downtown Los Angeles, as a result of accumulated trash and rat infestations,[7] and by a hepatitis A outbreak in San Diego that sickened nearly six hundred people and killed twenty.[8] San Francisco has become the poster child for unhygienic street living due to the proliferation of human feces and used drug needles littering so many of the city's sidewalks. San Francisco gained national notoriety in 2018 when city leaders felt compelled to establish a "Poop Patrol" for regular cleanup of waste after the city received nearly fifteen thousand complaints during the previous seven and a half months.[9] (And, because this is a city just up the peninsula from Silicon Valley, the problem even spawned the development of the colorfully named SnapCrap app to allow San Franciscans to more quickly and easily take a picture of sidewalk waste and report it to the city for cleanup.)

It is little wonder then, that for the first time, Californians rated homelessness as the number one issue facing the state in a September 2019 Public Policy Institute of California (PPIC) poll (tied with the perennial concern over jobs and the economy). "Democrats, Republicans, independents all had it in the first tier of concern," reported PPIC president Mark Baldassare. The related issue of housing was close behind.[10] Conditions have continued to deteriorate over the past few years. In a February 2023 PPIC poll, most Californians said homelessness was a big problem (70 percent of all adults, 76 percent of likely voters) or somewhat of a problem (26 percent of adults, 23 percent of likely voters). Those numbers represent a ten-percentage-point increase over the already high proportion of adults who cited homelessness as a big problem or somewhat of a problem in a May 2019 PPIC poll. In addition, the 2023 poll revealed that 70 percent of adults (73 percent of likely voters) observed that the presence of homelessness had increased in their local community over the past twelve months.[11]

Newsom, who as mayor of San Francisco in 2004 pledged to "abolish" chronic homelessness in the city within ten years,[12] devoted the vast majority of his 2020 State of the State address to the issue. He described the homelessness situation as "a blight on the soul of America," calling it a "disgrace that the richest state in the richest nation . . . is failing to properly house, heal, and humanely treat so many of its own people" and asserting that addressing homelessness "must be at the top of our agenda."[13]

At the State Level

Although homelessness actually has declined across the nation in recent years, with the numbers of homeless individuals falling from more than 647,000 in 2007 to approximately 582,500 in 2022 (a decrease of 10 percent), the homeless population has continued to increase in California, rising from about 139,000 to more than 171,500 during the same period (an increase of 23 percent).[14] Among the states to experience the largest increases in homelessness during the past fifteen years were Washington state, where the homeless population increased by 8 percent; New York, where it increased by 19 percent; California, which experienced a 23 percent increase; Louisiana, with a 34 percent increase; and Maine, which experienced a whopping 67 percent rise in homelessness. On the positive side, Florida, Georgia, Illinois, New Jersey, and Texas all experienced dramatic declines of between 39 and 50 percent in their homeless populations.[15] Even though only 12 percent of the nation's population resides in California,[16] the state now accounts for 30 percent of the nation's homeless population (New York has the second-highest percentage at 13 percent and is the only other state to top 5 percent). California also accounts for 45 percent of those experiencing chronic homelessness in the

United States and 49 percent of those experiencing homelessness who are unsheltered.[17] With 44 out of every 10,000 people in California experiencing homelessness, the state has the nation's highest rate of homelessness (Vermont, Oregon, and Hawaii also have rates of homelessness above 40 people per 10,000) and more than double the average national homelessness rate of 18 per 10,000.[18] Among other large states, Florida and Texas have below-average rates of 12 per 10,000 and 8 per 10,000, respectively.[19] Furthermore, the 67 percent of people experiencing homelessness who also are unsheltered in California represent the highest rate in the nation, followed by the rates in Mississippi (64 percent), Hawaii (63 percent), Oregon (62 percent), and Arizona (59 percent).[20]

At the Local Level

Almost one quarter of people experiencing homelessness in the United States reside in the nation's two largest metropolitan areas: Los Angeles City and County (11 percent) and New York City (11 percent).[21] And in terms of the share of the homeless population that also is unsheltered, three of the top five major metropolitan areas are located in California—Santa Clara County (77 percent), Alameda County (73 percent), and Sacramento County (72 percent). California's cities and counties also feature prominently in the "other largely urban" and "largely suburban" area categories.[22]

The Issue at Hand

Homelessness is an incredibly complex problem, with causes that are many and varied. Some of them are predictable (housing policies that restrict the supply of housing and otherwise raise prices, economic policies that make it difficult to earn a living), while others are not, including the loss of a job; mental illness or substance abuse, often the result of untreated childhood trauma; sudden health emergencies, including disability or the death of the head of a household; and even the preference of a subpopulation for a vagabond lifestyle or disconnection from traditional society. As such, and in light of the fact that different people respond in different ways to various approaches and incentives, no single "fix" will resolve all of the myriad underlying issues.

Merely throwing more money at the problem has clearly not been working—and California has thrown quite a bit of money at the problem in recent years. In fact, the California state government allocated nearly $24 billion total for homelessness and housing programs over five fiscal years, 2018–19 through 2022–23.[23] To make matters worse, the California State Auditor's office found that the state has not even been effectively tracking where all that money has been going, much less whether this spending has actually been fulfilling its intended purposes.

"The state lacks current information on the ongoing costs and outcomes of its homelessness programs, because [the California Interagency Council on Homelessness (Cal ICH)] has not consistently tracked and evaluated the state's efforts to prevent and end homelessness," the office asserted in an introductory letter to its April 2024 report. "Cal ICH has also not aligned its action plan to end homelessness with its statutory goals to collect financial information and ensure accountability and results."[24]

The State Auditor's office took Cal ICH to task not only for its lack of results but also for lacking even the curiosity and initiative to fulfill its mission in the future. The office noted that Cal ICH had produced just a single report, in 2023, covering financial information for the state's homelessness programs from fiscal year 2018–19 through fiscal year 2020–21; had not tracked any spending data since that time, "despite the significant amount of additional funding the state awarded to these efforts in the past two years"; and had no plans to produce any similar assessments in the future.[25] "Because Cal ICH does not analyze the available data to determine program effectiveness, it cannot provide critical information that state policymakers could use when prioritizing funding decisions for the myriad state homelessness programs," the State Auditor's office chided.[26]

Housing First

In recent years, federal, state, and local officials have rushed to adopt the "Housing First" approach to the problem, whereby people experiencing homelessness are placed in permanent housing. Although supportive services (e.g., mental health and substance abuse treatment, job and life-skills training, case management) are supposed to be offered, in practice they often are not. Accordingly, participating individuals have continued to struggle with the underlying causes of their homelessness. Housing First may help a certain portion of people experiencing homelessness, such as many of those who are experiencing chronic homelessness, but it may not be the best approach for many others, who would choose—and benefit from—more transformational interventions, including longer-term residential programs offering wraparound recovery services, workforce development, and training in other life skills that enable people to succeed. In fact, by establishing congregate developments housing individuals with continuing addiction and mental health challenges and failing to treat each person experiencing homelessness as a unique individual with unique needs, Housing First discourages many of its participants from achieving full success. In addition, an overly accepting or resigned attitude toward homelessness and related troubling issues—such as illicit drug use in public, encampments on public sidewalks, aggressive panhandling, and littering of used drug needles, bodily waste, and trash—has only exacerbated the problem.

Given those issues, a critical analysis of Housing First and other alternative approaches constitutes an important part of this book. In the following pages, we analyze the various causes of homelessness as well as potential solutions, in an effort to help devise more effective strategies to address the problem. Because California, San Francisco, and the larger Bay Area have become dramatic and visual representations of homelessness and its accompanying problems, special emphasis is placed on those areas. In Chapter 2, Lawrence J. McQuillan dives deeper into the numbers and the scope of the problem at both the state and local levels. Next, Hovannes Abramyan and Adam B. Summers consider the factors contributing to homelessness in Chapter 3, while in Chapter 4 Adam B. Summers takes a look at the Housing First approach—and why putting all of our eggs in that one basket might not be the best strategy for resolving the problem of homelessness. The related issue of harm reduction is addressed in Chapter 5 by Jonathan Hofer and Mary L. G. Theroux. In Chapter 6, Lawrence J. McQuillan examines the "homeless-industrial complex" and explains why California continues to fall behind on the homelessness problem despite significantly increasing the amount of taxpayer money spent on it. In Chapter 7, Scott Beyer and Christopher J. Calton discuss some alternative approaches and spotlight some successful programs both within and outside California. Finally, Mary L. G. Theroux and Adam B. Summers present recommendations and concluding thoughts in Chapter 8; a list of definitions of the terms used in discussing homelessness is contained in the appendix.

> ## *Our Definition of Success*
>
> The dominant approach to addressing homelessness in America, Housing First (see Chapter 4), is built on a slogan: "The solution to homelessness is housing." If a person experiencing homelessness leaves the streets because they become housed, that is counted as a successful outcome by Housing First advocates. This approach, however, ignores painful truths. For example, when government programs simply provide people with a roof over their head, these individuals often end up cycling in and out of homelessness—or worse—because the root causes of their homelessness are never addressed. As detailed in these pages, sadly, people die regularly in Housing First units from untreated substance use disorders.
>
> As an example of how poorly the Housing First definition measures success, an unemployed person who is a lifelong drug addict and formerly lived on the streets but now resides in a taxpayer-funded, government-provided permanent housing unit, with the expectation of doing so for the rest of their life, would be counted as a successful outcome by officials taking a Housing First approach.
>
> We reject that definition of success. We can—and must—do better.
>
> In contrast, by our definition, a successful outcome involves a formerly homeless adult fulfilling five aspirational goals:
>
> 1. (a) The person is housed legally or (b) living unhoused on private property without trespassing or creating a public nuisance (i.e., no longer homeless).
> 2. The person is not dependent on any substance to a degree that it prevents them from securing and keeping a job.
> 3. The person does not engage in property crimes or physical violence.
> 4. The person is employed and, ideally, self-sufficient, if they are of working age and are physically and mentally capable of employment.

5. If the person is not completely self-sufficient, then assistance, which could include cash assistance or a personalized treatment program, is provided by family, friends, or private/nonprofit charitable organizations that are not supported by taxpayers. Government assistance is limited to Social Security, Medicare, and unemployment benefits.

According to our definition, success is based on an assessment of the whole person within a social structure of secure property rights, market exchange, nonaggression, the rule of law, and individual rights and accountability.

Note that we do not expect more of a homeless or formerly homeless person than we expect of someone who has never experienced homelessness. For example, we do not expect lifetime sobriety of a formerly homeless person (although, for some people, sobriety may be necessary for the individual to fulfill all five conditions). Nor do we expect total self-sufficiency, as many people who have never experienced homelessness receive money or in-kind services from family or friends. We do, however, expect more than the deficient Housing First definition of "success": alive with a roof over one's head (which satisfies only criterion 1A in our definition above).

The significance of our definition of success will sharpen into view as readers progress through the book. We will reference the definition by citing "success" or "full success." This shorthand refers to an outcome that fulfills all five goals, recognizing that partial success or being "on the road" to full success is often the reality, especially in the short run.

Mary L. G. Theroux
Lawrence J. McQuillan
Jonathan Hofer
Christopher J. Calton
Adam B. Summers
Hovannes Abramyan
Scott Beyer

2

The Tragedy of Homelessness: By the Numbers

Lawrence J. McQuillan

Anyone who lives in or has visited the San Francisco Bay Area knows that homelessness is a serious "doorstep" problem. People sleeping on sidewalks and living in tent encampments serve as constant reminders of a failure to tackle the problem effectively. Indeed, homelessness in California is so pervasive that it is common to talk about it in terms of numbers and percentages, as this chapter does. But it is important to keep in mind that behind every number is an individual with a unique story—a husband, wife, father, mother, son, daughter, brother, sister, friend, or family member, all deserving of human dignity.

This chapter looks at the extent of homelessness in California, beginning with a statewide overview and the state's unique characteristics, and then drills down, presenting succinct summaries, to local cities and counties in the Bay Area. The focus is on California because, as the numbers will reveal, the Golden State is the epicenter of homelessness in America, in terms of both the severity of the crisis and its rapid growth in recent years. The data also show clearly that the current approach to addressing homelessness has failed, despite much hand-wringing by politicians and pronouncements by lawmakers that "we are fixing the problem" by throwing more taxpayer money at it.

California: The State of Homelessness

Total homelessness has trended upward in the Golden State during the mid-2010s and early 2020s.[1] As of December 2022, according to the US Department of Housing and Urban Development (HUD), 171,521 people were counted as experiencing homelessness in California and constituted 30

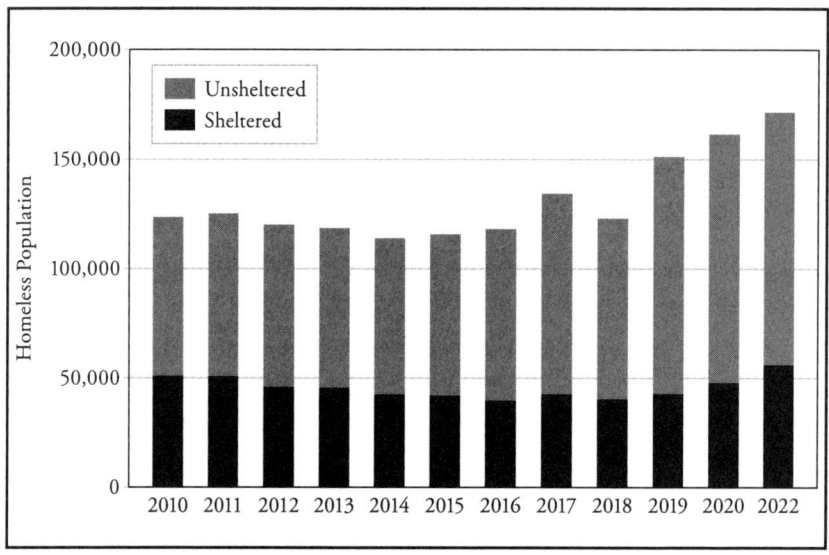

Figure 1. The Growing Problem of Homelessness in California, 2010–22

Sources: Matt Levin and Jackie Botts, "California's Homelessness Crisis—and Possible Solutions—Explained," *CalMatters*, December 31, 2019, https://calmatters.org/explainers/californias-homelessness-crisis-explained; US Department of Housing and Urban Development, Office of Community Planning and Development, *The 2022 Annual Homelessness Assessment Report to Congress*, December 2022, p. 16, https://www.huduser.gov/portal/sites/default/files/pdf/2022-AHAR-Part-1.pdf.

percent of the nation's total homeless population.[2] California is home to the largest homeless population of any state, numbering more than twice that of second-place New York. Ten years earlier, in 2012, 120,098 Californians experienced homelessness.[3] Figure 1 shows that homelessness was high but relatively stable in California from 2010 through 2016 before increasing dramatically thereafter. The data suggest a possibly new—and alarming—trajectory.

Tragically, California's entire homeless population now rivals in size the total population of prominent California cities. For example, there are now more people experiencing homelessness throughout California than the number of people living in Berkeley, Burbank, Inglewood, Pasadena, Sunnyvale, or Thousand Oaks.[4] In 2022, there were 115,491 *unsheltered* people experiencing homelessness and 56,030 *sheltered* individuals experiencing homelessness. If all of those people were in one location in California, they would represent the state's thirty-second-largest city, based on 2020 US Census Bureau population numbers.[5]

Shockingly, California is home to 12 percent of the nation's population, but the state accounts for about half of the unsheltered homeless people in the United States—people living on sidewalks, in vehicles, in parks, or in other public spaces.[6] In addition, 32 percent of the nation's unaccompanied youth experiencing homelessness and 32 percent of the nation's homeless veterans are located in California.[7]

Critical to the discussion herein is the fact that the homelessness figures most frequently cited are the result of counts conducted on a single night—a point-in-time (PIT) count—which, according to the National Law Center on Homelessness and Poverty and others, underestimates the true number of people experiencing homelessness.[8] The PIT approach, which is relied on to determine federal funding allocations, is wholly unscientific and should be reexamined. One reason for the undercount is that many people cycle in and out of homelessness throughout a calendar year. A point-in-time snapshot, therefore, captures only a fraction of the true extent of the problem. One study estimates that the number of homeless people is 2.5 to 10.2 times higher than point-in-time counts indicate.[9] Nevertheless, point-in-time figures generally are considered the best available data for comparison purposes. Moreover, despite their methodological limitations, point-in-time counts are extremely important because they shape funding, research, and policy decisions. HUD and other government agencies rely on PIT counts to measure changes in homelessness over time, which influence funding allocations.

The 2022 national point-in-time count was the first full tally of sheltered and unsheltered individuals and families experiencing homelessness since 2019 due to the COVID-19 pandemic.

San Francisco

The San Francisco Bay Area is a hot spot for homelessness, and the city of San Francisco is the national poster child for this humanitarian crisis. People experiencing homelessness and related quality-of-life problems seemingly are everywhere, with rampant public drug and alcohol abuse leading to public-health concerns of disease and sanitation. Nobody would wish this lifestyle on anyone, especially a family member or friend, yet it exists in the open throughout San Francisco and other parts of the Bay Area.

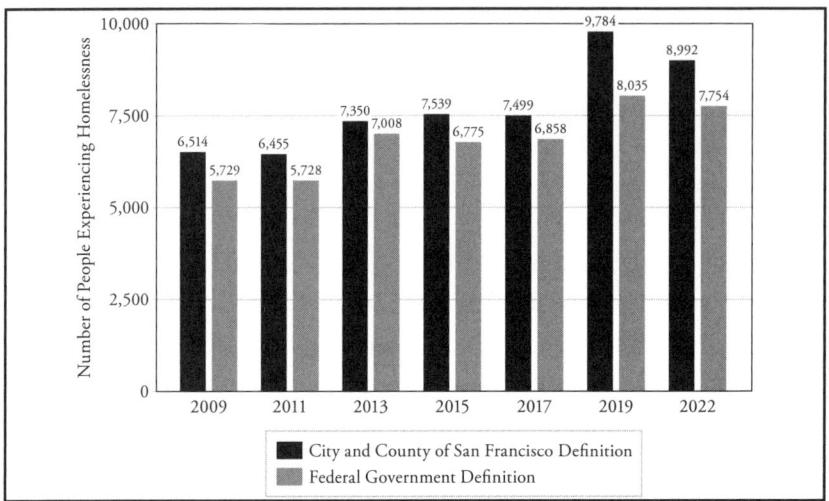

Figure 2. The Surge in San Francisco's Population of Those Experiencing Homelessness, 2009–22

Sources: City and County of San Francisco, Department of Homelessness and Supportive Housing, *San Francisco Homeless Point-in-Time Count Reports, 2009–2019*, https://hsh.sfgov.org/about/research-and-reports/archived-reports/#pit; City and County of San Francisco, City Performance Scorecards, Safety Net, "Homeless Population," https://sfgov.org/scorecards/safety-net/homeless-population; Applied Survey Research, *San Francisco Homeless Count and Survey: 2022 Comprehensive Report*, San Francisco Department of Homelessness and Supportive Housing, August 19, 2022, p. 14, https://hsh.sfgov.org/wp-content/uploads/2022/08/2022-PIT-Count-Report-San-Francisco-Updated-8.19.22.pdf; and Kevin Fagan and Mallory Moench, "New Data Shows 20,000 People Will Be Homeless in San Francisco This Year," *San Francisco Chronicle*, August 18, 2022, https://www.sfchronicle.com/sf/article/san-francisco-homeless-population-17380942.php.

San Francisco is unusual in that it is both a city and a county. Historically, San Francisco also has relied on a broader definition of homelessness than the federal HUD definition: Local officials include homeless people in jails, hospitals, and residential treatment centers in their homelessness counts. Regardless of the definition, as shown in Figure 2, homelessness has spiked in San Francisco. The city has experienced a 13 percent increase in homelessness since 2017 using the federal government's definition—and a 20 percent increase using the city's expanded definition of homelessness—with 8,992 people experiencing homelessness in 2022.

San Francisco has the largest homeless population of any city in the Bay Area. What is particularly troubling is that a majority (57 percent) of the city's homeless population is unsheltered, contributing to severe quality-of-life problems in particular neighborhoods.[10]

Oakland and San Jose

Homelessness is also surging in the Bay Area's other major cities, and at rates much higher than San Francisco's. As illustrated in Figure 3, Oakland's homeless population has soared by 83 percent, from 2,761 in 2017 to 5,055 in 2022. Unsheltered homelessness increased by 75 percent over five years, while sheltered homelessness doubled.

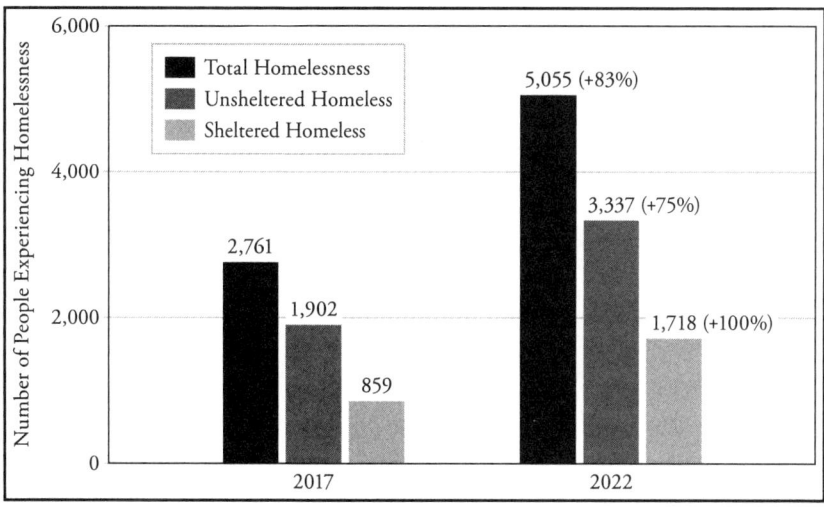

Figure 3. Oakland's Soaring Homeless Population, 2017 and 2022

Sources: Marisa Kendall, "Oakland's Homeless Population Grows 47 Percent in Two Years: New Data Underscores City's Homelessness Crisis," *Mercury News*, July 23, 2019, https://www.mercurynews.com/2019/07/23/oakland-saw-a-47-percent-spike-in-homelessness-this-year; Applied Survey Research, *Alameda County Homeless Count and Survey: Comprehensive Report, 2019*, EveryOne Home, August 15, 2019, https://everyonehome.org/wp-content/uploads/2019/07/2019_HIRDReport_Alameda_FinalDraft_8.15.19.pdf; and Applied Survey Research, *2022 Alameda County Homeless Count and Survey Comprehensive Report*, EveryOne Home, September 22, 2022, p. 23, https://homelessness.acgov.org/homelessness-assets/docs/reports/2022-Alameda-County-PIT-Report_9.22.22-FINAL-3.pdf.

Similarly, as shown in Figure 4, homelessness in San Jose—the nation's tenth-largest city—has jumped dramatically, increasing by 53 percent from

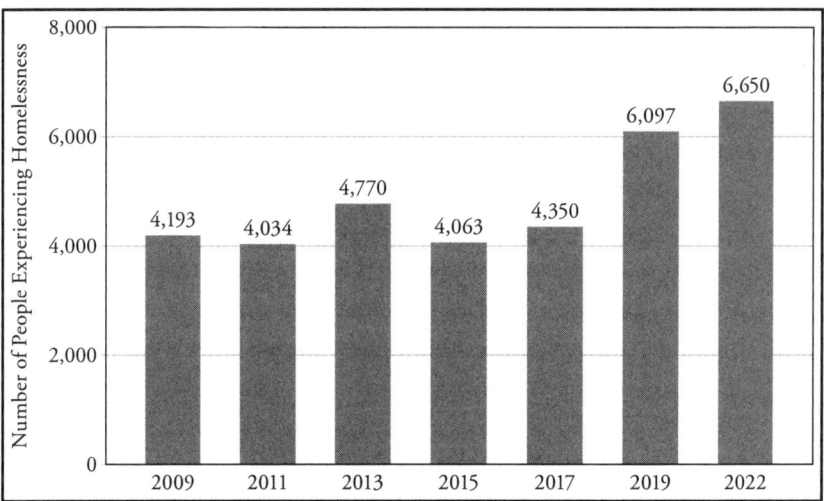

Figure 4. San Jose's Surge in Homelessness, 2009–22

Sources: Applied Survey Research, *City of San José Homeless Census and Survey: Comprehensive Report, 2019,* City of San José, https://www.sanjoseca.gov/home/showdocument?id=38890, and Applied Survey Research, *2022 County of Santa Clara Point-in-Time Report on Homelessness: Census and Survey Results,* Santa Clara County, 2022, p. 11, https://osh.sccgov.org/sites/g/files/exjcpb671/files/documents/2022%20PIT%20Report%20Santa%20Clara%20County.pdf.

2017 to 2022. In contrast, from 2009 to 2017, homelessness in San Jose was roughly stable. Overall, however, homelessness in San Jose has increased by 59 percent since 2009, from 4,193 in 2009 to 6,650 in 2022.

It is estimated that, taken together, more than 11,700 people experience homelessness in Oakland and San Jose on any given night. But, again, the true number of people experiencing homelessness throughout a calendar year may be many times larger than point-in-time counts indicate.

The San Francisco Bay Area

The San Francisco Bay Area comprises nine counties: Alameda, Contra Costa, Marin, Napa, San Francisco, San Mateo, Santa Clara, Solano, and Sonoma. Figure 5 presents data on homelessness for each county in both 2009 and 2022.

In three of the four most populous Bay Area counties—Alameda, San Francisco, and Santa Clara—homelessness has surged dramatically since

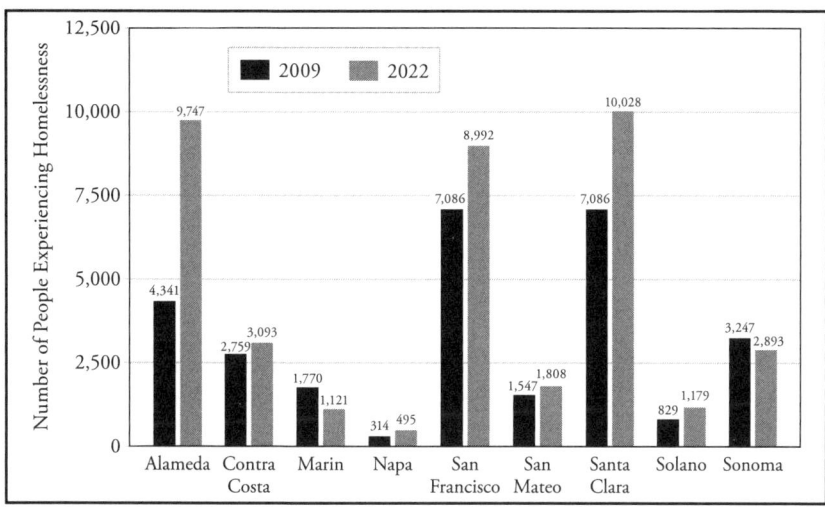

Figure 5. The Wave of Homelessness in San Francisco Bay Area Counties, 2009 and 2022

Sources: Kate Eby, "History of How Many People Are Homeless in the Bay Area," ABC7News.com, August 13, 2019, https://abc7news.com/5260657; City and County of San Francisco, City Performance Scorecards, Safety Net, "Homeless Population," https://sfgov.org/scorecards/safety-net/homeless-population; US Department of Housing and Urban Development, Office of Community Planning and Development, *The 2022 Annual Homelessness Assessment Report to Congress*, December 2022, dataset "2007–2022 Point-in-Time Estimates by CoC," https://www.huduser.gov/portal/datasets/ahar/2022-ahar-part-1-pit-estimates-of-homelessness-in-the-us.html; and Kevin Fagan and Mallory Moench, "New Data Shows 20,000 People Will Be Homeless in San Francisco This Year," *San Francisco Chronicle*, August 18, 2022, https://www.sfchronicle.com/sf/article/san-francisco-homeless-population-17380942.php.

2009. Napa and Solano Counties, on the other hand, experienced small increases, while in Marin and Sonoma Counties homelessness fell moderately. Marin County experienced the largest reduction (649 people). It is clear, however, that few counties can claim that they have a handle on the problem, especially the Bay Area's largest counties.

Overall, in the nine Bay Area counties combined, total homelessness increased by 39 percent, from 28,407 in 2009 to 39,356 in 2022. From 2017 to 2022 alone, total Bay Area homelessness increased by about 36 percent.[11] For comparison, consider that the total homeless population of the Bay Area (39,356) exceeds the entire population of upscale Beverly Hills (31,945).

People Experiencing Homelessness in California Who Are Also Unsheltered

A large percentage of people experiencing homelessness in California are unsheltered. Thus, homelessness is a highly visible aspect of daily life in California. Statewide, the percentage of people experiencing homelessness who also are unsheltered is 67 percent, the highest of any state.[12] Nationally, 40 percent of those experiencing homelessness are unsheltered, a striking difference.[13]

Unsheltered homelessness is a huge problem in the Bay Area as well, with 67 percent of its homeless population going unsheltered.[14] Among people experiencing homelessness in the region's major cities, 57 percent are unsheltered in San Francisco,[15] 66 percent in Oakland,[16] and 75 percent in San Jose,[17] which was home to the largest encampment of people experiencing homelessness in the continental United States, known as "The Jungle," until it was dismantled in 2014.[18] In Los Angeles, 68 percent of people experiencing homelessness are unsheltered,[19] many of them concentrated on Skid Row in downtown Los Angeles. In stark contrast to major California cities, 33 percent of people experiencing homelessness are unsheltered in Chicago, 27 percent in Denver, about 6 percent in New York City, and just 3 percent in Boston.[20]

Table 1. Rates of Homelessness and Unsheltered Homelessness in California, Florida, and Texas, 2022

	Homelessness per 10,000 residents	Unsheltered homelessness per 10,000 residents
California	44	30
Florida	12	5
Texas	8	4

Sources: US Department of Housing and Urban Development, Office of Community Planning and Development, *The 2022 Annual Homelessness Assessment Report to Congress*, December 2022, p. 16, and its full dataset, "2007–2022 Point-in-Time Estimates by State," https://www.huduser.gov/portal/sites/default/files/pdf/2022-AHAR-Part-1.pdf and https://www.huduser.gov/portal/datasets/ahar/2022-ahar-part-1-pit-estimates-of-homelessness-in-the-us.html; and."US States by Population," 2022, PopulationU.com, https://www.populationu.com/gen/us-states-by-population.

One obvious driver of the high rate of people experiencing homelessness who are unsheltered in California is the weather. California enjoys a moderate climate, which makes it possible to live unsheltered with fewer life-threatening weather conditions during the winter months and throughout the year. But the weather does not tell the whole story. Florida and Texas also enjoy moderate climates; yet, as shown in Table 1, each of those states experiences strikingly lower rates of homelessness and unsheltered homelessness than California.

Unlike the Golden State, Florida and Texas each have a rate of homelessness that is below the national average of eighteen people per ten thousand residents. Clearly, factors other than weather are needed to explain California's outsize homelessness rates. One such factor is California's—and especially San Francisco's—cultural permissiveness toward homelessness and its accompanying quality-of-life problems. San Francisco's political class tolerates homelessness and even subsidizes it, while many other cities do not.[21]

As a consequence of the large percentage of unsheltered people experiencing homelessness in California, many troubling antisocial behaviors are in public view, including defecation, urination, and needle use; substance abuse; severe mental illness; violence and other crimes; and unsanitary living conditions generally. The public-health implications are frightening, as exemplified by the spread of typhus and tuberculosis throughout homeless encampments and shelters in Los Angeles in 2019.[22] Merely sheltering people, if implemented incorrectly, can create other serious problems and may not reduce homelessness in the long run. Simply hiding the behaviors of people experiencing homelessness inside shelters or public housing may not improve matters, especially if underlying causes are not addressed (see Chapter 4). That said, in California, more than in many other places, the negative quality-of-life consequences of homelessness are in public view.

One Step Forward, Four Steps Back

Whether at the state level or in the Bay Area's cities and counties, homelessness has surged dramatically in recent years, accompanied by more severe quality-of-life problems. Figure 6 illustrates the sudden spikes in homelessness since 2017, ranging from a 20 percent increase in San Francisco to an 83 percent surge in Oakland.

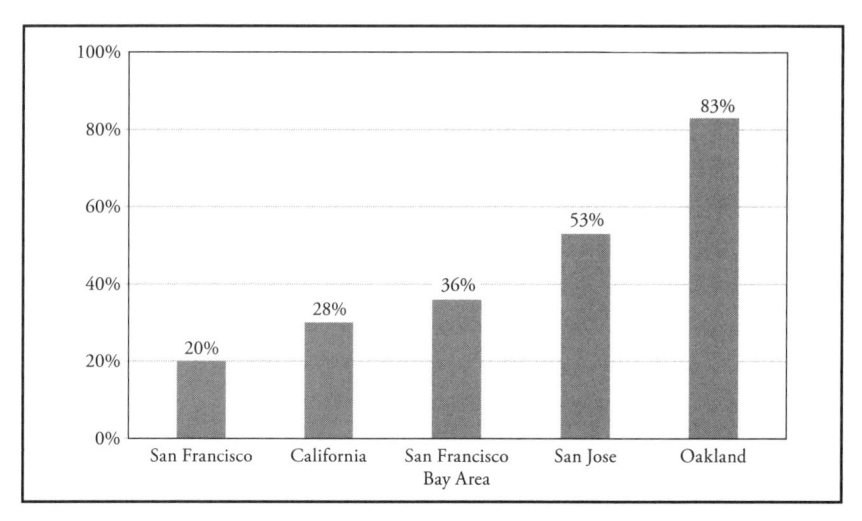

[Bar chart showing: San Francisco 20%, California 28%, San Francisco Bay Area 36%, San Jose 53%, Oakland 83%]

Figure 6. The Stunning Surge in California Homelessness, 2017–22

Sources: Figures 1–5.

The 20 percent increase in San Francisco's homeless population during the 2017–22 period tracks the experience in Los Angeles. Homelessness increased by 23 percent in the City of Los Angeles, with 41,980 people experiencing homelessness in 2022, and it increased by 20 percent in Los Angeles County, where a staggering 69,144 people experienced homelessness in 2022.[23] A noteworthy outlier is Sacramento County. Its homeless population increased a whopping 153 percent from 2017 to 2022 and, at 9,278 (with 72 percent unsheltered), is now larger than San Francisco's homeless population.[24] Sadly, seven of the eleven US cities and suburbs with the largest numbers of people experiencing homelessness are in California.[25]

Equally troubling is the continuous churn of people into homelessness. For every person experiencing homelessness who is newly housed each year in San Francisco and in Alameda County (where Oakland is located), three to four more people begin experiencing homelessness.[26] One step forward and four steps back is not a recipe for success. Clearly, the current Sisyphean approach to addressing homelessness has failed. In fact, the humanitarian crisis has gotten much worse, and to many people the problem now seems intractable and confounding.

To devise a plan that better addresses the growing tragedy of homelessness, we must first identify its main causes and contributing factors.

3

Factors Contributing to Homelessness
Hovannes Abramyan and Adam B. Summers

HOW IS IT that the San Francisco Bay Area, one of the nation's wealthiest metropolitan areas, with a median annual household income 72 percent higher than the national median,[1] finds itself with the third-largest homeless population in the country?[2] The data on homelessness offer some guidance for understanding the nature and origins of this epidemic of people experiencing homelessness in the Bay Area.

Composition of the Homeless Population in San Francisco

In August 2022, San Francisco released its most recent *Homeless Count and Survey*, a report on the numbers and composition of individuals experiencing homelessness within the City and County of San Francisco.[3] Although San Francisco realized a slight (3.5 percent) decline in the estimated number of people experiencing homelessness compared to the 2019 report, the total population is still 13 percent higher than it was in 2017.[4] The survey and other recent reports reveal several eye-opening aspects of homelessness in the region.

Age

The vast majority of people experiencing homelessness in San Francisco (75 percent) are 50 years old or younger, and almost half of the homeless population (49 percent) first experienced homelessness before the age of 25.[5] Seniors, however, are the fastest growing demographic among the state's homeless population.[6] And older people experiencing homelessness face particularly large challenges. According to a recent University of California, San Francisco (UCSF) study, people older than 50 experiencing homelessness in California face a 62 percent greater risk of death if they came into homelessness later in life, compared with those who became homeless earlier in life.[7] And according to another UCSF report, nearly half of all senior citizens experiencing homelessness became homeless after the age of 50.[8]

Gender

Most individuals experiencing homelessness who reside in San Francisco are men. Nearly six in ten (58 percent) identified themselves as male in the 2022 survey, while a little more than one third (34 percent) identified as female. The remainder identified as transgender (4 percent), nonbinary, or other than singularly male or female (2 percent), or were uncertain or refused to answer the question (3 percent).[9] The figures are very similar to those reported in the county's previous reports, signaling some consistency in the gender aspect of homelessness, although the individuals experiencing homelessness in 2022 were not necessarily the same people who were experiencing it in 2019 or prior years.

Race and Ethnicity

The majority of the homeless population in San Francisco is nonwhite. Despite constituting only 6 percent of the county's population, African Americans account for 35 percent of the total homeless population. Hispanic or Latino/a individuals of all races also are overrepresented among those experiencing homelessness, constituting 30 percent of the count but only 16 percent of the total county population. In contrast, it is estimated that about four in ten individuals experiencing homelessness are white (42 percent), even though more than half (51 percent) of the county's population is white. Asian Americans likewise are underrepresented among people experiencing homelessness, constituting only 7 percent despite representing more than one third of the total population (37 percent).[10] The demographic profile of San Francisco's homeless population demonstrates that the problem is neither distributed uniformly nor borne proportionally by all social groups. Rather, certain groups are more vulnerable to ending up on the streets. The reasons these groups are more susceptible to homelessness are varied, and they compound to create an epidemic that plagues the region.

Substance Abuse

Alcohol and illicit drug abuse are significant factors leading to homelessness. Although producing accurate estimates of substance abuse from self-reports collected in interviews is difficult (given the sensitivity of the topic and the fear of repercussions),[11] surveys such as those included in San Francisco's 2022 *Homeless Count and Survey* offer insightful (if necessarily conservative) estimates. The report finds that 12 percent of all individuals experiencing homelessness,[12] and nearly one fourth (22 percent) of those experiencing chronic homelessness,[13] identify drugs or alcohol as the primary cause of their condition. Put differently, a significant portion of San Franciscans experiencing homelessness attribute their homelessness directly to substance abuse before they ended up on the streets. For many of them, drugs and alcohol produced cascading negative effects on their careers, finances, and personal relationships. The issue is particularly acute in San Francisco, where Health Department officials estimate that drug addicts outnumber high school students,[14] and the gateway to homelessness appears to be as open as ever.

But drug and alcohol abuse are more pervasive and harmful among San Francisco's homeless population than even those numbers suggest. In the most recent survey, 52 percent of individuals experiencing homelessness self-reported alcohol or drug abuse—up from 42 percent in 2019[15]— and some independent estimates range even higher.[16] These estimates reflect the reality that often the depression and hopelessness associated with homelessness lead people to drug and alcohol abuse, rather than the other way around. This negative feedback loop of dependency impairs people's judgement and keeps them on the streets, despite any desire they may have to improve their situations. In some areas of San Francisco, such as the Mission, South of Market, and Tenderloin, substance abuse is both rampant and open, with fentanyl dealers lining the sidewalks and syringes commonly littering the ground, highlighting the extent of the problem.[17]

Mental Health Issues and Physical Disabilities

Tragically, a staggering number of people on the streets also suffer from physical or mental disabilities—problems that hinder successful reintegration into the workforce and society at large. More than a fifth (22 percent) of those experiencing homelessness report having chronic health problems, and a similar share (21 percent) have physical disabilities—including 13 percent who say they suffer from a traumatic brain injury.[18] While 7 percent attribute their homelessness primarily to a mental health issue,[19] 36 percent report a psychiatric or emotional condition, and 38 percent report having post-traumatic stress disorder.[20]

Although some of the people experiencing homelessness developed physical or mental disabilities while living on the streets, a large number of them found their way onto the streets following the deinstitutionalization movement that began in the 1960s. The Lanterman-Petris-Short Act of 1967, signed by then-Governor Ronald Reagan, ended the state's indefinite institutionalization of patients against their will for a host of mental health and developmental issues.[21] The act sought to end unjustified, indefinite (sometimes lifetime) commitments; protect individual rights by requiring judicial review of involuntary commitments; adopt the least restrictive means of treating people suffering from mental illness; and shift treatment from state institutions (and similar facilities), which had been criticized for being abusive and inhumane, to a community-based approach. The act also allowed law enforcement officers to apply for a seventy-two-hour involuntary hold (commonly known as a "5150," named after the section of the act that authorized it) for assessment and treatment at an appropriate facility for cases in which probable cause could be found that a person was suffering from a mental health condition that rendered him or her either a danger to themselves or to others, or else "gravely disabled." The dearth of effective community programs for treating the mentally ill, however, led many of them onto the streets or into the criminal justice system, from which they eventually were dumped onto the streets.[22] Thus, a significant share of the homelessness problem may be attributed to poor care options for mental illness. California has, however, recently established Community Assistance, Recovery, and Empowerment

(CARE) Court and expanded the definition of "gravely disabled," in an attempt to better address people dealing with mental illness and substance abuse issues (see Chapter 5).

Job Loss and the Lack of Affordable Housing

Many people experience homelessness for economic reasons. In fact, according to San Francisco's 2022 *Homeless Count and Survey*, the top two self-reported causes of a person's homelessness were largely financial: the loss of a job (21 percent) and eviction (14 percent).[23] Many factors contribute to such economic difficulties, as detailed below.

Cost of Living

Poverty in general and homelessness in particular are exacerbated by the high cost of living in California, particularly in the San Francisco Bay Area. Although the cost of living has affected nearly all residents in some form, its impact has been borne especially heavily by more economically and socially vulnerable people.

The costs are numerous, varied, and cumulative. For example, on top of facing the highest statewide sales tax in the nation (7.25 percent), Bay Area residents pay additional local sales taxes.[24] As of 2023, the combined sales tax rate in San Francisco is 8.625 percent, while in Alameda County it ranges from 10.25 percent to 10.75 percent, the highest in the state.[25] Californians as a whole also face the fifth-highest state and local tax burden in the country[26] and pay the highest gasoline taxes in the country.[27] When all sources of taxation are accounted for, Bay Area residents—especially those living paycheck to paycheck—are stretched thin and sometimes lack money for essentials. One of the most widely felt burdens is the high cost of housing in the Bay Area, which has grown well beyond the means of many ordinary residents, including families with children. Second only to New York City in rental rates, the San Francisco Bay Area has experienced multiple annual double-digit increases in rents in recent years, although rents appear to be stabilizing more recently. According to Zumper, a rental listing site, the median rent for a two-bedroom apartment in San Francisco currently is $4,000 per month, or

$48,000 per year.[28] That is 35 percent of the median annual household income in San Francisco ($136,692).[29]

Recent research demonstrates that housing costs are a major determinant of homelessness. For example, a December 2018 study by Zillow found that homelessness rises in places where rents consume more than 22 percent of disposable income and increases at an even higher rate when rent's share of income exceeds 32 percent.[30] A 2015 American Enterprise Institute policy paper also found that "a 10 percent increase in median rent is associated with a contemporaneous 4 percent increase in homelessness, which grows to 9 percent after one year."[31] The same link between a lack of affordable housing and homelessness exists locally as well, according to the Bay Area Council Economic Institute.[32]

Because most San Franciscans face very high rental costs, it is not surprising that the city is suffering such a great homelessness problem. Indeed, out-of-control housing prices have pushed many people to leave the Bay Area in favor of other, less expensive cities, such as Sacramento and Seattle.[33] But many others in the Bay Area's most vulnerable communities have been pushed onto the streets. According to the Bay Area Council Economic Institute's report, for extremely low-income households (those earning less than 30 percent of the area's median income), the high cost of housing "dramatically narrows the margin between housing insecurity and homelessness."[34] Such low-income households typically allocate the majority of their monthly incomes to rent, which often leaves them with less than $1,000 for other basic expenses.[35]

Supply Shortage

The sky-high housing costs in the San Francisco Bay Area are driven by a shortage in the supply of housing, relative to demand. Between the 1970s and 2000, thousands of single-room occupancy hotels were torn down and low-income apartments were taken off the market as part of an "urban renewal" movement.[36] These actions removed low-income housing from the market, providing fewer options for the economically disadvantaged and placing upward pressure on prices.[37] In more recent years, San Francisco has failed to add enough new housing units even to meet the demands of new jobs in the city, much less to tackle existing shortages. For example, between 2012 and

2022, the city added approximately 64,600 new jobs[38] but added only about 39,000 new dwelling units.[39]

The housing problem is well known and well understood, even if it has not been well addressed. The state's nonpartisan Legislative Analyst's Office (LAO) identifies the housing shortage as the key driver of the state's growing housing costs, especially in coastal communities such as the San Francisco Bay Area. As the LAO notes, the link between the supply of housing and the cost of housing is a matter of simple economics:

> Some of California's most sought after locations—its major coastal metros (Los Angeles, Oakland, San Diego, San Francisco, San Jose, and Santa Ana–Anaheim), where around two-thirds of Californians live—do not have sufficient housing to accommodate all of the households that want to live here. A shortage of housing along California's coast means households wishing to live there compete for limited housing. This competition bids up home prices and rents.[40]

Removing the governmental constraints that limit home building could have dramatic positive effects. A September 2019 report from the White House Council of Economic Advisers estimates that housing deregulation in eleven metropolitan areas with significantly supply-constrained housing markets would reduce overall homelessness in the United States by 13 percent. "Homelessness would fall by much larger amounts in these 11 large metropolitan areas; for example by 54 percent in San Francisco, by 40 percent in Los Angeles, and by 23 percent in New York City," the report concludes. "On average, homelessness would fall by 31 percent in these 11 metropolitan areas, which currently make up 42 percent of the United States homeless population."[41]

The high cost of housing in the San Francisco Bay Area not only pushes ever-larger shares of people toward homelessness, it also hinders any plausible opportunity for individuals experiencing homelessness to get back on their feet. When asked what kept them from securing permanent housing, nearly two thirds (63 percent) of individuals experiencing homelessness indicated that they would not be able to afford rent or did not have sufficient income.[42]

This, of course, assumes that enough housing units would be available to accommodate them in the first place.

Government Zoning and Land-Use Regulations

There are many regulatory hurdles that raise the costs of building new housing units and suppress housing development.[43] One primary example is zoning laws, which restrict the types and densities of housing development that may be built in various sections of the city or county. Land-use planning, permitting, and approval processes, including required environmental studies and, often, litigation, all drive up the cost of home building and lead to significant project delays, prompting many developers to give up in frustration or determine that projects are too risky or no longer profitable to build in such highly regulated regions. These and other regulatory hurdles limit the supply of housing, reduce consumer choice, and violate property rights by dictating what can—and what cannot—be built on a property owner's land.

The effects of such policies on housing prices are substantial. A 2006 Independent Institute report, for example, found that land-use regulation, "smart growth" policies, and other growth-management planning raised the median price of homes by more than $100,000 in dozens of US metropolitan areas—and the added price tag rose to between $160,000 and $850,000 in coastal California.[44] In the years that have followed, such "government planning penalties" have only become more costly and burdensome.

Inclusionary Zoning

In addition to standard "separation-of-use" zoning ordinances, many local governments also impose "inclusionary zoning," or affordable housing mandates, which require housing developers to either offer a certain portion of a new development's housing units at below-market prices or pay the government "in lieu" fees, which are supposed to be dedicated to affordable housing programs. Like many well-intentioned laws, however, the unintended consequences of such set-asides are largely the opposite of the intended effect: development is restricted, which makes housing even more expensive.

By making housing development less profitable, inclusionary zoning laws discourage home building, resulting in fewer housing units (including fewer affordable units) and higher prices for market-rate units, as developers try to make up for losses from the below-market-rate units. One study found that, after cities adopted inclusionary zoning laws, new housing production declined dramatically—by 31 percent in the first year, on average—and the cost of market-rate homes typically increased by tens of thousands of dollars. In some Bay Area cities, costs jumped by more than $100,000.[45] These negative effects far outweighed the measly 6,836 below-market-price units provided through inclusionary zoning across the entire Bay Area over a thirty-year period.[46] A similar analysis found that "cities that adopt below-market housing mandates actually drive housing prices up by 20 percent and end up with 10 percent fewer homes."[47]

A study of an inclusionary zoning law that went into effect in 2019 in Seattle, which also has suffered from significant housing supply and affordability issues, found "strong strategic substitution of new construction away from" neighborhoods subject to the inclusionary zoning mandate,[48] particularly for multifamily developments.[49] The negative effect on housing prices held even though the inclusionary zoning mandate was paired with a reform that allowed for greater housing density. "We interpret this result as evidence of [the law's] cost to developers outweighing its benefits," the researchers concluded.[50]

Such revelations prompted Jerry Brown, both when he was mayor of Oakland and when he was governor of California, to oppose inclusionary zoning mandates. As governor, in 2013 he vetoed Assembly Bill 1229, which would have expressly authorized local governments to impose inclusionary zoning mandates on new housing developments. "As Mayor of Oakland, I saw how difficult it can be to attract development to low- and middle-income communities," Brown wrote in his veto message. "Requiring developers to include below-market units in their projects can exacerbate these challenges, even while not meaningfully increasing the amount of affordable housing in a given community."[51]

Urban Growth Boundaries

Another type of zoning law that has significant ramifications for housing development is the urban growth boundary, which seeks to concentrate development in city cores within the boundary line, thereby ostensibly protecting farmland and open space outside the boundary. Such arbitrary boundaries limit the amount of developable land, encourage higher-density development, and drive up housing prices in city centers. As with other forms of zoning, growth boundaries limit consumer choice—and they even contravene consumer preferences, as many people prefer the larger, more affordable properties (particularly single-family homes) that are available farther from city centers.[52] Even people who prefer to live in the city near their jobs may be negatively affected, as the higher prices caused by urban growth boundaries force them farther away from the city center, leading to longer commutes, more traffic congestion, and added tailpipe emissions. Thus, as a 1999 Reason Foundation policy study concludes, urban growth boundaries raise housing prices, "produce lower-quality housing and amenities,"[53] and "[reduce] the quality of life for many people."[54]

Urban growth boundaries have been popular across the San Francisco Bay Area and are in effect in places such as Alameda, Contra Costa, Marin, and San Mateo Counties, as well as in the cities of Antioch, Fairfield, Fremont, Hayward, Napa, Richmond, San Jose, Santa Rosa, and Vallejo.[55] For this reason, development of vast swaths of the Bay Area is restricted, including much of the East Bay and South Bay.[56] Urban growth restrictions, promoted by environmental organizations such as the Greenbelt Alliance, seek to confine urbanization—but at the cost of a housing crunch that affects low- and middle-income residents disproportionately.[57] Moreover, zoning regulations that restrict the development of multifamily units, such as apartments, make matters worse. Supported by homeowners for the sake of boosting home values and keeping out unwanted newcomers, such zoning laws exacerbate the affordable housing crunch by preventing the supply of total housing units from increasing in order to meet communities' varied and changing housing needs.[58]

A Shortage of Housing but Not Land

It is not as if land were in short supply in the Bay Area.[59] Despite professed concerns about urban sprawl, only 18 percent of the region's approximately 4.5 million acres (roughly seven thousand square miles) is developed, with parks and open space accounting for more than one quarter of the land and with agricultural lands making up nearly half of the total.[60] But despite very low population growth, projected at only about 1 percent a year over the next twenty years,[61] "the competitive market for land no longer works, in large measure because of land-use regulation," concludes Wendell Cox, economic and demographic researcher and founding senior fellow at the Urban Reform Institute.[62] It should come as little surprise that Bay Area metropolitan areas have among the worst housing affordability multiples (defined as median house price divided by median household income) in the nation. The San Jose metro area posts an affordability multiple of 12.6, the worst of all US cities, followed by Honolulu (12.0) and San Francisco (11.8).[63]

It was not always this way, however. The sharp decline in housing affordability began in earnest only in the 1970s,[64] coinciding with the rise in stricter environmental and urban containment policies. "Before the evolution toward urban containment policies began, the median multiples in these metropolitan areas (and virtually all in the United States) were around 3.0 or less," Cox notes. "The decades-old Bay Area housing affordability crisis, and that of other urban containment metropolitan areas that are now seriously unaffordable (median multiples over 5.0) seeking to force higher densities, is more the result of policy than nature."[65]

Other Government Regulations

Numerous other state and local laws also reduce the supply—and increase the cost—of housing in California. Environmental regulations, such as the California Environmental Quality Act (CEQA), are exploited to slow or kill new developments by tying them up in red tape and litigation.[66] Prevailing (union) wage and solar panel mandates, high development impact fees, and a web of overly restrictive building codes and historic preservation rules at different levels of government stall housing construction and renovation and also increase the costs associated with building new housing.[67] Rent control policies (a common response to high housing costs) often do much more harm than good, leading to fewer units, poorer-quality housing (as units are allowed to deteriorate due to stiff competition for the below-market-rate units), and an increase in evictions, which is one of the main drivers of homelessness in San Francisco.[68]

Another impediment to home building is California's labyrinthine affordable housing financing process. Although affordable housing funding is handled by a single department in many large states, California has five different departments with financing responsibilities, each of which reports to different elected officials. "Developers have to file a series of applications to access a dozen different funding programs that . . . have their own regulations determining what projects win," according to the *Los Angeles Times*. "To make matters more confusing, there are three separate programs to finance homeless housing, and four geared toward affordable housing near mass transit—each with different rules."[69]

These obstacles to the construction of more housing hurt Californians broadly but are especially detrimental to those experiencing homelessness and those on the brink of homelessness.

Accommodating Policies Toward People Experiencing Homelessness

In addition to the aforementioned factors, homelessness is exacerbated by a resigned public attitude toward it, as well as related troubling issues such as open drug use and dealing on the streets and the widespread dangers of used drug needles, human feces, and other public filth. The surge in these conditions has made San Francisco the poster child for both homelessness and the failure to deal with the problem effectively. Given the city's generous public services; state laws such as Propositions 47 and 57, which essentially decriminalize public drug use and petty crime; and city policies institutionalizing street encampments, it should come as little surprise that people who wish to engage in such behavior—and take advantage of available public services—gravitate to San Francisco. During the early 2000s, San Francisco reconsidered such policies and eventually cut direct cash payments to those experiencing homelessness, with proponents such as then-Mayor Gavin Newsom suspecting that they were causing an influx of people experiencing homelessness into the city from neighboring counties.[70]

In recent years, programs in San Francisco that provide people experiencing homelessness with a range of free services and resources likewise have come under attack, being labeled "magnets" for those individuals.[71] For example, a controversial policy by the San Francisco Department of Public Health to provide limited amounts of free tobacco, drugs, and alcohol to quarantined individuals experiencing homelessness during the COVID-19 crisis has generated a great deal of opposition from people alleging that, in enabling destructive habits, the city has gone too far to accommodate those experiencing homelessness (see more on this in the "Project Roomkey: Another Application of Housing First" text box in Chapter 4).[72]

The data provide some evidence to support the claim that San Francisco's permissive attitude is making the city a magnet for people experiencing homelessness. The 2022 survey of the city's homeless population found that more than a quarter (28 percent) reported living outside the city when they most recently became homeless. The figure includes 24 percent who traveled to San Francisco from another county in California and 4 percent who came from out of state.[73] In addition, 17 percent of those experiencing homelessness reported that they had been in San Francisco for less than a year, and about half (49 percent) said they had been in the city for less than five years.[74] As a 2016 *San Francisco Chronicle* editorial lamented, the city suffers from "an influx of about 450 chronically homeless people a year [and] needs to shed any perception that it is a sanctuary for people who are unwilling to participate in programs designed to get them off, and keep them off, a life in the streets."[75]

Although a significant share of San Francisco's homeless population migrated from elsewhere, the vast majority (71 percent) reported living in the city when they most recently became homeless[76]—indicating that the epidemic is still largely a homegrown problem, resulting from substance abuse, physical or mental health problems, a systemic housing shortage, and other economic factors. But whether the individuals experiencing homelessness are locals or newly relocated, a new approach is needed to ensure that public intoxication, camping on public sidewalks, aggressive panhandling, and other disruptive behaviors are not viable options.

Mitigating homelessness will also require a change in housing policies and a dedication to more effective substance abuse and mental health treatment.

4

Housing First Puts People's Most Critical Needs Last

Adam B. Summers

ONE OF THE primary approaches to addressing the homelessness problem currently favored by government policymakers and some homelessness advocates (particularly those who participate in government-funded efforts) is "Housing First," a form of permanent supportive housing. As the name implies, this approach emphasizes placing people experiencing homelessness in housing immediately, with the idea that access to supportive services and connections to the community-based programs they need to keep their housing and avoid returning to homelessness will follow. In practice, however, such services are often either not provided or not accessed by most residents. As a result, the underlying issues that led to their homelessness remain unaddressed, and many people end up returning to the streets. A similar approach, known as "rapid rehousing," provides short-term rental assistance and various wraparound services for up to two years. Like Housing First, such services are optional and offered without preconditions.

In contrast, transitional housing programs and transformational housing programs rely on an approach known as "housing readiness," which aims to provide temporary housing and wraparound services to help individuals experiencing homelessness address underlying issues until they reach the point at which they are able to secure permanent housing and achieve full success. Such programs may last up to about three years. Critically, transitional housing programs typically include wraparound recovery, job training, and other services, and often require participants to maintain sobriety or fulfill other expectations in order to continue in the program. As noted above, although such services may be offered by Housing First programs, to the extent that they are not accessed, participants in Housing First do not confront the underlying causes of their homelessness effectively (see Table 2). Historically, transitional housing programs have been "high barrier," meaning that only those ready to commit to sobriety and a rigorous program will utilize the programs. These programs sometimes have established draconian consequences for even fairly minor offenses. Participants might be kicked out with nowhere to go solely for missing a class, for example. Failing alcohol or drug tests likewise routinely would result in participants being expelled, generally meaning they return to life on the streets. Many transformational housing programs are more flexible, however. Model programs, such as Haven for Hope (see Chapter 7) and The Salvation Army's The Way Out program, for example, take a more tolerant approach and work with participants facing challenges to create plans for getting back on track. For those who determine that they truly are not yet ready for a transformational program, a soft landing is provided at a lower-barrier facility.

History of the Housing First Policy

The Housing First model was developed during the late 1980s and 1990s, although its popularity among policymakers did not take off until the model was embraced by President George W. Bush's administration in 2004. At the time, this approach was tailored toward people experiencing chronic homelessness, which consisted primarily of single men with substance abuse, mental illness, or physical disability issues.

The federal government's support for Housing First programs expanded significantly during President Barack Obama's administration. The Homeless Emergency Assistance and Rapid Transition to Housing (HEARTH) Act of 2009 changed the US Department of Housing and Urban Development's definitions of homelessness and chronic homelessness and established the Continuum of Care Program, which consolidated three existing homelessness grant programs. According to the National Alliance to End Homelessness, a "continuum of care (CoC) is a regional or local planning body that coordinates housing and services funding for homeless families and individuals."[1] The HEARTH Act also changed the Emergency Shelter Grants Program, renaming it the Emergency Solutions Grants Program and allowing funds to be allocated to homelessness prevention and rapid rehousing, in addition to emergency shelter services.[2] This effectively facilitated a change to more of a Housing First approach and resulted in fewer federal funds for short-term emergency shelter and related services. In 2013, HUD essentially adopted Housing First as the solution for all people experiencing homelessness by including it in the department's Notice of Funding Avail-

Table 2. Comparison of Homelessness Assistance Program Approaches

	Transitional Housing	Housing First & Permanent Supportive Housing	Rapid Rehousing
Housing Type	Short-term (programs may last up to three years)	Long-term (unlimited)	Short-term rental assistance (up to two years)
Services	Typically requires sobriety, participation in services	Optional, with focus on harm reduction	Optional, with focus on harm reduction
Primary Focus	Underlying issues that lead to one's homelessness	Housing	Housing

ability, which details the requirements that applicants must meet to receive grants. This policy continued during President Joe Biden's administration. The State of California followed suit, adopting Housing First as its policy in 2016 when the legislature and Governor Jerry Brown approved Senate Bill 1380, which declared, "It is the intent of the Legislature to adopt a 'Housing First' model for all state programs funding housing for people experiencing homelessness or at risk of homelessness."[3] Many local governments, including those of Los Angeles, San Francisco, and Sacramento, have also adopted the Housing First approach.

This policy shift has had severe ramifications for the provision of services to individuals experiencing homelessness. It now is effectively impossible for transitional housing programs or other models to receive government funding in Housing First jurisdictions, unless they are paired with a rapid rehousing program. (See Chapter 7 for more on how this requirement impairs the emergence of successful alternative programs.) Current policy has forced many programs to face difficult decisions about whether to lose or forgo funding and scale back operations or switch to the Housing First model. It is little

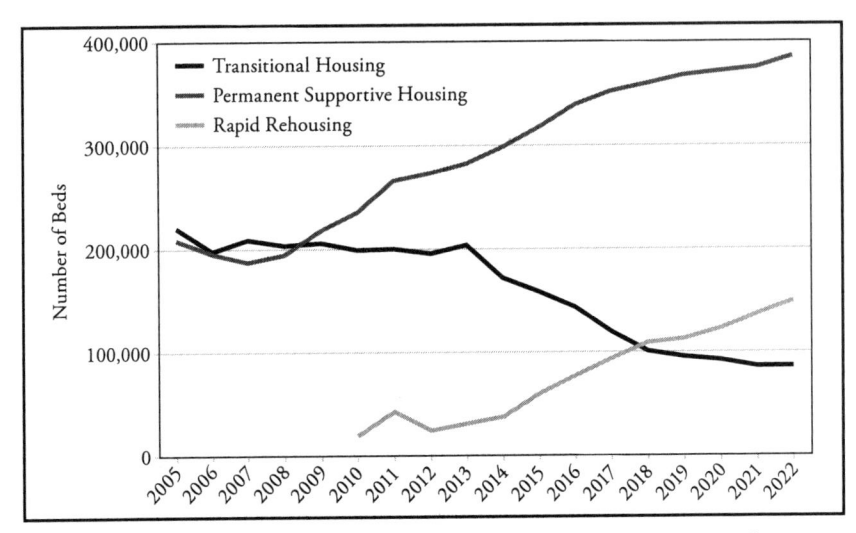

Figure 7. Number of US Beds to Assist Individuals Experiencing Homelessness (by Program Type), 2005–22

Note: Does not include "other permanent housing," emergency shelter, or safe haven beds.

Source: US Department of Housing and Urban Development, Homelessness Assistance, Continuum of Care Program, "Housing Inventory Count Reports," accessed April 12, 2024, https://www.hudexchange.info/programs/coc/coc-housing-inventory-count-reports/?filter_Year=&filter_Scope=NatlTerrDC&filter_State=&filter_CoC=&program=CoC&group=HIC.

surprise, then, that Housing First programs have flourished ever since, while transitional housing programs have gone into steep decline. Nationally, the number of permanent supportive housing (PSH) beds rose by a striking 85 percent, from nearly 209,000 beds in 2005 to more than 385,000 in 2022. Meanwhile, the number of transitional housing beds dropped a precipitous 61 percent, from approximately 220,000 to less than 86,000 in the same period. The number of rapid rehousing beds also has risen substantially, from fewer than 20,000 in 2010 to more than 149,000 in 2022 (see Figure 7). A similar pattern has emerged in California, although the increase in Housing First beds there has been even more dramatic. The number of transitional housing beds fell 55 percent, from nearly 34,000 in 2005 to roughly 15,000 in 2022, while the number of PSH beds has increased 127 percent, from roughly 32,000 to more than 72,000, and the number of rapid rehousing beds now exceeds 29,000 (see Figure 8).

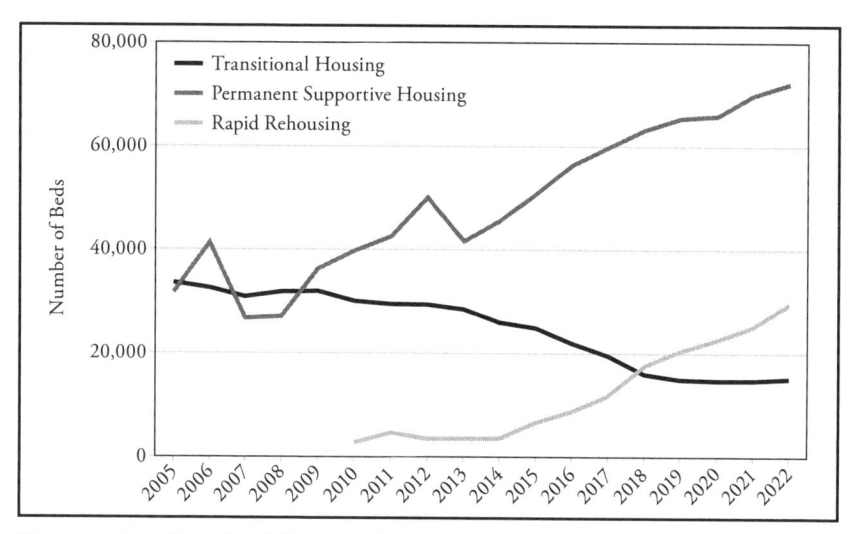

Figure 8. Number of California Beds to Assist Individuals Experiencing Homelessness (by Program Type), 2005–22

Note: Does not include "other permanent housing," emergency shelter, or safe haven beds.

Source: US Department of Housing and Urban Development, Homelessness Assistance, Continuum of Care Program, "CoC Housing Inventory Count Reports," accessed April 12, 2024, https://www.hudexchange.info/programs/coc/coc-housing-inventory-count-reports/?filter_Year=&filter_Scope=State&filter_State=CA&filter_CoC=&program=CoC&group=HIC.

Housing First Criticisms

Despite its political popularity, evidence of Housing First's effectiveness in meeting the needs of people experiencing homelessness and reducing region-wide homelessness is mixed at best. Homelessness did decline during the late 2000s and early 2010s, lending some initial support and enthusiasm for the Housing First strategy. The explosion of homelessness in recent years, however—even as Housing First has continued to be the predominant policy (preferred by HUD and numerous state and local governments) and spending on homelessness has ballooned—calls the efficacy of the approach into serious question.

There is some evidence that Housing First can have some positive outcomes, particularly with respect to housing retention. A 2013 American Public Health Association article written by several Pathways Vermont researchers reported that their organization's Housing First program realized a housing retention rate of 85 percent over three years by adopting "hybrid assertive community treatment-intensive case management teams."[4] A 2016 *Journal of Community Psychology* article also found that, for participants in a Housing First program targeted at chronic street homelessness or limited homelessness populations with serious mental health issues, 90 percent of residents were housed after one year, versus 35 percent for a comparison group. In addition, the participants experienced significantly shorter spells of homelessness or hospitalization in psychiatric facilities.[5] Moreover, a 2017 study reported in *PLOS ONE* found that participants in Vancouver, British Columbia, Canada, who (1) were experiencing homelessness or were precariously housed with histories of homelessness, (2) suffered from mental illness and moderate or severe disabilities, and (3) experienced other problems, such as substance abuse or legal issues, spent much more time in stable housing during a two-year period—74 percent of the time, compared with 26 percent for the "treatment-as-usual" group.[6]

The One-Size-Fits-All Approach Is Ineffective

There is no convincing evidence, however, that Housing First is effective when applied to the entire homeless population, as governments at the federal, state, and local levels have claimed. Indeed, even some of the studies supportive of Housing First have cautioned against interpreting the results too broadly or exaggerating the benefits of the approach.[7]

"Many of the claims about Housing First overreach what the evidence actually says," warned a 2012 report for the Australian Housing and Urban Research Institute. "While much can be learned from Housing First, it is also clear that in the process of transferring Housing First to Australia important findings have been ignored, factors contributing to its success have been oversimplified, and claims about its effectiveness overstretched."[8]

A review of multiple studies and articles supportive of Housing First revealed numerous methodological flaws: "Low retention rates, failure to collect data consistently across experimental conditions, and vulnerability to recall bias all weaken the current studies' ability to fairly assess Housing First programs."[9] Other commentators have questioned the objectivity of certain Housing First studies, noting that they generally are conducted by a relatively small group of academics, many of whom have ties to organizations that advocate for Housing First policies.[10]

Many other studies have identified shortcomings in Housing First programs themselves. A study of chronically unsheltered individuals in Boston, published in April 2021 in *Medical Care*, for example, found that housing retention was 82 percent after one year but fell dramatically to 36 percent after five years and to just 12 percent after ten years.[11]

"Long-term outcomes for this permanent supportive housing program for chronically unsheltered individuals showed low housing retention and poor survival," concluded researchers from the Harvard T. H. Chan School of Public Health, Boston Health Care for the Homeless Program, and Massachusetts General Hospital in Boston. "Housing stability for this vulnerable population likely requires more robust and flexible and long-term medical and social supports."[12] Moreover, the Boston researchers found that the supposedly "permanent supportive housing" was anything but permanent for a large portion of the participants. "Nearly half in our study required [more than one] apartment to remain housed, with many requiring 3–6 apartments. While only 8 persons were evicted, 28 tenants were moved a total of 45 times to avoid eviction," they found.[13] The researchers concluded, "Each subsequent housing relocation increased the risk of a tenant returning to homelessness. Three or more housing relocations substantially increased the risk of death."[14]

In addition, a 2018 National Academies of Sciences report concluded, "Overall, except for some evidence that PSH improves health outcomes among individuals with HIV/AIDS, the committee finds that there is no substantial published evidence as yet to demonstrate that PSH improves health outcomes or reduces health care costs."[15]

Other studies have found that Housing First generally performs no better than other approaches for treating substance abuse or mental illness,[16] and it tends to be more expensive than alternative approaches.[17] And a 2017 Washington Legal Clinic for the Homeless study criticized the local government of Washington, DC, for its overreliance on the related approach of rapid rehousing, finding that

- 45 percent of families in such programs ended up in eviction court,
- only 10 percent of families were able to increase their incomes over a one-year period,

- only two out of every five families were able to maintain their housing without assistance, and
- four out of five reported poor conditions in their apartments.[18]

According to a 2015 study by Kevin Corinth, permanent supportive housing is correlated with a very small immediate reduction in the homeless population, but even this effect disappears after one year.[19] Moreover, relying solely on this approach, one would have to add at least 12.6 PSH beds to reduce the homeless population by one person in the long run.[20] Thus, Corinth concluded, "investment in permanent housing may lead to small short-run reductions in homelessness, but if there are no long-run effects, limited funds will be tied up in serving people who otherwise could have escaped homelessness with more temporary assistance."[21]

"Permanent supportive housing . . . is not associated with any long-run reduction in homelessness," Corinth added. "The muting effect driven by the non-chronically homeless suggests that PSH should be better targeted to the chronically homeless, although the lack of affirmative evidence that PSH reduces even the chronically homeless population suggests that plans to end chronic homelessness using PSH should be more modest."[22]

Housing First might be an appropriate approach for some subpopulations of the homeless, such as individuals experiencing chronic homelessness, who were the program's original targets, or others so traumatized and distrustful of public officials or service providers that they would not otherwise agree to participate in higher-barrier programs, such as transformational housing. It appears, however, that Housing First's benefits have been exaggerated and that it has been overprescribed for the entire homeless population at large. Addressing the needs of various populations dealing with different causes of homelessness and different severities of underlying issues is, of course, a complex problem, and any one-size-fits-all approach is likely to be counterproductive and fail to serve certain portions of the homeless population effectively. Thus, policymakers responsible for funding homelessness programs should recognize that homelessness is an individualized problem that needs to be addressed on an individualized basis. They should focus on rewarding successful outcomes—whether the approach used is Housing First, transitional housing, or another model—and leave private-sector and nonprofit organizations free to determine how best to meet the needs of people experiencing homelessness in their communities.

Neglecting Care of the Individual

Perhaps the most damning criticism of Housing First is that it largely neglects the "supportive" component as originally designed, leaving unaddressed the trauma, substance abuse, and other root causes that lead people into homelessness and thus preventing them from escaping it. Housing First applies a Band-Aid to a severe wound. By not emphasizing long-term stabilization, Housing First too often serves merely as a revolving door between housing and homelessness. As a Salvation Army officer who works directly with people experiencing homelessness said, "They're inside, but culturally homeless."[23] Such harms are not easy to quantify, nor are the effects of a successful transformational program. But a lax attitude on the part of Housing First programs toward treatment and life-skills training and their tolerance of destructive behaviors—even if such behaviors are reduced modestly—still facilitate the cycle that robs individuals of their dignity and prevents them from realizing their full success. (See the "Our Definition of Success" text box in Chapter 1 for a complete description of the elements of "full success.")

"Since HUD started emphasizing 'Housing First' over services and not requiring participation in programs, national homelessness has increased," said Robert Marbut, founding president and CEO of the successful Haven for Hope transformational housing facility in San Antonio, Texas (spotlighted in Chapter 7). "It's not working. We've got to get back to addressing the root causes of homelessness, and engaging people in services—not enabling them."[24]

The late Bob Coté, a man who, after experiencing homelessness, got off the streets and went from participant in to leader of Denver's Step 13 Evolution Process (later renamed the Step Denver transitional housing program), likewise criticized the optional services approach. Coté touted the very high success rate of his "no drugs, no booze, find a job" program (profiled in Chapter 7). "My biggest adversaries are government homeless shelters that don't ask people to do anything for themselves and Social Security Disability programs that allow people to continue the same mistakes they've been making," he told columnist John Fund.[25]

The Housing First approach "is basically saying the cause and solution of homelessness is housing, regardless of [one's] behaviors," added Paul Webster in October 2019 when he was vice president of Solutions for Change in San Diego County. (Webster later became senior policy adviser at the US Department of Housing and Urban Development.) "This takes away the incentive to become self-sufficient" and eliminate sociopathic behavior in order to become a productive member of society, he added.[26] By funding exclusively Housing First and permanent supportive housing programs, Webster continued, policymakers are rewarding failed behavior and effectively crowding out preventive programs for people who are on the brink of homelessness, while they still have custody of their children.

Housing First forces a cycle of waiting until people are desperate enough to need more services and more dramatic interventions, resulting not only in higher costs to governments (and, ultimately, taxpayers) but also a "catastrophic loss of human potential." Moreover, transitional housing programs are not "tough love," as they sometimes are described; they simply prohibit self-destructive behavior. Such programs help people reach full success, rather than treating them as victims, Webster noted.[27]

Then there is the question whether people who have severe mental health issues or are addicted to drugs or alcohol can even make rational, self-interested decisions about the kinds of treatment and other services they require. Many people may be afflicted with anosognosia, a misperception or lack of awareness of one's condition, which affects a substantial portion of people with mental health issues.[28] Drew Pinsky, MD, a board-certified physician and addiction medicine specialist who has spent most of his career working in a psychiatric hospital, stresses that "motivated care" is preferred to "mandated care" and recommends presenting people suffering from anosognosia with limited choices: "Sorry, you can't live in the street. We're going to arrest you for drug use. But you don't have to go to jail; you can go to this drug treatment facility."[29]

For individuals who are truly unable to care for themselves, conservatorship may be the best answer, for, as Pinsky also notes, letting people stay on the street "is a death sentence."[30] Although confining people to treatment facilities against their will should be an absolute last resort, it may be a crucial option in extreme cases when someone has broken laws repeatedly or is deemed by a judge to represent a serious threat to public health or otherwise pose a significant danger to themselves or others. As such, conservatorship laws should be reexamined to determine whether they strike the right balance between individual rights and the health and safety of others. (See Chapter 5 for more about changes to California conservatorship laws in recent years.)

Housing First Is Expensive and Inefficient

Even if the Housing First approach worked for everyone, it simply would not be financially or practically feasible, given that the demand for affordable housing far outstrips the supply. This is particularly true in California, where state and local government policies have reduced the supply of housing and dramatically increased the costs of building new housing—affordable or otherwise. As noted in Chapter 3, policies such as zoning restrictions; environmental regulations; high development impact fees; prevailing (union) wage mandates; lengthy and labyrinthine planning, permitting, and approval processes; and litigation all serve to raise housing prices or prevent needed housing from being built in the first place. And this is especially true for Housing First units that are scattered about, as opposed to units grouped into a single facility, which take advantage of lower transaction costs and economies of scale.

According to a 2020 *Los Angeles Times* report, even "affordable" housing developments in California could cost $500,000, $700,000, or even close to $1 million per unit. At that time, the average cost to build a government-subsidized apartment for low-income residents in the state was $500,000. Even after adjusting for inflation, that price tag was 26 percent higher than it was just a decade earlier.[31] Costs have only increased since then. A follow-up *Los Angeles Times* report two years later noted that a number of affordable housing projects in the Bay Area had eclipsed $1 million per unit—with some San Francisco Housing Authority sites topping $1.2 million a unit—and in Southern California, an apartment development in Hollywood cost $848,000 per unit.[32]

Speaking of the Greater Los Angeles area, residents of Los Angeles approved Proposition HHH in the November 2016 election to provide $1.2 billion in subsidies for supportive housing for individuals and families experiencing homelessness. But after three years, according to a 2019 report from City of Los Angeles Controller Ron Galperin, only one project had been completed, and the median cost of the units was more than $531,000—nearly the same as the median condominium sales price in the city at the time ($546,000). That price tag was far more than the $350,000–$414,000 cost that the city touted prior to Proposition HHH's passage. The report estimated that more than one thousand units funded by Proposition HHH would top $600,000 per unit, and one project would exceed an average of $700,000 for its forty-one units—more than the median price of a single-family house in Los Angeles County ($628,000). Moreover, the controller found, developers were spending approximately 40 percent of their budgets on "soft costs," such as development fees, consultants, and financing—about three and a half times the cost of land and nearly as much as the cost of actual construction (labor and materials), which eats up nearly half of total project costs.[33]

A follow-up controller's office report in 2022 found that although some progress had been made in construction, with 1,142 units completed five years after Proposition HHH's approval by voters, project costs had continued to grow and timelines continued to expand. Average per-unit costs had grown to just shy of $600,000 by 2021, with 14 percent of units under construction exceeding $700,000 a unit and one project expected to cost nearly $837,000 per unit.[34] The controller found that Los Angeles's notoriously expensive building climate had been exacerbated by factors such as "prevailing wage requirements, financing complexity, land use issues, project labor agreements, and building characteristics (e.g., enhanced accessibility standards)"[35]—most of which, it should be noted, are due to unwise government policies. It took an average of 3.4 years to complete finished projects, and that timeline was expected to grow to 4.3 years for projects under construction.[36] As a result, the controller recommended further streamlining the city's permitting process and directing more Proposition HHH funding to interim housing projects in order to reduce costs and make housing available more quickly.[37]

"We can all look ourselves in the mirror and say if the price of these units keeps going up, whether it's $400,000 or $550,000, we're going to run out of money for these kinds of things from a purely public sector, philanthropic stance," said Gary Painter, director of the Sol Price Center for Social Innovation at the University of Southern California. Painter also decried project delays that "cause some of these projects to take five to seven years when they should, if everything was moving smoothly, take 12 to 18 months."[38]

These high costs and lengthy project timelines make Housing First an untenable solution, on its own, for addressing homelessness and housing affordability adequately. The inability of Housing First to put much of a dent in homelessness in San Francisco and Los Angeles—despite many years of such efforts—and the difficulty of getting new units built in the first place demonstrate that this strategy cannot effectively be scaled to such large populations. We simply do not have the time or the money to build a new home for every person experiencing homelessness. Even at an average rate of $500,000 per unit (which, by now, is probably rather conservative), and even assuming that we could build every unit needed right away (because costs will only increase the longer it takes to build new units), providing housing for the estimated 171,521 Californians currently experiencing homelessness would carry a price tag of roughly $86 billion. Furthermore, even if we could somehow provide such a substantial amount of money and get enough new housing units built, merely warehousing a certain segment of the population out of public view, effectively making them permanent wards of the state dependent on taxpayers, does not serve the interests of those in need of help or the interests of local residents and taxpayers (see "Our Definition of Success" in the introduction). Furthermore, an approach centered on "a permanent home for every person experiencing homelessness" encourages more people to participate in the future, creating an endless cycle of dependency and rising costs for taxpayers.

People experiencing homelessness would thus be better served if Housing First was implemented on a more modest scale, targeting the subpopulations best suited to it and taking advantage of other more efficient and cost-effective solutions as well. Unfortunately, spending more money while falling further behind has become the norm.

Project Roomkey: Another Application of Housing First

In early April 2020, California Governor Gavin Newsom announced the launch of Project Roomkey. The program was intended to protect the most vulnerable people experiencing homelessness from the coronavirus outbreak and prevent further spread of the disease by getting them off the streets or out of crowded shelters and isolating them in hotel and motel rooms, many of which were vacant because of state and local government lockdowns in response to the pandemic.[39] Those eligible for the program included people experiencing homelessness who had tested positive for COVID-19 but did not require hospitalization, those who had been exposed to the disease, and those who were asymptomatic but who were at high risk due to age (sixty-five or older) or underlying health conditions. The Federal Emergency Management Agency (FEMA) covered 75 percent of state and local governmental costs, which, in addition to the rooms, included expenses for support services such as meals, security, and custodial services. Local governments and community groups were responsible for providing health care, behavioral health, and case management services.

At a May 29, 2020, press conference, Governor Newsom announced that the state had met its initial goal of securing at least 15,000 hotel and motel rooms, which he reported had a 60 percent occupancy rate.[40] In a separate but similar effort, the state embarked on a plan to purchase approximately 1,300 trailers and deploy them to local governments for the same purpose.

Although Project Roomkey may have been a temporary arrangement (the hotels' lease contracts initially ran for three months but later were extended, with FEMA announcing in December 2020 that it would continue to fund such "shelter-in-place" programs throughout the duration of the COVID-19 emergency),[41] as opposed to permanent supportive housing, the program incorporated PSH's Housing First harm reduction approach, which offered housing without any sobriety or other treatment requirements. This led to some controversy when it was reported in May 2020 that San Francisco was delivering and administering alcohol, cannabis, and methadone to drug addicts staying in Project Roomkey facilities.[42]

In an article for *City Journal*, reporter Erica Sandberg detailed shocking conditions at hotels used to temporarily house people experiencing homelessness in San Francisco, including high-end lodgings such as the InterContinental San Francisco and InterContinental Mark Hopkins. The results included "destroyed rooms," "rampant illegal drug use," "used syringes . . . discarded haphazardly," a lack of mental health treatment, disorganized operations, "deeply demoralized" city staff, and several deaths within just a few days, including "a non-guest [who] was recently found dead in the hallway, still clinging to a crack pipe."[43]

"You are talking drug-fueled parties, overdoses, deaths. People are being assaulted. You have sexual assaults going on. It is pandemonium," Sandberg said during a July 2020 Fox News Channel interview. "It is extremely bad and it needs to stop."[44]

The San Francisco Police Department even arrested two people for operating a meth lab in a room at a hotel used for housing individuals experiencing homelessness and others at risk of contracting the coronavirus.[45]

There were cost and efficiency considerations as well. The program was not fiscally sustainable, Abigail Stewart-Kahn, the interim director of the San Francisco Department of Homelessness and Supportive Housing, told KQED in November 2020. The average room cost of $260 per night was at least three times the $70 to $90 daily cost for other types of housing.[46] Nonetheless, the city extended its homeless hotel program until early 2022.[47]

Despite all that spending, Project Roomkey's results were rather dubious. Although the program did temporarily get many people experiencing homelessness off the streets and out of crowded shelters during the coronavirus pandemic, after six months only 5 percent of clients had found a permanent home. More than three times that number (16 percent) returned to homelessness; an additional 39 percent left the program, and caseworkers did not know where they went. In addition, strained caseworkers struggled to manage the high demand, with an average of thirty-six Project Roomkey clients for every caseworker—more than double a typical caseload.[48]

Still other problems arose in California hotels, such as suicide attempts, concerns about access to mental health treatment, limited access to personal protective equipment for workers, lax security, and a spike in police activity (which was five times greater than in the previous year) at a San Diego hotel used for COVID-19 isolation, including people experiencing homelessness.[49] Despite the free lodging, meals, laundry service, and other amenities, the program experienced an attrition rate of at least 20 percent, and about one third of the remaining guests ignored shelter-in-place rules and stayed outside all day.

Other such programs around the country experienced similar problems. New York City likewise operated a program to temporarily house people experiencing homelessness in hotels. At one point, nearly one in every five hotels in the city housed people experiencing homelessness.[50] The city decided to shutter its program, however, following a sharp increase in crime in and around the participating hotels and reports about the high costs of the program, estimated at as much as $28 million per month (over and above the substantial federal subsidies provided through FEMA).[51]

As if all of this were not bad enough, San Francisco used confidentiality clauses in hotel contracts and emergency disaster laws to prevent reporters from entering properties housing people experiencing homelessness, thus keeping the public in the dark about which hotels were participating in the program and what their new guests had been doing during their stays.[52]

"What keeps me up at night is what happens when [shelter-in-place measures] recede," said Kathleen Clanon, MD, medical director of Alameda County Care Connect, a program of the county's Health Care Services Agency to coordinate health care and social services, in a May 2020 webinar hosted by then-Assemblyman Bill Quirk (D-Hayward).[53] Clanon indicated that she would like to keep some of those hotel properties for long-term housing of people experiencing homelessness but conceded that doing so still would not be enough to address the problem adequately.

Yet that is just what California decided to do. In addition to the $150 million the state made available to local governments in March 2020 for using hotels and motels to house people experiencing homelessness who were also at high risk for COVID-19, the state budget that Governor Newsom signed at the end of June 2020 included $550 million in federal Coronavirus Relief Fund money to purchase and rehabilitate hotels, motels, vacant apartment buildings, residential care facilities, and tiny homes for the purpose of housing individuals experiencing homelessness. The federal funds came with the caveats that they were to be allocated for one-time capital expenditures, such as building acquisition and improvements—not ongoing operational expenses—and that they had to be spent by December 30, 2020. The accelerated timeline prompted the state to exempt such projects from California Environmental Quality Act (CEQA) review. In addition, $50 million of state funds were dedicated to ongoing support services for the program, and another $300 million in general state homelessness funding could also be allocated for the same purpose.

To reflect an intention to continue the homelessness housing program after the coronavirus pandemic had passed, the program's name was changed from Project Roomkey to Project Homekey. Governor Newsom included an additional $750 million for the Homekey program in his initial fiscal year 2021–22 budget proposal.[54] Then a historic projected budget surplus and the promise of tens of billions of dollars more from the federal government via the American Rescue Plan coronavirus relief package, signed into law in March 2021, allowed Newsom to expand his proposal significantly. Under the state budget signed by Newsom in July 2021, California allocated $12 billion for homelessness programs during the ensuing two years, including $5.8 billion to expand Project Homekey, which was estimated to add 42,000 homeless housing units, and $150 million to stabilize and rehouse Project Roomkey clients.[55]

"We've long dreamed about scooping up thousands of motel rooms and converting them into housing for our homeless neighbors," Newsom said in a statement. "The terrible pandemic we're facing has given us a once-in-a-lifetime opportunity to buy all these vacant properties, and we're using federal stimulus money to do it."[56]

As of fiscal year 2023–24, the state had spent more than $3.6 billion on Project Homekey over three rounds of funding.[57] In the March 2024 election, Californians very narrowly (with just 50.2 percent of the vote) approved Proposition 1, a $6.4 billion bond measure that would allocate an additional $2 billion for Homekey projects and new affordable housing construction, with the remainder to go toward the construction of mental health care and drug or alcohol treatment facilities.

The California State Auditor's office deemed the Homekey program "likely cost-effective," because acquiring and refurbishing old hotels and motels is cheaper than building brand new "affordable" housing units. Homekey projects cost an average of $144,000 per unit, compared to a range of $380,000–$570,000 for new affordable housing projects built in 2019.[58] The auditor's analysis, however, was based on just eight projects that received funding during the first round of Homekey funding, and the data were five years old. At an Assembly Budget Subcommittee on Accountability and Oversight hearing in March 2024, Department of Housing and Community Development Director Zachary Olmstead pegged the cost of the average Homekey project at about $325,000 per unit over the previous year. That is still cheaper than new construction, especially in coastal areas, where affordable housing costs are currently in the range of $450,000 to $700,000 per unit.[59]

There are only so many underutilized hotels and motels available for purchase, however, so the project is likely to house only a fraction of the homeless population in the state. Moreover, as with other Housing First "solutions," the failure to ensure that participants are receiving needed support services or that sobriety requirements are enforced means that the underlying causes of participants' homelessness often go unaddressed.

Many of those who are housed in Project Roomkey or Homekey units have their own criticisms of the programs, too. Inconvenient locations and strict and inflexible rules such as curfew, a prohibition on guests, and not being able to have a key to one's own space have made life miserable for many residents and made it difficult for some to hold a job to help them escape from homelessness.

"We were sold on the idea that we were to be given hotel rooms that would function like kitchenless apartments," John C., a homeless man in Los Angeles, told the *California Globe*. "As someone who had been living on the street since 2015, that sounded great. I was working a night shift at a convenience store at the time, and I was close to getting a real apartment of my own. Project Roomkey dashed all of that."

"First of all, they don't care where you need to be, and where they put me in a motel was even farther away from my work," he explained. "Work, which, by the way, I wasn't allowed to go to anymore because it meant giving up my job because of the curfew. We really thought they would care about us, but nope. Several of us actively working to get out of our position either had to quit our jobs to get this housing or quit the housing to keep our jobs."[60]

"All they do is get us off the streets for a bit with this Project, it seems," added Trevor, a homeless man in Los Angeles who stayed in Project Roomkey housing during 2020 and 2021. "And they spent billions on it? It's crazy. They spend all that money getting us into these motels, but then don't follow through on additional help, or sabotage what we had going, then act surprised when we're back on the street. It's crazy."[61]

Some even described Homekey housing as prisonlike.

"I feel like as if I did something wrong. I'm a criminal. I committed a crime, and I'm in jail, or I feel like, I'm . . . I don't want to say how it really makes me feel. It makes me feel useless, worthless," Karyn Goldstein, a Project Homekey resident in Chatsworth, told Spectrum News 1.[62]

Such experiences prompted Goldstein, along with other homeless individuals and activists, to form an organization called Unhoused Tenants Against Carceral Housing.

Los Angeles homeless advocate and housing placer Logan Kramer summed up residents' frustrations and the fundamental problems with the Roomkey/Homekey approach in a separate *California Globe* article:

> [Governor] Newsom is mostly focused on homeless and chronic homeless housing and is ignoring the ways to get rid of this long-term. First off, homeless people don't really trust these types of hotel housing sites. They need flexible hours for work, or need more accessible locations so commutes aren't long and they can build lives again. But these sites have curfews and assignments not based on their needs. He's kind of just saying, "Here is your free housing. Be grateful." But people need more than just a place to sleep to get over homelessness. All Newsom is doing is making the problem less visible.[63]
>
> It seems that more Californians may be coming to similar conclusions. The near defeat of Proposition 1 may be evidence that Californians are beginning to sour on continually throwing more money at the problem and doubling down on a Housing First–only strategy that clearly is not working.
>
> Only time will tell if the continuing worsening of the homelessness problem and changing political tides will lead to a switch to more productive solutions.

5

The Promise and Pitfalls of Harm Reduction for Reducing Homelessness

Jonathan Hofer and Mary L. G. Theroux

THE HARM REDUCTION concept and its associated set of practices have gained significant national traction as an approach to support individuals—both housed and unhoused—with substance use disorders or co-occurring mental health conditions. Harm reduction strategies have gained prominence as they have been coupled with the Housing First approach favored by the federal government and many state and local governments.

Harm reduction strategies have even been sold as a means of helping to "end homelessness." In 2007, for example, the Greater Victoria Coalition to End Homelessness in British Columbia, Canada, was notable for its efforts to bring multiple government agencies together to integrate "harm reduction into strategies to end homelessness."[1]

As harm reduction strategies have evolved, it has become increasingly evident that although some services have notable successes, others have struggled to make positive impacts. The question arises: What is the role of harm reduction as it pertains to individuals experiencing homelessness?

The term "harm reduction" is applied in two distinct ways, both captured in the National Harm Reduction Coalition's definition. First, "harm reduction is a set of practical strategies and ideas aimed at reducing negative consequences associated with drug use." Second, "harm reduction is also a movement for social justice built on a belief in, and respect for, the rights of people who use drugs."[2] Those two definitions present quite different ideas, because drug use can be deleterious to people other than those who use drugs (e.g., their families and their broader communities) and also because sometimes restricting the rights of people who use drugs can reduce harm (e.g., punishing drunk driving).

Because many of the individuals experiencing homelessness—particularly those experiencing chronic homelessness—suffer from substance use disorders, our focus sharpens on the outcomes of harm reduction as it relates to homelessness and the Housing First approach, where the need for innovative solutions and reforms is urgent.

Research has highlighted the significant overlap between homelessness and substance use disorders, with estimates indicating that up to two-thirds of homeless individuals experience problematic substance use disorders.[3] Moreover, as noted in Chapter 3, among a subset of the total homeless population, people experiencing chronic homelessness, 63 percent reported drug or alcohol abuse.[4] According to one public-health researcher who has conducted surveys of drug users in San Francisco for the past quarter century, the percentage of people responding to the surveys who are homeless has risen from roughly 25 percent when he first began his research a quarter century ago to about 80 percent today.[5] Among veterans, two of the most salient risk factors associated with homelessness, even more than insufficient income, are substance use disorders and mental illness.[6]

In addition, substance use disorders and mental illnesses are both causes and results of homelessness.[7] Certain drug-use patterns, such as sharing syringes, speedballing (mixing stimulants, such as methamphetamine, with depressants, such as heroin), and sharing cookers (containers used for mixing or heating illicit substances), are especially associated with higher rates of infectious disease transmission.[8]

Within the broad scope of harm reduction, the Drug Policy Alliance describes several key goals and features of the approach, which are representative of the strategies commonly advocated. These strategies include the following:

- improving access to drugs that reverse opioid overdoses, such as the generic drug naloxone
- operating supervised consumption services (SCSs), also referred to as supervised injection facilities (SIFs), which are "legally sanctioned facilities designed to reduce the health and public order issues often associated with public drug consumption by allowing onsite, supervised use of drugs"[9]

- encouraging drug checking, also referred to as adulterant screening, which refers to policies that permit the use and distribution of drug-testing supplies to assist individuals in identifying specifically what a particular substance contains[10]
- protecting individuals who report illicit drug use to emergency services (including self-reporting)
- expanding syringe access in order to lower the transmission of infectious diseases
- reducing the stigma associated with recreational and "problematic" drug use

Naloxone

The late twentieth and early twenty-first centuries witnessed a surge in the prescription of opioids, resulting in what some have termed the "most severe public health crisis in US history."[11] According to the Centers for Disease Control and Prevention, "The number of people who died from a drug overdose in 2021 was more than six times the number in 1999. The number of drug overdose deaths increased by more than 16 percent from 2020 to 2021. Over 75 percent of the nearly 107,000 drug overdose deaths in 2021 involved an opioid."[12] In a medical context, opioids are a class of drugs that act on a person's opioid receptors and that are primarily used for pain management. Common examples include morphine, codeine, hydrocodone, heroin, and fentanyl. With the development of potent prescription pain relievers, such as OxyContin, came an increase in opioid prescriptions.[13] Opioids began to be prescribed more liberally for managing various forms of pain, resulting in a rise in addiction rates. During the same period when opioid prescriptions were surging and causing a profound public health crisis, significant steps were taken to enhance the availability of naloxone, a life-saving agent capable of reversing opioid overdoses.

In 2023, the US Food and Drug Administration approved a first-ever, over-the-counter four-milligram naloxone nasal spray.[14] Naloxone, commonly referred to by the brand name Narcan, is an agent that can reverse the effects of an opioid overdose. Previously, naloxone availability varied widely. In some states, such as California, "standing orders" allowed for naloxone to be distributed through programs or pharmacies.[15] Elsewhere in the United States, however, naloxone was available only by prescription, limiting its accessibility. Now that it is available over-the-counter, patients can access naloxone in supermarkets, in convenience stores, and through online distributors, improving its availability in areas with limited health care resources.[16]

A 2019 study noted, "Homeless individuals had disproportionately higher adjusted risk of opioid-related outcomes."[17] Opioid misuse and overdoses have been significant issues since the US opioid crisis began in the late 1990s, leading to large numbers of deaths every year.[18] Efforts by state and federal governments to combat the opioid crisis have produced only limited successes. Over the past decade, a particular concern has been the drug fentanyl. Fentanyl is a highly potent synthetic opioid, and many fatal overdoses are attributed to its misuse. In some instances, individuals may be unaware that they are consuming it because their drug of choice has been "laced" with fentanyl to increase the intended drug's potency, or cross-contamination has occurred. Given its high potency, fentanyl is likely to exacerbate the quality-control problems of illicit drug suppliers and may make certain drug habits, such as consuming drugs in combination, more dangerous.

In order to facilitate access to drugs that reverse opioid overdoses, the Drug Overdose Prevention and Education Project, an initiative funded by the City and County of San Francisco, distributed more than fifty thousand doses of naloxone in 2020. About 8 percent of those fifty thousand doses were administered to individuals experiencing opioid overdoses. For some unknown subset of those cases, the overdose might have otherwise proved fatal.[19] In 2021, San Francisco furnished 33,495 naloxone kits, in addition to the emergency-use packs available from other sources. That same year, 9,492 overdose reversals were reported, more than double the 2020 figure.[20]

Unfortunately, the distribution of all of those naloxone kits has not been able to prevent the trend of increased overdose deaths, mostly from fentanyl. Overdose deaths have ballooned from 222 in 2017 to 811 in 2023—a staggering 265 percent increase.[21] The drug-overdose death toll is more than the number of people who died in San Francisco from the coronavirus outbreak during the same period.[22] As the *New York Times* reports, "San Francisco's overdose death rate is higher than West Virginia, the state with the most severe crisis, and three times the rates of New York and Los Angeles."[23] Given the vastly stronger toxicity of fentanyl and the speed with which a fentanyl overdose can lead to death (compared with, for example, a heroin overdose), the likelihood of a successful fentanyl poisoning intervention often is small.

The isolation imposed by San Francisco's Shelter-in-Place Hotel Program during the COVID-19 pandemic may have been an additional contributor to the recent higher overdose death rate, because someone equipped with naloxone may not have been in the immediate vicinity of a victim. An April 2021 *City Journal* article revealed that nearly three quarters of these 2020 drug-overdose victims "perished while isolated inside hotel rooms and supportive housing provided by the city. Six died in the Hotel Whitcomb, a designated Shelter-in-Place hotel, in a single month."[24] As a result, calls for the establishment of supervised consumption sites have been on the rise. While naloxone undoubtedly has saved lives, it is not a permanent substitute for addiction recovery, especially in light of widespread fentanyl use.

Supervised Consumption Sites

Supervised consumption sites are defined as sterilized venues with professional supervision where individuals consume previously obtained drugs. Sites generally make available clean paraphernalia such as syringes or cookers and check drugs for adulteration, in addition to simply monitoring individual drug users.

Supervised consumption sites have produced some well-documented benefits. For people who utilize supervised consumption sites, there is diminished risk of fatal overdoses and HIV transmissions.[25] In the twelve weeks following the opening of North America's first supervised consumption site in Vancouver, British Columbia, Canada, on September 22, 2003, public injection of drugs and biohazardous waste in Vancouver declined.[26] The reduction in waste observed in this study, however, may have been influenced by inclement weather that resulted in fewer people spending time outside.

Although the potential for crime reduction is a key intention behind the implementation of some supervised consumption sites, no long-term evidence clearly supports this outcome.[27] Rather, results have been largely mixed. In 2023, the City of Vancouver declined to renew a lease for an overdose-prevention center, citing negative effects on the community and noting issues of public disorder outside the site.[28] Yet, in New York City, a 2023 study of both overdose-prevention centers and syringe-service programs found no statistically significant increases in reported crimes or emergency service calls.[29]

Service providers who do not refer individuals to other services, such as medical treatment or substance use counseling, for further assistance, risk merely perpetuating these individuals' substance use disorders, rather than reducing the harm of drug use. For example, individuals experiencing homelessness can be offered drug paraphernalia, drug checking, or access to supervised consumption sites, but they may not be provided with opportunities for programs offering recovery services. One former addict who had lived on the streets and experienced San Francisco's harm reduction programs reported that, although drug paraphernalia was supplied by city workers, he never was offered a treatment bed or assistance with quitting.[30] Fortunately, with the encouragement of a neighborhood police officer, he eventually was able to complete The Salvation Army's rehabilitation program.

Although supervised consumption site interventions have achieved commendable outcomes, it is essential to address other important, less rosy dimensions of such programs. Supervised consumption sites are touted widely as effective means of reversing overdose deaths, usually supported by few to zero instances of deaths within the centers themselves. In looking at overall drug-overdose deaths, however, unless such centers are coupled with immediate access to recovery services, the establishment of the centers can correlate with *increases* in overdose deaths. Drug deaths in Vancouver, for example, more than doubled from 2016 to 2022, from 231 to 550, despite the city's twelve overdose-prevention sites.[31] And overdose deaths in the year that San Francisco's Tenderloin Center operated increased slightly from the year before, from 640 to 647.[32] Of course, correlation does not necessarily imply causation, and it is possible that conditions could have been worse without supervised consumption sites; nevertheless, the overdose numbers from Vancouver after the implementation of supervised consumption sites paint a bleak picture.

Moreover, studies that assert large declines in overdose deaths from supervised consumption sites may suffer from making inappropriate causal claims. In particular, two disparate populations often are compared: individuals who attend supervised consumption sites frequently and those who attend infrequently. The differences observed between these two populations *may* be attributed to the supervised consumption site, although it is not now apparent that the supervised consumption site, rather than other factors, is making the key difference.

Opening a supervised consumption site could have the unintended consequence of increasing the nominal homeless population in a given city or region by encouraging migration to areas offering consumption sites or other harm reduction programs. A Simon Fraser University study reported an association between "increases in the use of public services" and the migration of mentally ill individuals and individuals experiencing homelessness.[33] This is not to suggest that supervised consumption sites necessarily promote drug tourism; however, cities must be realistic in acknowledging that harm reduction services do not automatically mean that the number of unsheltered people will decline. Supervised consumption sites may be costly for cities to operate and may not be substantially cheaper than providing treatment options.

Wound Management Clinics

People who inject drugs are at a high risk for bodily injury and disease. Injection-related injuries, such as "abscesses and vascular damage, can result in significant morbidity and mortality if untreated."[34] A meta-analysis has shown that people who inject drugs have a mortality rate that is approximately thirteen times higher than those who do not use drugs.[35] Not only do infections resulting from injection-related injuries lead to higher mortality rates for the drug-injecting population; hospitalizations resulting from injection-related injuries also impose a sizable cost on the health care system.[36]

Such diseases and injuries are a particular concern for people experiencing homelessness. It has been observed that homelessness may be associated with risky injection-related behavior, such as the sharing of drug paraphernalia and unsafe disposal of needles, cookers, or other materials.[37] Wound management clinics generally have been helpful in this regard.

Wound management clinics are specialized health care facilities where health care professionals assess, treat, and monitor various types of wounds, particularly soft tissue infections, providing specialized care to promote healing and prevent complications. A cohort study of the Integrated Soft Tissue Infection Services Clinic in San Francisco found that opening the clinic "resulted in a 47 percent decrease in surgical service admissions and an estimated savings of over $8 million for costs related to [cutaneous injection-related infections]." The study also reported that a wound management clinic in Oakland "found that the average cost per individual treated . . . was $5, substantially lower than equivalent hospital costs of $185 and $360."[38] Wound care may be offered by some supervised consumption sites, but such services are not necessarily universal.

Although offering wound management services may lead to beneficial health outcomes relative to not having such services, maintaining wound management services that are detached from other support programs may not give an individual the best chance of recovering. Some individuals may be unaware of the risks associated with certain consumption practices and may not seek out services. People experiencing homelessness may face barriers in reaching clinics, especially for injuries or diseases that require more than a single treatment. A detection problem may also complicate personal decision-making. An individual with symptoms of infection may not be able to recognize their symptoms or identify their cause, thus dismissing their severity and failing to seek treatment. A potential follow-up problem arises as well, because it may be difficult to track down people experiencing homelessness for future care, especially if they have no permanent address or mobile phone. Therefore, pairing wound management services with other services, such as outreach and transportation, likely facilitates care and improves patient outcomes.[39] A potential solution is to intervene for related ailments as soon as possible, such as when service providers are first introduced to an individual and are able to have necessary services on standby.

Syringe Exchanges

Another type of harm reduction service that has shown some success is syringe exchange programs. At the height of the HIV/AIDS crisis in San Francisco, for example, syringe exchanges were a successful private endeavor that complemented public substance use disorder interventions.[40] The most notable instance of private provision of syringes was by the all-volunteer group Prevention Point, which distributed injection and hygiene supplies. It has since organized community efforts to clean up used, discarded syringes and other biohazardous materials.[41]

The National Research Council and Institute of Medicine Panel found that, after the introduction of a syringe exchange program, reported needle sharing among injection drug users declined sharply, from 66 percent to 35 percent between 1987 and 1992. Moreover, participants who utilized the program more than twenty-five times during the previous year were less likely than the control population to share syringes.[42] And a meta-analysis of twenty-eight studies found that needle exchange and syringe programs were associated with lower rates of hepatitis C acquisition in Europe.[43]

Despite the notable positive public-health outcomes of such programs, it is imperative that communities avoid the temptation to conclude that syringe exchange services are sufficient by themselves and thus fail to address the complex needs of individuals, especially people who are searching for stable housing. Another potential shortcoming of syringe exchanges is the issue of medical litter. The City and County of San Francisco has implemented a syringe exchange program in an attempt to minimize harm to drug users and the general public. The city "exchanged" 5.8 million syringes in 2018, although there often was no requirement to turn the used ones in.[44] The city ended up collecting 3.8 million (66 percent) of those syringes, leaving approximately 2 million syringes unaccounted for.[45]

After San Francisco's 2018 efforts to distribute syringes, the *San Francisco Examiner* reported: "Of the collected syringes, 3.1 million were returned to syringe access sites, 59,000 were dropped off at syringe disposal kiosks, and 107,136 [were] picked up through cleanup sweeps."[46] That year, Mayor London Breed proposed spending an additional $13 million over two years for the city's street-cleaning efforts, in part owing to the high concentrations of medical litter.[47] As the San Francisco example illustrates, distributing clean, new syringes without requiring that they be exchanged for used syringes can result in an increase in biohazardous waste and can negate the declines in medical litter observed in syringe exchange studies such as the aforementioned Vancouver case study. In other words, syringe exchange programs amounting to syringe distribution programs can generate adverse effects for the general population.

Legal Environment of Care

Recovery from substance use disorders often requires motivation and support, as many individuals may not choose to seek help on their own. San Francisco has implemented harm reduction strategies involving the provision of drug paraphernalia and information on its use. But in severe cases of disability or impairment, outside intervention may, unfortunately, become necessary.

In 2014, Californians passed Proposition 47, which reduced, to "cite and release," the penalties for possession of controlled substances such as methamphetamine, cocaine, and heroin and theft of less than $950 per crime, among other offenses.[48] The downgrading of such crimes from felonies to misdemeanors has prompted local police and district attorneys to stop prosecuting many of these cases. In addition, it has resulted in the discontinuation of the practice of courts offering rehabilitation, rather than incarceration, for individuals charged with crimes related to substance use disorders, such as serial theft to support one's drug habit. Studies generally have shown that drug courts offer promising results, particularly in reducing recidivism and lessening future substance use disorders.[49] Since the passage of Proposition 47, however, the number of individuals who utilize drug courts has declined. A 2020 paper by the Center for Court Innovation found that 67 percent of drug courts in California saw their caseloads drop after the passage of Proposition 47.[50] In Los Angeles County, for example, the number of clients referred to the county's Department of Health by drug courts decreased from 3,399 admissions in fiscal year 2013–14 to 2,820 admissions in fiscal year 2015–16.[51]

In addition, California's Lanterman-Petris-Short Act of 1967 severely limited hospital commitments through court order. Although the law has the noble aim of trying to prevent the undue commitment of patients, especially in its expansion of the role of psychiatrists in identifying inappropriate involuntary commitments, it has had the unfortunate result of removing options other than the street for many people with mental disorders experiencing homelessness.[52] Legislation such as California's Senate Bill 1045 and Senate Bill 40 have attempted to address the needs of individuals suffering from mental illnesses who pose a risk of harm to themselves or others or who are "gravely disabled." SB 1045, passed in 2018, created a "pilot program that allows for the conservatorship of adults with serious mental illness and substance use disorder treatment needs."[53] Under a conservatorship, a person, called a conservator, is appointed by a judge to make decisions on behalf of the conservatee.[54] In 2019, SB 40 was signed into law, revising the role of outpatient treatment included in SB 1045 and reducing the conservatorship period to a maximum of six months.[55]

The laws' extremely narrow qualifications, however, have prevented such measures from actually being applied. Nearly six years after the passage of SB 1045, use of the conservatorship program targeting mentally ill residents suffering from substance use disorders and living on the city's streets remained low. In San Francisco, only one petition for homelessness-related conservatorship was filed in 2021, and just two people were placed in that status in 2022.[56] By 2023, fourteen individuals were notified that they were on a path to "housing conservatorship," but as of the publication of the San Francisco Housing Conservatorship Program's 2023 *Annual Evaluation Report*, no petitions for housing conservatorship were awaiting court approval.[57] When SB 1045's pilot program was implemented, the San Francisco Department of Public Health had "estimated [that] approximately 50–100 individuals [would be] eligible" for the program.[58] Supervisor Rafael Mandelman, a supporter of the legislation, stated, "I said at that time that even if SB 1045 only helped one person, I believed it was worth doing. And I still believe that, but I didn't think it would actually literally be just one person."[59]

In 2022, California lawmakers passed legislation establishing the Community Assistance, Recovery, and Empowerment (CARE) Court, a civil court process designed to provide comprehensive care and support to individuals dealing with severe mental health and substance use disorders.[60] CARE Court is intended to focus on addressing mental health issues "upstream," with the goal of preventing conservatorships and institutionalization. This initiative allows individuals, families, clinicians, and first responders to refer people who are struggling with schizophrenia spectrum or psychotic disorders. The law provides for early interventions and community-based care plans, which encompass various mental health and substance use disorder treatment services, along with social services, housing, and wellness and recovery support. The CARE Act, in an effort to emphasize accountability, provides for fines for local governments that fail to comply with the framework's requirements.

The proceeds of the fines are directed toward supporting the affected individuals. The legislation received bipartisan and near-unanimous approval in the California Senate and Assembly and is supported by substantial funding for the state's homelessness and mental health programs.

The year following the CARE Act's passage, in 2023, Senate Bill 43 was signed into law. Most notably, SB 43 expands the definition of "gravely disabled" in existing statutes and codes for the purpose of determining eligibility for involuntary commitment and treatment. The definition now encompasses individuals who, due to severe substance use disorders or co-occurring mental health issues, cannot provide for their personal safety or necessary medical care, in addition to basic personal needs such as food, clothing, and shelter. The bill also adds chronic alcoholism as a condition that can result in "gravely disabled" status, while also expanding the data collection responsibilities of the California Department of Health Care Services. SB 43 will allow medical records statements from health practitioners and clinical social workers to be admissible in conservatorship proceedings.

The pairing of CARE Court and SB 43, on its face, may appear contradictory: The intention of the CARE Act is to reduce conservatorships, and SB 43 seemingly allows for expanded use of conservatorships. The CARE Court framework, however, may be best thought of as an early intervention, while the modifications to conservatorship in SB 43 are intended more for last-resort interventions. Although the overall effects of CARE Court and SB 43 are unclear given their recent adoption, it is obvious that conservatorship should be considered only in the most extreme cases, in which people experiencing homelessness have a diminished capacity to reason or understand the consequences of their actions. CARE Court may be an upgrade in this respect. However, because CARE Court allows individuals to submit a petition on behalf of others, there is a potential civil liberties risk that unwilling participants may be deprived of their due process rights.[61] Thus, strict safeguards must accompany the use of conservatorships and alternative court systems to prevent abuse and ensure that conservatorships are authorized only in the most extreme cases.

Amid discussions of early and last-resort interventions in addressing homelessness, it is crucial to spotlight innovative programs such as Haven for Hope's jail diversion initiative, a noteworthy example of a community-driven effort transforming the landscape of jail bookings in San Antonio, Texas. Individuals are screened for diversion eligibility by Bexar County's Population Impact Control Unit.[62] Once approved for release by a judge, the individuals are accommodated at the Haven for Hope facility, where they receive substance abuse treatment and mental health services, if needed.[63]

The diversion program has shown considerable success. The year following its inauguration in 2009 saw a substantial decline in jail bookings—3,323 fewer—which continued in subsequent years: There were 5,360 fewer bookings in 2018 than in 2010.[64] Collaborative efforts—including San Antonio's IMPACT (Integrated Mobile Partners Action Care Team) Project, in which street teams deployed by the police and fire departments offer to connect people experiencing homelessness to support services; Haven for Hope's Jail Release Program (JRP); and the Center for Health Care Services' Jail Diversion Program—have contributed to this positive trend.

Haven for Hope's JRP, which was established in collaboration with the University Health System, the Center for Health Care Services, and Bexar County, has produced some impressive results. The JRP aims to curtail jail recidivism, reduce preventable hospital admissions and emergency room visits, and enhance the overall circumstances of participants. "Since its inception, over 300 JRP participants have completed the program" and transitioned to community housing, according to a Haven for Hope fact sheet.[65] The data also underscore the economic benefits of such diversion programs, as the reduction in jail bookings alleviates some of the public funding burden. Remarkably, the JRP has reduced emergency room visits and hospital admissions substantially, resulting in an approximate cost savings of $80,000 per JRP participant.[66] The outcomes for people entering Haven for Hope from the court program reportedly are as good as for individuals entering voluntarily.[67] (See Chapter 7 for more information on Haven for Hope and its service offerings for people experiencing homelessness.)

Localities seeking effective strategies for addressing homelessness and enhancing community well-being should consider San Antonio as a model. Jail diversion programs with a partner like Haven for Hope showcase the positive impact that comprehensive diversion programs can have, both in improving individuals' lives and using scarce public resources more efficiently.

68 | Beyond Homeless

A Better Path to Recovery

As explained in Chapter 4, Housing First incorporates a harm reduction approach to treatment. But this often ranges from no supportive services at all to the provision of paraphernalia without treatment services. The focus on rapid housing placement can lead to inattention to individualized needs. Since Housing First adopts a more macro view, rather than an individualized, bespoke approach to recovery, Housing First may not effectively cater to individuals with complex needs, such as severe mental health issues or chronic substance use disorders.[68] Neglecting the unique needs of the homeless population, particularly those suffering from substance use and addiction, increases the risk of relapse, housing instability, and poor health outcomes.

Because many Housing First units prioritize harm reduction over effective support for vulnerable residents suffering from unaddressed trauma, addiction, or mental health issues, many Housing First buildings become the subjects of frequent calls for emergency services. By neglecting to treat underlying issues that led some residents to become homeless in the first place, Housing First facilities risk becoming places where the homeless merely come to die more slowly. Furthermore, graduates from a sixty- or ninety-day recovery program may be placed in a mixed Housing First community among active drug users, undermining their efforts to stay clean and contributing to a "washing machine" effect, in which individuals cycle between the streets, social service programs, and housing. A more comprehensive approach would integrate mental health services, substance use disorder treatment, employment assistance, and social assistance to ensure that individuals experiencing homelessness receive the tailored and multifaceted support they require.

There have been some attempts to pair Housing First with integrated mental health and addiction services. Such an effort was made in Canada, where it was dubbed the "Housing First Plus" program. The program produced significant benefits in assisting people with serious mental illness to exit homelessness, although researchers noted that the practical difference was minuscule relative to the "treatment-as-usual" control group, which could receive any other housing and community support services.[69]

Research has shown consistently that individuals experiencing homelessness are at a greater risk of various health issues, including chronic medical conditions, mental health disorders, and substance use–related complications.[70] When provided with access to recovery services, individuals with substance use disorders can receive vital support in managing their conditions and achieving sustained recovery. Combining housing options with mental health services and other interventions can produce better outcomes for people who are experiencing homelessness or who are marginally housed. A 2011 meta-study concluded that "coordinated treatment programs for homeless persons with concurrent mental illness and substance misuse issues usually result in better health and access to health care than usual care."[71] Usual care refers to either no intervention or an intervention that is not typical of harm reduction, such as a referral to a social worker.

Addictionologist Drew Pinsky, MD, favors therapeutic harm reduction that "helps people get their lives back," but not by "putting people on medication that keeps them permanently ill."[72] Harm reduction interventions have the potential to reduce the rate of adverse medical events from substance abuse, but not all harm reduction practices include connecting the individual with additional therapeutic help. Failing to do so can undermine an individual's rehabilitation significantly.

Integrated environments of care are needed to optimize harm reduction strategies. Addictions, traumas, and illnesses vary widely. Because of these differences, services such as syringe exchange programs and supervised consumption sites do not fully address the diverse array of obstacles a person may encounter. As Pinsky asserts:

> Four walls is not a treatment for psychiatric illnesses. Any legitimate environment of care always includes the necessary services to manage psychiatric patients. Wraparound services are synonymous with comprehensive psychiatric services, which people don't seem to understand. They include a psychiatrist, a psychologist, a medical doctor, a social worker, a drug counselor, a vocational rehab therapist, and an occupational therapist.[73]

He adds, "There are dedicated services and beds for the homeless left unused and there is plenty of money to provide these services."[74] For harm reduction to be helpful to those experiencing homelessness, those support services must be utilized. Under current approaches, the onus rests largely on individuals to somehow become aware that such services are available and then choose to seek them out and gain access.

Given the fragmented nature of available resources, individuals experiencing homelessness with substance use disorders often face significant barriers when attempting to access recovery services. They must navigate a complex array of services that frequently are spread out across the city and may not be well coordinated. This scenario raises the "transaction costs" associated with seeking recovery services—the various barriers and inconveniences that individuals experiencing homelessness with substance use disorders encounter, including transportation expenses for people who do not have reliable transportation options, time constraints, paperwork burdens, and other logistical obstacles.

Logistical barriers, particularly transportation barriers, can lead to "rescheduled or missed appointments, delayed care, and missed or delayed medication use. These consequences may lead to poorer management of chronic illness and thus poorer health outcomes."[75] Some individuals may require multidimensional support, such as mental health counseling and vocational training; but mental health services, for example, may be located in an entirely different part of the city and siloed from vocational training services. As a consequence, many individuals may be deterred from accessing the support they need. While some programs and services provide transportation, it may not be conveniently available and, again, the onus of taking advantage of this service falls on the individual. To overcome such obstacles, an integrated approach that combines various recovery services under one roof and fosters effective coordination among providers is essential. Programmatic integration would not only streamline access to recovery services but also reduce the burdens on individuals facing homelessness, increasing the likelihood of successful engagement in recovery programs.

A "one-stop shop" model that houses all recovery services under one roof and coordinates recovery strategies in combination with sheltering could offer numerous benefits to homeless individuals with substance use disorders. Such an approach can provide a more user-friendly experience for clients, as it facilitates access to a comprehensive range of services and support at a single location. The potential reduction in transaction costs associated with seeking recovery services is substantial. Moreover, an integrated model encourages a client-centered approach, whereby service providers can collaborate efficiently, share information, and develop personalized recovery plans tailored to each individual's needs.[76] By creating a coordinated network of support, individuals experiencing homelessness can receive more effective and efficient care, leading to more active engagement in recovery programs and greater chances of successful long-term outcomes.

Such a model presents a compelling approach to addressing homelessness and substance abuse, particularly due to its potential to foster experimentation and innovation while providing greater accountability. Given the evolving nature of harm reduction strategies and the uncertainty surrounding their effectiveness in various circumstances, a one-stop shop model allows for flexibility and the exploration of various interventions without being subjected to path dependence for less effective harm reduction strategies, and the model optimizes interventions that are effective. Note that such one-stop facilities need not be publicly funded, though they may house public agencies offering support services. In fact, private or nonprofit management is preferable, as this freedom to control the purse strings without special-interest or other political pressures and motivations provides considerably stronger incentives to maximize efficiency and focus on results-driven approaches. Because they must compete for funding based on demonstrated outcomes, nonprofits are compelled to prioritize effectiveness and continually improve their services, ultimately benefiting individuals by pairing harm reduction strategies with comprehensive recovery programs.

Conclusion

Addiction and recovery specialists generally favor harm reduction strategies—so long as they are employed as means of reducing or eliminating dependence on substances. Although the intentions of harm reduction advocates might be beneficent, the unfolding reality tells a more intricate tale about the results. Such strategies, which might fall under the umbrella of harm reduction, may not be attuned properly to homelessness reduction.

Paired recovery and harm reduction programs ought to be thought of not as binary either-or choices, but rather as parallel and complementary approaches. Some harm reduction interventions may be stopgap measures that prevent, stop, or slow health decline until the person is ready to enter treatment and achieve full recovery. Harm reduction has had notable successes: (1) making available overdose reversal agents; (2) lowering rates of hepatitis C acquisition; (3) lowering net costs compared to equivalent hospital treatment; (4) lowering average cost per individual treatment; (5) decreasing surgical service admissions related to various injection-related infections; and (6) lowering rates of HIV transmission. Harm reduction as practiced within the Housing First approach, however, neglects crucial areas of need. To be an effective means of reducing homelessness, especially among people experiencing chronic homelessness, harm reduction needs to be practiced as its name implies, with the aim of actually reducing the long-term harm of substance use disorders. A comprehensive approach that provides recovery services in addition to shelter will promote well-being and enable individuals to achieve full success as defined in Chapter 1. Programmatic changes are needed because if spending was the solution to homelessness, the problem would have been solved years ago.

6

The Homelessness-Industrial Complex: Spending More but Falling Further Behind

Lawrence J. McQuillan

Homelessness has spawned a vast network of well-intentioned programs that are staffed by sincere individuals who want to solve the problem. While these staffers' hearts may be in the right place, their organizations and bureaucracies have become entrenched interests—a homelessness-industrial complex that too often perpetuates an ineffective status quo. Those experiencing homelessness are not well served, and may even be harmed, by the current strategies and dominant Housing First approach.

It is difficult to know exactly how many agencies, programs, and taxpayer dollars target homelessness, because the programs are overlapping, intersecting, and opaque. Add in other systems, such as police, firefighters, hospitals, courts, emergency medical services, and the like, which expend resources on people experiencing homelessness but cover many other people as well, and the calculus gets even more complicated. A cynic might argue that the lack of transparency is intentional and intended to limit public oversight and provider accountability. Regardless of the motives, a full accounting is impossible. In 2020, then–California Assemblyman David Chiu (D-San Francisco) admitted, "No one today can tell me how much money is being spent on homelessness in California on all levels."[1] Sadly, the relevant information is still lacking today.

This chapter explores spending on homelessness in one key city, San Francisco, to provide a glimpse into the complexities, dollar amounts, and incentives at work. We begin with the tangled web of homelessness spending in San Francisco and then explore spending contributions by the federal government and the State of California that find their way to the City by the Bay. Keep in mind that money spent on homelessness *programs* is not the same as money spent on *people* experiencing homelessness—a crucial distinction—because not all of the money spent "on homelessness" reaches unhoused people.

Spending by the City and County of San Francisco

In most cities and counties nationwide, including San Francisco, services for people experiencing homelessness typically are coordinated by local governments: city and county agencies. In fiscal year 2022–23, the City and County of San Francisco budgeted $672 million for programs specifically targeting individuals experiencing homelessness.[2] (San Francisco's fiscal year runs from July 1 through June 30.) Responsibility for the oversight, coordination, and implementation of those programs falls to the city's Department of Homelessness and Supportive Housing (HSH), which employs a full-time staff of about 100–110 people.[3]

Among its main activities, HSH funds permanent housing, builds and operates shelters, subsidizes rental payments, and, perhaps most important, contracts with external nonprofit service providers. In a press release announcing the launch of HSH in 2016, the office of then-Mayor Ed Lee stated, "Through the provision of coordinated, compassionate, and high-quality services, the Department of Homelessness and Supportive Housing strives to make homelessness in San Francisco rare, brief, and one-time."[4] None of those aspirational goals has been achieved, even though HSH has spent more than $3.3 billion since its inception in 2016.

The black line in the top graph of Figure 9 (see p. 85) shows that HSH spending swelled by 278 percent between fiscal years 2013–14 and 2022–23, from $178 million to $672 million—a staggering increase. Because HSH was launched in 2016, spending amounts before 2016 are estimates prepared by the Mayor's Office based on homelessness programs that existed at the time but were scattered across various city departments.

HSH delivers many of its core services through nonprofit service providers; thus, a large part of HSH's budgeted funds passes through the department to nonprofit suppliers (and to some for-profit companies). For example, in fiscal year 2021–22, 40 percent of HSH's budgeted funds were passed along directly to nonprofit service providers.[5] That percentage has been as high as 85 percent in recent years.[6]

As of January 2023, HSH had awarded more than four hundred active contracts and grants, primarily to nonprofits.[7] The largest contract recipients were the Tenderloin Housing Clinic ($170 million), Episcopal Community Services of San Francisco ($160 million), Five Keys Schools and Programs ($130 million), Bayview Hunters Point Foundation for Community Improvement ($83 million), and Tides Center ($70 million).

Sadly, the *San Francisco Standard* reported that $88 million worth of contracts remaining on HSH's books (as of January 2023) had been awarded to organizations whose nonprofit statuses had been "revoked, suspended, or tagged as delinquent by the state Attorney General's Office," making these organizations ineligible by state law to receive or spend funds.[8] HSH has maintained more contracts with out-of-compliance nonprofits than any other city department, a black eye for the department. Between July 1, 2022, and January 5, 2023, HSH paid $13 million to nonprofits that had lost their good standing with the California attorney general. This lack of oversight is consistent with the findings of a 2020 city audit that "the department [HSH] does not sufficiently monitor provider contracts to ensure service goals are met," nor does it have "documented policies defining program monitoring."[9] In other words, HSH throws money at nonprofits without knowing whether they are achieving performance goals or even whether they are operating lawfully and eligible to receive HSH contracts.

In addition to accessing government programs that specifically target the city's homeless population, people experiencing homelessness in San Francisco also may participate in a number of other, more broad-based programs. For example, San Francisco spends nearly $600 million annually on its Behavioral Health Plan, which offers an array of specialty behavioral health services, including drug treatment programs, for people with few resources. Individuals experiencing homelessness can access those services.[10]

Unhoused individuals likewise may participate in San Francisco's County Adult Assistance Programs (CAAP); CAAP provides cash and other benefits to low-income adults without dependent children (and thus serves as the city's "welfare system" or "General Assistance").[11] The maximum benefit for San

Francisco residents currently is $712 per month, with eligibility renewable every six months.

HSH's spending spiked in FY 2020–21, when it grew to $852 million from $368 million in FY 2019–20; spending then moderated to $672 million in FY 2022–23. The sudden jump was due to two factors. First, tax revenue began to flow into the Our City, Our Home (OCOH) Fund to be spent on homelessness programs, specifically permanent housing, mental health, homelessness prevention, and shelter and hygiene services. In September 2020, the California Supreme Court sided with the 61 percent of San Francisco voters who supported Proposition C, a 2018 measure authorizing the city to impose a gross receipts tax on businesses with annual revenue greater than $50 million for the purpose of funding programs for those experiencing homelessness. At the time, projections were that Proposition C would add another $250–$300 million per year to San Francisco's homelessness programs. Fiscal year 2020–21 was the first year that the new tax revenue could be spent.[12] It was anticipated that 37 percent of annual HSH funding would come from OCOH's revenue stream by fiscal year 2023–24.[13] Second, at the same time, San Francisco (and other cities) began receiving additional money from the state and federal governments to manage the impacts of COVID-19 on the homeless population (see the discussion in the text box, "Project Roomkey: Another Application of Housing First," in Chapter 4).

In reality, the total amount of money spent on homelessness in San Francisco each year might be closer to $1 billion, according to Chris Megison, president and CEO of Solutions for Change, a Southern California nonprofit that works to solve family homelessness. "Add private donations and state and federal funding, and you're probably pushing a billion dollars [a year] spent on homelessness in San Francisco," Megison told the *Marina Times*.[14] By some estimates, the total even *exceeds* $1 billion per year.[15] These estimates, now at least several years old, appear rather conservative today, particularly given the myriad programs across city departments that are accessible to people experiencing homelessness, as well as the large donations from private companies, foundations, and individuals that bypass city coffers and go directly to nonprofits.

According to the *San Francisco Chronicle*, there are approximately one hundred nonprofit groups in the Bay Area that provide services to people experiencing homelessness.[16] Many of these groups receive multimillion-dollar donations from private sources. For example, in 2017, Tipping Point Community, which provides unrestricted funding to Bay Area nonprofits fighting poverty, committed $100 million to an effort to cut in half the number of people experiencing chronic homelessness in San Francisco within five years.[17] (The venture failed to achieve its goal; in fact, chronic homelessness in San Francisco increased by 26 percent from 2017 to 2022.) In 2018, Cisco Systems committed $50 million to fight homelessness in Silicon Valley, while Airbnb pledged $5 million to combat San Francisco's homelessness.[18] In 2019, Airbnb donated $2 million, and Twilio contributed an additional $700,000 to Rising Up, a public–private partnership intended to reduce youth homelessness in San Francisco by 50 percent by 2023 through temporary housing subsidies and job placement services.[19] Rising Up secured $6 million in private funding in 2019.[20] (The effort failed to achieve its goal, as youth homelessness in San Francisco decreased by 3 percent from 2019 to 2023, not by 50 percent.) Also in 2019, YouTube's CEO and Google.org gave a total of $1.35 million to the San Francisco nonprofit Hamilton Families to combat homelessness.[21] The list goes on. The upshot is that HSH controls the bulk of homelessness spending in San Francisco, but not all of it.

Spending Contributions by the Federal Government

Some of the money spent on homelessness in San Francisco comes from the federal government or, more precisely, from federal taxpayers. The primary federal effort for combating homelessness is the Continuum of Care (CoC) Program administered by the US Department of Housing and Urban Development (HUD).

A CoC is a local or regional geographic area within a state where governments and nonprofit organizations coordinate service delivery and funding, with the goal of reducing the area's homeless population. A CoC can be a major city, a city plus its suburbs, a county, a combination of counties, or a combination of cities or towns. The United States has 387 CoCs; 44 of them are located in California.[22] The City and County of San Francisco is its own CoC (designated CA-501). The San Francisco CoC is governed by the Local Homeless Coordinating Board (LHCB), which oversees the federally funded programs there and advises the CoC's designated "lead agency," in this case HSH, to "ensure a unified homeless strategy that is supported by the mayor, the Board of Supervisors, city departments, nonprofit agencies, people who are homeless or formerly homeless, and the community at large."[23] That is a big ask.

In fiscal year 2021–22, HUD allocated $2.8 billion for Continuum of Care Program Competition Awards, which are competitive grants awarded to thousands of local homelessness projects across the country.[24] (The federal government's fiscal year runs from October 1 through September 30.) According to HUD, the awards program is "the largest source of federal grant funding for homeless services and housing programs servicing people experiencing homelessness."[25] Of that $2.8 billion, California's 44 CoCs received a combined total of $526 million to fund 773 homelessness projects. The San Francisco CoC received $51.4 million, which was allocated to forty different homelessness projects.[26] The largest grant was $15 million for rental assistance intended to prevent homelessness.

Since fiscal year 2013–14, annual CoC funding to San Francisco has increased by 126 percent, from $23.5 million to $53 million in fiscal year 2022–23 (HUD grants to San Francisco's CoC are represented by the dark gray line in the top graph of Figure 9 [see p. 85]). HUD grants pass through HSH, the San Francisco CoC's lead agency, to the grant recipients; therefore, the money is included in the city's spending figures discussed earlier in this chapter—a disclaimer to prevent double counting.

In addition, people experiencing homelessness may benefit from other federal programs, many of which also serve the general public. There are *thirty-five* other federal programs that support people experiencing homelessness, according to the US Interagency Council on Homelessness, which coordinates the collective federal response to homelessness.[27] Many of those federal programs have familiar names.

For example, Medicaid (called Medi-Cal in California) provides free or low-cost health care coverage to low-income people of all ages and is funded jointly by the federal government and state governments. Each state operates its own program within federal guidelines, and annual eligibility renewal is required for recipients.

The Supplemental Nutrition Assistance Program (SNAP), known in California as CalFresh (and previously known as the Food Stamp Program), issues monthly electronic debit cards that allow low-income people to buy food.[28] The maximum monthly benefit for an individual currently is $281.[29]

Another program, the Special Supplemental Nutrition Program for Women, Infants, and Children (WIC), provides low-income pregnant women and women with infants or children under five years old with specialized food assistance, counseling, and health care referrals. WIC is federally funded from general revenues. Federal WIC funds are transferred to state health departments, which typically allocate the funds to local WIC clinics. WIC provides a minimal average monthly benefit of about $57 per participant for the food portion of WIC's benefits.[30]

Supplemental Security Income (SSI) provides monthly cash assistance to low-income elderly, blind, or disabled people. Currently, the basic monthly SSI payment for an individual is $943.[31] The SSI program is federally funded from general revenues. Recipients of SSI are automatically eligible for CalFresh food benefits.

Social Security Disability Insurance (SSDI) distributes cash to people who are younger than their full retirement age, have accumulated a sufficient number of work credits, and no longer can support themselves through work due to severe physical or mental impairments. Currently, the average monthly SSDI benefit is $1,538.[32] SSDI is funded by the federal payroll tax. Note that the average benefit from either SSI or SSDI is considerably larger than the maximum CAAP welfare payment, which encourages claims of disability by people experiencing homelessness and by others. The list of alphabet-soup federal programs goes on.

Spending Contributions by the State of California

Finally, much of the money spent on homelessness in San Francisco comes from the state government or, more precisely, from state taxpayers. The light gray line in the top graph of Figure 9 (see p. 85) shows the taxpayer money spent by the State of California on programs for people experiencing homelessness in San Francisco, based on the findings of a 2023 report published by the California Interagency Council on Homelessness (Cal ICH).

The Cal ICH assessment—the most comprehensive examination of state homelessness programs ever conducted by the State of California—identified

Table 3. California State Spending on Homelessness Programs by State Agency and Fiscal Year (in Dollars)

Agency	Total Funding FY 2018–19	Total Funding FY 2019–20	Total Funding FY 2020–21	Total Funding All Years
California Community Colleges Chancellor's Office (CCCCO)	0	9,000,000	9,000,000	18,000,000
California Department of Corrections and Rehabilitation (CDCR)	0	0	5,222,660	5,222,660
California Department of Social Services (CDSS)	150,000,348	268,894,240	205,863,914	624,758,502
California Governor's Office of Emergency Services (Cal OES)	34,974,012	55,492,786	77,359,096	167,825,894
California Housing Finance Agency (Cal HFA)	20,467,800	32,859,565	25,861,291	79,188,656
California Interagency Council on Homelessness (Cal ICH)	500,000,000	750,000,000	300,000,000	1,550,000,000
California Tax Credit Allocation Committee (TCAC)	377,205,008	646,228,768	1,002,606,389	2,026,040,165
Department of Health Care Services (DHCS)	381,978,199	352,228,151	380,769,296	1,114,975,646
Department of Housing and Community Development (HCD)	806,027,537	1,363,280,042	1,842,422,692	4,011,730,271
Total	2,270,652,904	3,477,983,552	3,849,105,338	9,597,741,794

Source: California Interagency Council on Homelessness, *Statewide Homelessness Assessment (July 1, 2018–June 30, 2021): Report to the Legislature,* February 2023, p. 29.

thirty-five state programs that have a "primary focus on providing resources directly to people experiencing or at risk of homelessness" during the three fiscal years running from 2018–19 to 2020–21.[33] (The fiscal year for the State of California runs from July 1 through June 30.)

Table 3 shows that the State of California spent $9.6 billion over three fiscal years on thirty-five homelessness programs administered across nine state agencies—a staggering amount of taxpayer money. Spending grew by 70 percent over just three years, demonstrating the state government's ever-growing desire to intervene in the homelessness crisis. Of the $9.6 billion total, 62 percent went to housing construction, rehabilitation, and preservation, more than six times the amount that went to services for unhoused people.[34]

Several major programmatic developments over this three-year period drove ever-increasing state spending on homelessness. Governor Gavin Newsom signed the fiscal year 2019–20 state budget authorizing a historic $1 billion in new aid to fight homelessness, including $650 million to local governments for emergency aid in the form of the Homeless Housing, Assistance, and Prevention program.[35] These funds were intended to open emergency shelters, build permanent housing, and provide rental assistance.[36]

In July 2019, Newsom created a task force of thirteen "regional leaders and statewide experts"—primarily politicians—to advise his administration on how best to spend money appropriated in the state budget to "combat homelessness."[37]

Despite a slimmer state budget, thought to be needed to plug a projected $54.3 billion budget deficit (owing to the coronavirus outbreak and the government's subsequent shutting down of large swaths of the economy), the fiscal year 2020–21 budget still contained $900 million for homelessness efforts, including $600 million to acquire hotels, motels, and other buildings to house individuals experiencing homelessness (see the "Project Roomkey: Another Application of Housing First" text box in Chapter 4 for more details), and an additional $300 million in general homelessness aid to local governments.[38] Governor Newsom's initial fiscal year 2021–22 budget proposal included $1.75 billion for homelessness initiatives, including an additional $500 million for the Homekey program (which grew out of the Project Roomkey program), $250 million for residential facilities, and $750 million for behavioral health programs.[39] But the budget deficit expected during the coronavirus outbreak did not materialize. In fact, the stock market remained remarkably strong, and in May 2021 Newsom announced a projected budget surplus of $76 billion (covering the 2020–21 and 2021–22 fiscal years).[40] The surplus, combined with an additional $26 billion in federal funds from the American Rescue Plan relief package, prompted Newsom to pursue an even more ambitious—and costly—homelessness agenda.

The state budget Newsom signed in July 2021 contained $12 billion in funding for homelessness programs over the next two years (fiscal years 2021–22 and 2022–23), including $5.8 billion to purchase more hotels and similar properties for permanent housing under the Homekey program, $2 billion in grants to local governments, $1.75 billion for affordable housing construction, and $150 million to stabilize participants in Project Roomkey hotels.[41]

Returning to the 2023 Cal ICH assessment report, the $9.6 billion spent on homelessness programs by the State of California has gone to a wide variety of recipients:

> Cal ICH staff identified 16 different types of recipients that were allocated funding by state homelessness programs. These recipient types include: 44 Continuums of Care (CoCs), 58 Counties, 39 Cities, one City/County [San Francisco], 14 Tribes and Tribally Designated Housing Entities (TDHEs), one County/Tribe (applying jointly), 678 Developers, 189 Providers, 29 Nonprofits, 22 Administrative Entities, 14 Community Colleges, 11 Housing Authorities, one Housing Commission, 66 Sponsors, and 43 Sponsor/Developers. Sponsors and Sponsors/Developers refer to the entities that apply for and are awarded tax credits for the development of affordable housing.[42]

Regarding San Francisco, significant spending assistance provided in 2018 by then-Governor Jerry Brown did not prevent a surge in homelessness.[43] San Francisco received $28 million from Brown's 2018 package of $500 million, titled the Homeless Emergency Aid Program,[44] "designed to provide direct assistance to cities and counties to address the homelessness crisis throughout California."[45] San Francisco also received $1.6 million in 2018 from the $53 million California Emergency Solutions and Housing Program to fund "activities to assist persons experiencing, or at risk of, homelessness."[46]

During the more recent surge in state homelessness spending under Governor Newsom, more than $567 million of the $9.6 billion was funneled to the San Francisco area: $135.8 million in FY 2018–19, $219.7 million in FY 2019–20, and $211.9 million in FY 2020–21, an increase of 56 percent over just three years (see the light gray line in the top graph of Figure 9 on p. 85).[47] As with money from the federal government, state funding sent to San Francisco's HSH is included in the city's figures discussed earlier in this chapter—again, a disclaimer to prevent double counting. Keep in mind that some of that $567 million is in the form of tax credits—often called "tax expenditures"—to local developers that build affordable housing.

In addition to the thirty-five homelessness-specific programs noted in the assessment report, other state government programs support people experiencing homelessness in addition to the broader public. For example, the State Supplementary Payment (SSP) is a state program that gives additional cash to low-income elderly, blind, or disabled people who participate in SSI. Currently, the maximum SSP monthly payment for individuals is $220.[48]

Temporary Assistance for Needy Families (TANF), called CalWORKs in California, is a "welfare-to-work" program. It is federally funded by block grants to states, although states also must kick in funds. Typically operated by county welfare departments, TANF distributes cash to low-income families with children, and it encourages employment, two-parent families, and childbirth after marriage. The median monthly TANF benefit is $498, with time limits on the number of consecutive months an individual may receive assistance as well as a lifetime limit.[49] In fiscal year 2017–18, CalWORKs also set aside $85 million to help prevent homelessness by providing temporary housing, rental assistance, and counseling services.[50]

The basic unemployment insurance (UI) program temporarily replaces about half of a jobless individual's previous wages for up to twenty-six weeks in California, subject to a maximum benefit amount of $450 per week.[51] Employers pay into the system on behalf of their employees.[52] The state operates the program and covers the benefits provided. The federal government, however, also taxes employers to help cover the administration costs of the program and any extended weeks of benefits granted during recessions. States also can borrow from the federal trust fund to cover regular UI obligations.

The Mental Health Services Act (MHSA) is funded by a 1 percent income tax surcharge on personal incomes above $1 million per year. The tax was approved by California voters in 2004 (Proposition 63). Revenue from the tax is distributed monthly to counties for the purpose of funding programs, facilities, and housing that benefit people with mental health issues, including people experiencing homelessness. Table 4 shows that San Francisco has benefited considerably from MHSA's tax transfers, by as much as $60 million in a single fiscal year.

Table 4. Total State Revenue and Transfers to San Francisco from California Mental Health Services Act Taxes, Fiscal Years 2019–23 (in Millions of Dollars)

	FY 2018–19	FY 2019–20	FY 2020–21	FY 2021–22	FY 2022–23
Total Revenue	1,968.5	1,770.3	2,891.7	3,042.6	1,977.5
San Francisco's Share	38.2	35.3	58.1	60.7	39.3

Source: California State Controller, "Mental Health Service Fund," fiscal years 2018–19 through 2022–23, accessed September 23, 2024.

Based on past experience, there is no reason to expect that the massive infusion of new taxpayer money into this alphabet soup of homelessness programs will end—or even slow—the homelessness crisis. On the contrary, evidence suggests that this humanitarian tragedy will only grow, given the current programmatic and policy approaches. This evidence has not stopped California's mayors from going, hat-in-hand, to Sacramento to lobby for more state taxpayer money for their local homelessness programs. In May 2023, the Big City Mayors coalition met with Governor Newsom to demand $2 billion in annual ongoing funding for such programs. The coalition also demanded funding for 2,300 housing units under the Homekey program.[53] In California, it is common for every level of government to blame the other levels of government for failing to do enough to solve homelessness. Not surprisingly, pointing fingers has not solved the problem, nor is it a substitute for effective solutions.

Good Intentions Are Not Enough

The bottom graph in Figure 9 shows that homelessness in San Francisco has increased by 22 percent since fiscal year 2013–14 despite skyrocketing spending (see the top graph of Figure 9). HSH spending increased by 278 percent

The Homelessness-Industrial Complex: Spending More but Falling Further Behind | 85

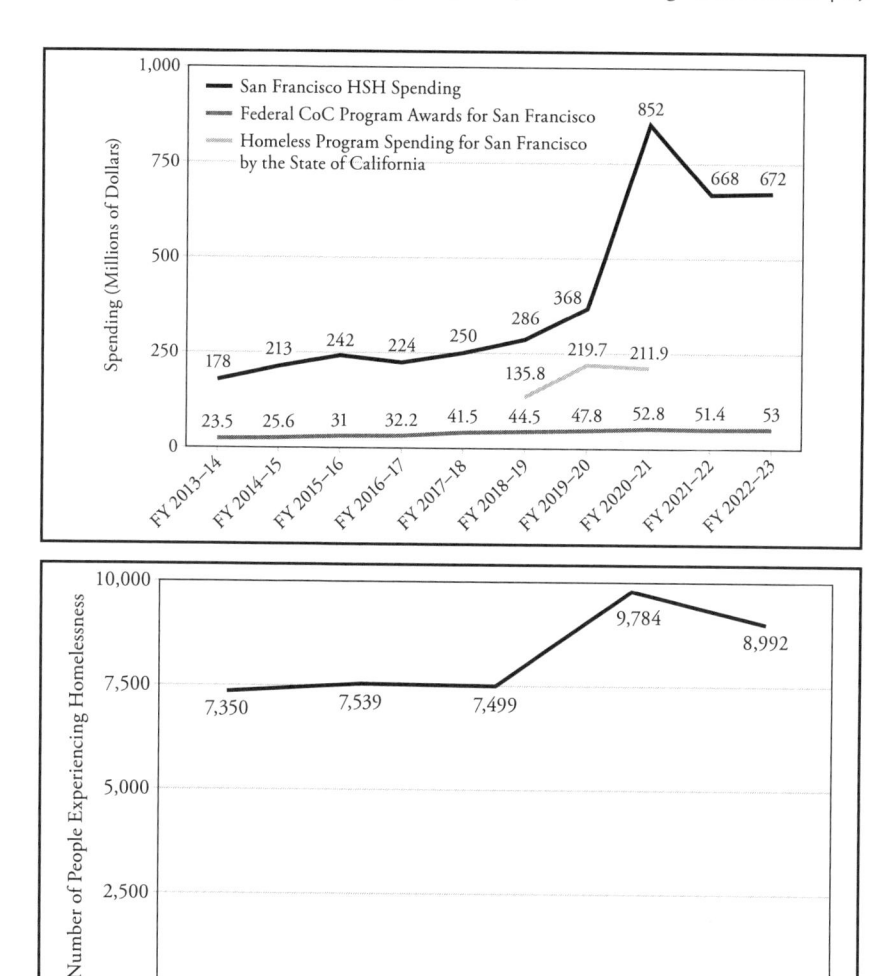

Figure 9. Spending More but Falling Further Behind on San Francisco Homelessness, 2013–23

Notes: (1) The San Francisco Department of Homelessness and Supportive Housing began operations on July 1, 2016. Homelessness spending prior to that date was scattered across various city departments. The spending amounts listed for "HSH" in the years before fiscal year 2016–17 were calculated by the Mayor's Office to present comparable figures over time. (2) HSH spending spiked in fiscal year 2020–21 because that was the first year that "Our City, Our Home" funds for homelessness programs were allocated. The fund was established with the passage of Proposition C in 2018 but could not be distributed sooner due to court challenges. State and federal funds allocated to mitigate the effects of COVID-19 on the homeless population also boosted spending at this time.

Sources: San Francisco Board of Supervisors, Budget and Legislative Analyst's Office, "Performance Audit of the Department of Homelessness and Supportive Housing," August 6, 2020, p. 4 (fiscal year 2013-14), https://sfbos.org/sites/default/files/BLA_Performance_Audit_Homelessness_%26_Supportive_Housing_080620.pdf; San Francisco Department of Homelessness and Supportive Housing, "Historic Spending on Homeless Services in San Francisco," fiscal years 2014-15 and 2015-16, accessed February 20, 2020, https://web.archive.org/web/20200220115945/http://hsh.sfgov.org/overview/budget/; San Francisco Department of Homelessness and Supportive Housing, "HSH Budget," fiscal years 2016-17 through 2022-23, accessed March 19, 2024, https://hsh.sfgov.org/about/budget/; Heather Knight, "What It Really Costs to Help the Homeless. And How Businesses Can Do More," *San Francisco Chronicle*, August 24, 2018, https://www.sfchronicle.com/bayarea/heatherknight/article/Businesses-must-contribute-more-to-city-s-13178743.php; San Francisco Department of Homelessness and Supportive Housing, *Fiscal Year 2019-20 and 2020-21 Budget, Local Homeless Coordinating Board*, July 1, 2019, https://hsh.sfgov.org/wp-content/uploads/2019/07/2019-HSH-Budget-Presentation-for-LHCB_07.01.19.pdf; US Department of Housing and Urban Development, HUD Exchange, "CoC Award Summary Reports by Component and Program Type," CA-501: San Francisco CoC (2013-22 reports), https://www.hudexchange.info/programs/coc/awards-by-component/?filter_Year=&filter_Scope=CoC&filter_State=CA&filter_CoC=CA-501&program=CoC&group=AwardComp; US Department of Housing and Urban Development, HUD Exchange, "Fiscal Year 2019 Continuum of Care Competition Grants: Homeless Assistance Award Report," CA-501: San Francisco CoC, https://files.hudexchange.info/resources/documents/2019-california-coc-grants.pdf; California Legislative Analyst's Office, "The 2015-16 Budget: California Budget Plan," October 19, 2015, https://lao.ca.gov/Publications/Report/3302; Liam Dillon, "Billions of Dollars to Help California's Homeless Population Are Piling Up—and Going Unspent," *Los Angeles Times*, March 25, 2018, https://www.latimes.com/politics/la-pol-ca-slow-homelessness-spending-20180325-story.html; Benjamin Oreskes, "Even If California Spends Millions More on Homelessness, Here's Why Few Will Notice," *Los Angeles Times*, May 24, 2019, https://www.latimes.com/local/lanow/la-me-ln-state-homeless-count-newsom-housing-funding-grants-20190524-story.html; Office of Governor Gavin Newsom, "Building Off Historic Investment and Action to Help Cities and Counties Tackle Homelessness, Governor Newsom Signs Series of Bills Addressing Homelessness," September 26, 2019, https://www.gov.ca.gov/2019/09/26/building-off-historic-investment-action-to-help-cities-and-counties-tackle-homelessness-governor-newsom-signs-series-of-bills-addressing-homelessness/; Kate Eby, "History of How Many People Are Homeless in the Bay Area," ABC7News.com, August 13, 2019, https://abc7news.com/5260657/; Severin Campbell, *Performance Audit of the Department of Homelessness and Supportive Housing*, prepared for the Board of Supervisors of the City and County of San Francisco by the San Francisco Budget and Legislative Analyst, August 6, 2020, p. 4, https://sfbos.org/sites/default/files/BLA_Performance_Audit_Homelessness_%26_Supportive_Housing_080620.pdf; Applied Survey Research, *San Francisco Homeless Count and Survey: 2022 Comprehensive Report*, San Francisco Department of Homelessness and Supportive Housing, August 19, 2022, p. 14, https://hsh.sfgov.org/wp-content/uploads/2022/08/2022-PIT-Count-Report-San-Francisco-Updated-8.19.22.pdf; Kevin Fagan and Mallory Moench, "New Data Shows 20,000 People Will Be Homeless in San Francisco This Year," *San Francisco Chronicle*, August 18, 2022, https://www.sfchronicle.com/sf/article/san-francisco-homeless-population-17380942.php; and California Interagency Council on Homelessness, *Statewide Homelessness Assessment (July 1, 2018–June 30, 2021): Report to the Legislature*, February 2023, p. 180, https://bcsh.ca.gov/calich/documents/homelessness_assessment.pdf.

during the same period, while federal contributions to San Francisco's CoC increased by 126 percent.

Similarly, the State of California's homelessness spending for San Francisco increased by 70 percent during the shorter sample period covered by the 2023 Cal ICH assessment report of FY 2018–19 through FY 2020–21, while San Francisco's share of state spending increased by 56 percent. Yet San Francisco's homeless population increased by 30 percent during this same period. Over a longer period of five fiscal years, 2018–19 through 2022–23, the California state government allocated nearly $24 billion total for homelessness and housing programs, yet homelessness increased statewide by 40 percent during this same period.[54]

Surely, nobody can claim with a straight face that homelessness has increased in San Francisco and across California because of a lack of resources or a lack of awareness of the problem. It is more plausible that homelessness increased because increased government spending subsidized counterproductive behaviors and sustained programs that did not address effectively and efficiently the root causes of homelessness. We must stop measuring success by dollars spent; otherwise, we will continue to spend more while falling further behind.

Proponents of the existing government-dominated Housing First approach will say that more time or more funding is needed before others pass judgment. But proponents have been saying the same things for years, and despite being given significantly more money over the past ten years, the problem has only escalated in San Francisco and across California.

In San Francisco's five-year strategic plan update on homelessness, published in 2019, the city announced a number of specific goals, including

- reducing chronic homelessness by 50 percent by December 2022;
- ending family homelessness by December 2022;
- reducing youth homelessness by 50 percent by December 2022; and
- ending large, long-term encampments for those experiencing homelessness by July 2019.[55]

Yet today in San Francisco, hundreds of encampments thrive, thousands of people remain chronically homeless and the total is increasing, and hundreds of families with children still experience homelessness and the total has surged. Whenever the city misses a homelessness benchmark deadline like those above, which occurs regularly, officials simply extend the target date and throw more money at the problem; there is no accountability for failure.

Continually, government initiatives are being created, and more taxpayer money is being spent, yet the problem escalates. The logical conclusion is that ineffectiveness is the result of design problems, not awareness problems or money problems. Indeed, the State Auditor's office described California's efforts to combat homelessness as "uncoordinated" and "disjointed" in a February 2021 report.[56] And a subsequent report, in April 2024, criticized the state for not even effectively tracking whether the billions of dollars it spent to try to prevent and end homelessness were actually helping to achieve those goals.[57]

The failure to adequately address homelessness is not due to a lack of government programs or inadequate taxpayer funding. Governments keep spending more to address the crisis, and the crisis keeps getting worse. Rather, failure is due to (1) faulty public policies regarding homelessness and (2) flawed programmatic designs characterized by mistaken priorities and little effective oversight and accountability. Governments across California are spending record amounts of taxpayer dollars on such programs, yet homelessness continues to thrive, along with its accompanying quality-of-life problems. We are only falling further behind.

A large and tangled web of government agencies, nonprofit service providers, charitable foundations, and government spending programs all share the goal of "ending homelessness." Unfortunately, these programs often fail to provide successful interventions for people who already are experiencing homelessness or to adequately address the factors that lead to homelessness, especially substance abuse, mental health issues, and a lack of affordable housing.

The current approach fails to tackle the problem successfully, and it offers perverse incentives to service providers. The more that programs fail, the more taxpayer money is poured into them. Organizations receive more money and power when the problem grows. As Chris Megison of Solutions for Change contends, based on San Francisco's experience and the enormous amounts of money dedicated to the problem, "There shouldn't be a single person left in that city [San Francisco] who says [reducing homelessness is] about more money."[58] Some commentators argue, in fact, that government money exacerbates the problem by subsidizing counterproductive behaviors among certain segments of the homeless population (see Chapters 3–5) and by attempting to treat the symptoms of homelessness, rather than addressing its underlying behavioral causes effectively. The best hope for many people experiencing homelessness is for "management" of the crisis to evolve beyond the failed one-size-fits-all Housing First model of government-centered control to alternative approaches with better success rates.

San Francisco is, of course, just one city in California. Homeless encampments also continue to thrive in Los Angeles, Oakland, Sacramento, and San Jose, despite new government initiatives. We can add to those urban areas the dozens of counties and hundreds of towns and cities across the state that operate homelessness programs to arrive at the true financial toll. That is only part of the story, however. An even larger toll is paid by communities that endure the negative quality-of-life consequences of homelessness and by the individuals experiencing homelessness themselves, who continue to suffer trauma, despair, and unfulfilled potential. Billions of dollars have been spent on well-intentioned programs staffed by sincere individuals, yet homelessness has only gotten worse. The dominant Housing First approach has proved itself incapable of solving all manner of problems for everyone experiencing homelessness.

It is time to implement and scale up alternative designs based on successful, innovative approaches to better address homelessness in the San Francisco Bay Area, across California, and throughout the United States.

7

Alternative Models: Improving Outcomes with Housing Readiness

Scott Beyer and Christopher J. Calton

As DISCUSSED PREVIOUSLY, two main models are used to address homelessness: Housing First, which prioritizes permanent supportive housing, and housing readiness, which focuses more on transitional/transformational housing. This chapter takes a closer look at the housing readiness model and some of the organizations that have been implementing it successfully, as well as one provider that felt compelled to change its successful housing readiness program as a result of governmental Housing First diktats.

Although Housing First programs often fail to remedy the underlying causes of homelessness, such as addiction and mental illness, housing readiness works from the premise that people experiencing homelessness have far greater potentials. Housing readiness facilities adopt multiphase processes intended to help participants gain greater personal responsibility and reach their full success.

Upon beginning a housing readiness program, participants typically receive on-campus temporary housing and are enrolled in programs designed to help them recover from addictions, prepare for employment, and acquire basic life skills. As participants progress, they will find employment and move to off-site transitional housing. Once they have graduated and attained stable financial footing, they will move into more permanent housing. To its critics, the downside of housing readiness is that it imposes barriers to entry, such as sobriety requirements, and "cherry-picks" people who are already willing to help themselves. But such programs have proved to be quite effective at transforming people's lives and preventing them from becoming perpetual taxpayer dependents. The following are just a few successful examples, both in California and across the country.

Haven for Hope

One of the most successful—and comprehensive—programs in the country for people experiencing homelessness is Haven for Hope in San Antonio, Texas. This twenty-two-acre megafacility for people experiencing homelessness is often compared to a college campus. Its roots go back to 2005, when founder William Greehey, who also was the founding CEO and chairman of Valero Energy Corporation, sought to discover the best practices utilized by transformational programs across the country and establish a "one-stop shop" to provide personalized services for people experiencing homelessness. Greehey then raised more than $101 million—approximately 60 percent of which came from the private sector—to build the campus.[1]

Haven for Hope has modified its approach somewhat over the years, adopting what David Huete, vice president of transformational services, calls "a true trauma-informed" plan that serves individuals on a case-by-case basis.[2] While Haven for Hope maintains a transitional, goals-based orientation, it does not apply the same measures to all clients, in contrast to Housing First models. Its personalized approach grew out of experimentation with serving new clients, such as prisoners.

Haven's prison outreach program, which is relatively new, is tailored for people experiencing homelessness who have been arrested for crimes such as public substance abuse. The program assists individuals with high recidivism rates and involves staff members who have been imprisoned themselves. "Many of the individuals that are referred to us by the county have over 50 arrests a year," Huete noted. Inmates are sent to Haven for Hope directly after being released from jail and get help finding housing and counseling on how to avoid jail reentry. "It's transformative for them to come into a stable shelter situation," Huete said.[3]

Haven for Hope also offers specific programs for specific populations, such as veterans and single mothers. "There's a lot of on-ramps to homelessness," Huete added, "and at Haven, we like to have a lot of off-ramps . . . [providing] a buffet of services."[4]

Although Haven for Hope is primarily a transformational facility, it incorporates a low-barrier emergency shelter known as the Courtyard. Also known as the South Campus, the Courtyard is a covered outdoor area with attached secure indoor sleeping areas. The facility also offers three hot meals a day, showers, restrooms, storage lockers, laundry facilities, mail service, and outreach services including peer support, case management, housing navigation, and medical and mental health services. In recent years, Haven for Hope has expanded its services to include an acute care clinic, substance abuse recovery services, ID recovery assistance, job coaching and placement, financial sustainability counseling, and benefits assistance.[5] This facility alone has dramatically reduced the nighttime presence of people experiencing homelessness throughout downtown San Antonio.

Those staying in the Courtyard are urged to commit to recovery and enter Haven for Hope's Transformational Campus, which offers long-term housing with no time limits and individualized supportive services for addiction recovery, education, life skills, and employment. The Transformational Campus also offers childcare, legal services, health and mental health care, and animal kennels.

Haven for Hope's ultimate goal is for its clients to exit homelessness and leave the campus. To aid in this effort, the organization partners with a network of third-party service providers outside of the central facility who offer transitional housing, supportive housing, and more. Haven for Hope has 51 campus partners (30 with designated spaces), 30 referral partners, and 7 community partners, or a total of 88 partners.[6] Since 2010, more than 7,000 people have exited the Transformational Campus to find permanent housing, with 91 percent remaining stable and not returning to homelessness after one year. Approximately 1,700 individuals now live at the Transformational Campus and the Courtyard, working to make the shift to a self-supporting lifestyle.

Haven for Hope's private sector–led model has provided greater incentives and opportunities to pursue strategies that improve the organization's efficiency. One of these strategies is to ensure accountability for the third-party service providers on which it relies, a feature that often is lacking in the awarding and continuation of government grants by public sector agencies.

"We did end relationships with poor performing organizations," said Scott Ackerson, a licensed master social worker (LMSW) and Haven for Hope's former vice president of strategic relationships, who continues to work with the organization as a consultant. "We also put a stipulation into our [memoranda of understanding] with partners that they were required to follow principles of evidence-based practices adopted by Haven to provide services as a formal partner of Haven."[7]

A study of Haven for Hope's practices commissioned by the Kronkosky Charitable Foundation found that from 2007 through 2019 the organization generated net benefits to the community in the range of $2.9 billion to $8.3 billion, with an average of $5.6 billion, translating to $29 in benefits for every dollar spent.[8] In addition to the value of providing services such as housing and health care, the study estimated that Haven for Hope produced $142 million in benefits from reduced criminal activity and that children served by Haven for Hope programs would realize an additional $89 million in lifetime earnings (along with additional beneficial ripple effects for the broader economy) because they would avoid disruptions from bouncing repeatedly from school to school, thereby enhancing their educational outcomes and improving their earning potential.[9] The study also noted that, as of 2019, Haven for Hope had not evicted any clients from the facility.[10]

Haven for Hope also has realized significant efficiencies from its systems-based colocation model, under which its 285,000-square-foot facility serves as a home for multiple service providers who share space on the campus. According to Katherine Gonzalez, who conducted her doctoral research on Haven for Hope, this integrated system is the foundation of the organization's success. Other cities that wish to replicate Haven for Hope's model may not have enough land available for a twenty-two-acre campus, she notes, but they can still adopt its method of coordinating the work of different nonprofit organizations and government agencies to collaborate efficiently in serving the needs of the homeless population.

"Haven's role as a system coordinator provided the platform necessary to spark innovation," Gonzalez explained.[11] The health care services available to Haven for Hope's residents illustrate what these innovations can look like.

Between April 2015 and March 2016, Haven for Hope was the largest source of medical 911 calls in San Antonio, causing the fire department to form a "terrible impression" of the campus, according to one Haven for Hope staffer: "The fire department didn't care that the call was made, but they cared that the fire truck and an ambulance would make it all the way here, and then they would have to go to the hospital, taking them out of the community for other response."[12]

To ease the strain on emergency resources, Haven for Hope partnered with Southwest Texas Regional Advisory Council (STRAC), a unit of the Department of State Health Services, to open an acute care station on the campus. The station is staffed seven days a week by rotating paramedics who operate a mobile integrated health unit to respond to emergency medical calls from Haven for Hope residents. The on-site paramedics are better able to triage patients, treating the less urgent cases at the scene or providing patients with taxi vouchers to hospitals or referrals to be seen at primary care clinics the next day. In 2017, before the initiative took effect, 70 percent of emergency calls originating from Haven for Hope resulted in ambulance transports to downtown hospitals; in 2018, after the mobile health unit was implemented, the transport rate for Haven for Hope emergency calls had been reduced to just 17 percent. With the cost of a single ambulance transport and emergency room visit amounting to $900 and $1,000, respectively, the collaboration between Haven for Hope and STRAC saved the city more than $665,000 in 2018 alone.[13]

Cooperation between Haven for Hope and the San Antonio Police Department likewise has helped to reduce the burden on county jails. In most places, explained Ackerson, any conflict between a homeless individual and law enforcement officers ends with the police dropping the person off at some random shelter with a spare bed—or putting them in jail. But in San Antonio, officers know to transport cooperative individuals to Haven for Hope. Once there, clients can shift to whichever campus program they need. This option helps to avoid the burden of lugging themselves and their belongings to multiple locations.

For providers, Haven for Hope offers the benefit of centralization within one facility. If San Antonio's homeless service infrastructure were dispersed across dozens of buildings—a common scenario in other US cities—dozens of organizations would have to engage in site selection, lease or purchase agreements, maintenance, and other legal matters. Haven for Hope prevents such duplication by making space for third-party providers on its own campus, thereby both increasing convenience for clients and reducing costs for service providers.

The colocated agencies at Haven for Hope usually pay $1,200 annually to access Haven for Hope's office space, internet, parking, and other operational amenities. Colocation means that many providers, from a local mental health service agency to an LGBTQ youth homeless shelter, can operate what is effectively their organizational headquarters at Haven for Hope.

Having multiple specialists at one site enables cross-collaboration, which has improved practitioner training, trauma-informed care, and client caseload management. Colocation also reduces transaction costs by connecting clients to providers more efficiently and providing a single-entry portal for accessing multiple services.

Contrast the efficiency and cost savings that Haven for Hope has delivered to San Antonio with New York City, where the absence of coordination among mental health providers has been found to produce suboptimal homeless care,[14] or with California cities such as Los Angeles and San Francisco, where single-room occupancy (SRO) units and other supportive housing formats have flooded certain areas with crime and the units can be miles from needed health care providers.[15] The latter problem seems innate to the Housing First model, because it is impossible to provide proper security and treatment when untreated people experiencing homelessness are scattered in rooms and buildings all around town, rather than concentrated in a single campus.

Ackerson said that Haven for Hope's expansive colocation model was inspired by Father Joe's Villages, a 2,000-person campus in San Diego. The Salvation Army is also looking to begin using such a model, with a planned 20-acre, $95 million campus in Dallas capable of housing 600 people, including 150 emergency shelter beds, 150 beds for its substance abuse treatment program, 250 transitional housing units, and 20 apartments for families.[16]

As illustrated above, Haven for Hope has made the most of its economies of scale to effectively and efficiently improve the lives not only of people experiencing homelessness who use its services but also of others living in the surrounding community. Haven's model could—and should—be replicated in many other cities across the country.

Step Denver

Step Denver may be one of the better-known housing readiness organizations because of its history and longtime former leader. Step 13 Evolution Process (later renamed) opened in Denver, Colorado, in 1983 with the mission of helping men experiencing homelessness overcome addiction. Its executive director was Bob Coté, who once was an alcoholic himself (and one of Step 13's original residents)[17] but fought through to recovery on his own willpower. He believed that others could do the same.

Coté developed messaging for Step Denver that was both philosophically conservative and critical of other groups providing services to individuals experiencing homelessness. Back then, providers were (as many are now) more likely to enable people's addictions than to help them recover. Coté's answer for addicted men was simple: overcome substance abuse, as he had, by getting a job. This tough-love approach helped thousands of men and won Coté accolades from think tanks and politicians, including George H. W. Bush, who as president honored Coté.[18] But by the time Coté died in 2013, his strategy had become somewhat antiquated.

New research had surfaced about addiction, which by then was understood to be a disease that could be tackled not just by willpower but through specific medical interventions and counseling. After discussing a new direction, Step Denver's board agreed to roll out programs that mixed Coté's gospel of self-reliance with a scientific approach and hired Paul Scudo as the organization's new executive director.

Step Denver has found great success with this hybrid approach. It starts when local men experiencing homelessness are referred to Step Denver by probation officers, correctional facilities, shelters, or word of mouth. On day one of entry, participants sign contracts stating that, in exchange for accessing Step Denver's resources, they will live their lives based on the "Four Pillars" of sobriety, work, accountability, and community.[19] During week one, participants meet with a peer recovery coach, get job training, and become in-house custodians (to redevelop their work ethic). Beginning the following week, they are expected to seek employment. All men must leave Step Denver's facility each morning by 7:30 a.m. to work at a job or look for one. They are not allowed to return until 4:30 p.m. and must be back no later than 6:45 p.m. because nightly programs start at 7:00 p.m. The programs include addiction recovery talks, peer meetings, further job training, and sessions that teach family values, personal finance, and physical health.

Once participants begin receiving money from their jobs, they pay Step Denver $250 per month for continued room and board. "That doesn't even scratch the surface of our costs," says Scudo. "That's more about the accountability piece of our program—having the individual relearn that they have to pay for where they live."[20]

Participants stay in Step Denver's primary facility for six months, then transfer to sober-living homes off-site for their final eighteen months in the program. When they graduate and reenter society after those twenty-four months, they must have full-time jobs and be completely self-supporting—receiving no money from family, church, or government.

"You're required to be personally responsible for your choices, your actions, your behaviors, and your outcomes. And you cannot blame or make excuses any longer," says Scudo.[21]

Step Denver has used its hybrid model for eight years. The organization serves 275 men annually, on average, and boasts an impressive graduation rate of 70 percent. Once participants have become alumni, many of them return to help Step Denver's new entrants. In all, Step Denver transforms nearly 200 men annually who otherwise would be on the streets, in jail, or in dysfunctional, dependent relationships. Moreover, Step Denver achieves all of its success without any government funding. The organization's budget is financed entirely by individual contributions and private and nonprofit foundations.

Union Rescue Mission

Union Rescue Mission (URM), located in the middle of downtown Los Angeles's Skid Row community, is perhaps the nation's largest emergency shelter. Founded in 1891, the faith-based organization has been dedicated to feeding "both the body and the soul" of homeless individuals and families for more than 130 years.[22]

To Reverend Andy Bales, who led the organization from 2005 through 2023, URM's raison d'être never could be fulfilled under the Housing First model. "Shelter alone would mean the mere warehousing of precious human beings made in the image of God," the reverend said in 2009, offering a lonely voice against the Housing First initiatives that were spreading through California. Under Bales's leadership, URM remained committed to providing a "continuum of housing within the much needed continuum of care."[23]

URM's "continuum" of services might be likened to a stairway that residents climb toward self-sufficiency. The stairway begins with the provision of temporary emergency shelter and services to meet each person's most pressing needs, such as food, clothing, and medical care. These emergency services offer a doorway for a number of transitional services.

Single men can enroll in URM's long-term transformational program, which requires participants to complete an intensive one-year training program. "These men attend hundreds of programming hours," Bales explains, including "classes on relationships, overcoming addictions, anger management, Bible study; hours in our Learning Center; in physical education; in work therapy and volunteering through the Mission."[24] URM's commitment to individual development recognizes the psychological value of fostering a sense of accomplishment, with graduates donning caps and gowns to mark their successful completion of the demanding curriculum.

The next step on the stairway is a six-month apprenticeship program, in which participants remain at the mission while employed or attending school. The transformation ends with a three-month transitional-living period while graduates seek permanent employment and independent housing. The transformational program shepherds hundreds of men to independent living every year.

Single women with children can participate in a similar program at URM's Hope Gardens Family Center, where they enjoy refuge from the dangers of Skid Row. In addition to educational and rehabilitation services, the center offers childcare and youth development activities that include tutoring, mentoring, leadership training, and recreational events. The center also is home to a permanent community of single, elderly women. For families that include fathers, the Angeles House offers comparable services with the requirement that families save 30 percent of their incomes to facilitate their transition to permanent housing.

For individuals who are unwilling or unable to commit to the intensive transformational program, Bales launched the Gateway Project in 2011. Under this initiative, men and women who utilize emergency services are given the opportunity to receive ongoing shelter and services for $5 per day. The purpose behind these modest fees, which fall far short of covering the costs of the services provided, is not to generate revenue, but to imbue residents with a sense of responsibility and self-empowerment. "Men and women who contribute to their own well-being gain a greater sense of control over their circumstances, as well as a greater confidence that they can overcome their present circumstances," the organization asserts.[25]

The common theme that unites the variety of URM's programs is the belief that the transition from homelessness to sustainable self-sufficiency requires a holistic approach that addresses the needs of the mind, body, and spirit together. This approach contrasts starkly with Housing First, which Bales believes nurtures permanent dependence—or, as he describes it, "survival and subsidy."

Because government grants for homelessness services require organizations to adopt the Housing First model, Bales's refusal to compromise URM's mission has left the organization entirely cut off from taxpayer support. "We're completely privately funded," Bales explained during an interview in 2023. "We don't take any federal, state, or local funding because, if we did, we couldn't focus on recovery and sobriety and safety and peace."[26]

For an organization with annual operating expenses topping $45 million, the refusal of taxpayer-financed subsidies is astonishing, but the reverend recognizes that URM's unwavering commitment to providing services that produce long-term results is precisely what attracts private donors. "When people hear that somebody is going to turn their life around, they get excited and they support us," he explains, adding that "people aren't excited about paying tax dollars to sustain somebody in a tax dollar situation that's unsustainable, that costs too much to do, and then leaves them in a perpetual victimhood."[27]

The Salvation Army

The Salvation Army operates a national network of Adult Rehabilitation Centers (ARCs). Each year, the facilities help more than 150,000 people combat addiction, restore their families, and build their work and social skills. ARCs accept homeless and non-homeless people. Like those at Union Rescue Mission, the services are faith-based, as caseworkers rely on the Christian faith to help people find purpose beyond drugs and alcohol. Accordingly, the centers do not rely on government funding.[28] Instead, they leverage private donations and sales from Salvation Army thrift stores, which employ people participating in the rehab programs. The Salvation Army also operates homeless shelters that are not explicitly faith-based.

The Salvation Army is merely one of the better-known of many faith-based organizations that serve individuals experiencing homelessness, including Catholic Charities, Jewish Family Service, ICNA Relief (a faith-based Muslim group), and the Deseret Industries thrift shops of the Church of Jesus Christ of Latter-day Saints. According to researchers from the Baylor Institute for Studies of Religion, such faith-based organizations account for a majority of emergency shelter beds in some cities.[29]

Major experimentation often takes place in the faith-based facilities—a real marketplace for service delivery—given that they follow their own methods and beliefs, rather than top-down government protocols. The Baylor study estimated that these housing readiness–style, faith-based organizations generate $119 million in taxpayer savings over the first three years after program participants graduate.[30]

Solutions for Change

California has the largest crisis in the country in terms of the sheer magnitude of individuals experiencing homelessness. So it is perhaps fitting that a fully developed housing readiness model has arisen there, in the form of Solutions for Change. The state government's decision to support the Housing First approach exclusively would end up harming the organization, however, making Solutions for Change's experience a cautionary tale about accepting government funding—and the strings that come attached to it.

Based in San Diego County, Solutions for Change was founded in 1999 by Chris and Tammy Megison, a couple dedicated to social entrepreneurship who wanted to end family homelessness. The focus of the organization's treatment is on housing families, with the most common participants being single mothers with children. Solutions for Change's operations are similar to Step Denver's, despite its focus on families, rather than men only.

Solutions for Change originally was based on a 1,000-day "empowerment academy" known as Solutions University, which requires that participants sober up and find jobs. During the first 150 days, participants live on-site and take part in a life training program that teaches them skills such as how to market themselves to employers, raise a family, and overcome addictions. During the next 150 to 200 days, participants work full-time while still living on campus and paying 30 percent of their incomes in rent. For the remainder of the program, they live off campus in Solutions for Change's transitional housing. When the 1,000 days end—or often before then—participants are expected to find their own housing and become self-supporting. In five years, Solutions University has graduated roughly 800 families, positively affecting the lives of between 2,500 and 3,000 people. The recidivism rate for drug use among participants who complete the program is just 7 percent, compared with 74 percent for similar local organizations.[31] "We are recidivism busters," says Chris Megison.[32]

Solutions for Change has achieved its positive results on a $6 million annual budget, $100,000 of which comes from San Diego County, with the remainder being raised from foundations, individual donors, and private revenue streams. The ability to help so many people so effectively on such a modest budget is impressive. Megison offers three key reasons for Solutions for Change's successes.[33]

First, Solutions for Change taps an active alumni network for its Solutions University—including "alumni" who technically still are enrolled in the thousand-day program. Once participants graduate from the campus facility to transitional housing, they return to help with new entrants. These returning alumni not only allow Solutions for Change to operate with fewer full-time staff members, but also help to build the community orientation needed to stave off recidivism. Alumni know that they are accountable to both the people who got them through the program in the first place and the new entrants, who are relying on them to be that same pillar of stability.

Second, Solutions for Change runs Solutions Farms, one of the largest aquaponics operations in the western United States. Although most Solutions University participants find outside employment during their thousand days in the program, others work on the farm. The revenue from selling the water-grown produce is used to underwrite operations elsewhere in the program.

Third, Solutions for Change operates Solutions in the Community, a real estate arm that builds affordable housing for participants. Those units house participants during the transitional stage, while at the same time generating another revenue stream for funding the organization's operations. Unlike Step Denver, whose leaders feel that the organization does not have the bandwidth necessary to scale up, leaders at Solutions for Change want to expand beyond

San Diego County. In early 2019, Megison told *World* magazine that he is working to build facilities in ten different communities.[34]

Funding Issues

A common feature of most of the housing readiness programs described above is that they receive little, if any, money from taxpayers. The reason for this funding model, as Solutions for Change would come to discover, is that along with taxpayer support come bureaucratic rules and political priorities that may not align with and may even be counterproductive to its recipients' aims.

Dating back to the George W. Bush administration, Housing First has been the federal government's model of choice for homelessness services provision. But the federal government has embraced the principle so dogmatically that it has excluded experimentation with potentially more successful alternatives. Just ask Megison. He refused the government's mandate to suspend work and sobriety requirements as conditions for participant entry, because doing so would contradict Solutions for Change's approach to homelessness. Megison also did not want new tenants openly using drugs on campus around the mothers and children living there, calling that idea "insane."[35]

As a result, Solutions for Change sacrificed $600,000 a year in federal funding. Megison thought that eschewing federal grants with such strings would be enough. But then San Diego County informed him that some of the residents' participation in Solutions University, with its drug-testing requirements, violated state and federal Housing First mandates. It turned out that some Solutions for Change residents at one of the organization's permanent supportive housing facilities received federal Housing Choice Voucher Program (also known as Section 8) rent subsidies, which triggered the Housing First requirements. As a result, the funding for those housing units would be lost.[36] Although the rent subsidies for existing beneficiaries were not withdrawn, the county refused to issue vouchers for the property's new residents.

The decision affected only one of the buildings owned by the organization, but Megison realized that disputes over Housing First's regulations would be an ongoing issue. So, after fighting with the government for about a year and a half, Solutions for Change made the difficult decision to end its mandatory Solutions University program, the cornerstone of its rehabilitative programming for participants living in permanent supportive housing, although services continue to be offered on a voluntary basis.

"There are more than enough residents who are disappointed that the units will no longer be a part of the program," Solutions University graduate Christa Medeiros, who later was hired by Solutions for Change as an empowerment coach for residents, told the *San Diego Union-Tribune*. Medeiros added that addiction had been the root cause of her own homelessness and that while in the program she would not have been comfortable living next to someone who was still using drugs.[37]

The exclusive government focus on Housing First, including its prohibition on mandatory drug testing, contains "a strong bias against accountability," Megison said. "We're still fighting to keep them sober, but we don't have all our weapons, those tools," he added. "The state has stripped the ability of management to keep these places from becoming taxpayer-funded drug housing."[38]

The *San Diego Union-Tribune* article contrasted Solutions for Change's situation with the San Diego Rescue Mission, another local organization dedicated to addressing homelessness. The Rescue Mission offers a year-long residential program called Mission Academy. The organization is allowed to require participants to attend classes and be tested for drugs because it does not accept any government funding.[39]

Solutions for Change has not been forced to end its programming completely, however. It continues to operate a revised Solutions Academy at its transitional housing facility on the main campus, which does not have the same government funding problems as do its permanent supportive housing facilities. Because transitional housing generally is limited by law to two years, Solutions Academy now runs for seven hundred days. In addition, the organization has modified transitional housing to on-campus housing. The program continues its vocational focus and retains its drug-testing and class participation requirements.

Megison came away from the experience with an understanding of the deep flaws in the federal Housing First approach. He calls many of the participants in his program "Housing First refugees," who have described fleeing horrible conditions at Housing First facilities.[40] Moreover, Megison compares the Housing First approach to a hospital that treats broken legs by administering painkillers rather than resetting bones.[41]

"We [at Solutions for Change] see homelessness as a symptom," Megison said in an interview. "For the vast majority of people who become homeless, it's a consequence of other things that happened to them. So, whereas the government has gone all in on treating homelessness with housing, we see that as treating the symptoms of the underlying problem.... The government has created a multibillion-dollar symptom relief model."[42]

Both Megison and Paul Scudo of Step Denver believe that their programs, in contrast to Housing First, address the problems underlying homelessness. The people who enter their programs actually want to improve themselves and are given access to the resources and community support necessary to do so, in order that they may emerge from homelessness through the strength of their own efforts. Those two programs enable hundreds of people each year to improve their lives considerably and overcome homelessness, and that number swells to many thousands when similar organizations nationwide are considered.

"We need to go back to a menu of options. That's been taken from us. There's no choice anymore," Megison said. "We need a menu of options, and one of those options needs to be personal accountability and solving the root causes [of homelessness]."[43]

Government funding is not the best answer to the homelessness problem, given the reduced incentives of taxpayer-funded organizations to produce positive results, compared with privately funded organizations, and the corrupting influences and inefficiencies of the strings that come with government funding. Funding dollars should flow to innovative and efficient organizations based on program *effectiveness* and *results*, not on program *design* that complies with popular fads and government mandates.

8

Recommendations and Conclusions
Mary L. G. Theroux and Adam B. Summers

HOMELESSNESS IS SUCH a complicated and vexing problem because it has many different causes. And even when resources and successful programs are available, many people experiencing homelessness will choose not to take advantage of them. Too often, people will say that homelessness is just a substance abuse problem, just a mental illness problem, or just a housing problem. Too often, some homelessness reform advocates and politicians place their faith in finding a silver bullet and myopically try to enforce a one-size-fits-all policy. It is a mistake to think that placing people in housing will end homelessness, as many of them will end up back on the streets, especially if the underlying causes of their homelessness are not addressed. Precisely because people are different, face different challenges, and begin—and continue—to experience homelessness for different reasons, a multifaceted and individualized approach to the problem is essential. One lesson that we should have learned by now is that homelessness, at its core, is not a problem caused by the underfunding of government programs. Despite dramatic increases in funding and billions of dollars spent in recent years—with the money coming from taxpayers, nonprofit organizations, and private charities—the homelessness problem in California, and particularly in the San Francisco Bay Area, continues to worsen.

Although politicians and well-intentioned advocates for individuals experiencing homelessness may make grandiose and ambitious claims about "ending homelessness," it is better to be more realistic about whom we can help and how.

"There's a mythology that you can—quote, unquote—end homelessness at any moment, but there are new people coming in, suffering through the cycles of their lives," Gavin Newsom acknowledged while he was mayor of San Francisco. "It's the manifestation of complete, abject failure as a society. We'll never solve this at City Hall."[1]

Nevertheless, a number of things can be done to help many more people experiencing homelessness overcome their obstacles and get back on the path toward achieving full success. Our recommendations generally fall into two main categories: (1) recommendations related to policies addressing those currently experiencing homelessness and (2) recommendations related to housing policies that may affect homelessness rates and push more people into homelessness in the future if left unaddressed.

Homelessness Policy Recommendations

Public policies that seek to reduce homelessness have been stuck in a status quo rut, mired in a myopic, and even dogmatic, view that the Housing First approach is the primary and best solution to the problem. Yet, even as the state and many local governments have adhered to this approach and have continued to throw ever-larger amounts of money at the problem, it has only worsened. The status quo does a disservice not only to taxpayers but also to the many people experiencing homelessness who could have benefited significantly from alternative approaches. The following are several recommendations to improve policies to better meet the needs of people experiencing homelessness without breaking the bank.

Allocate resources based on demonstrated performance metrics and positive outcomes.

Performance metrics that gauge success by outcomes must be identified, and data tracked accordingly, in order to direct resources to programs that serve various segments of the homeless population more effectively, regardless of the particular methods or approaches utilized to achieve success. Because private programs accountable to their donors tend to have greater incentives to demonstrate success, it would be more effective to allocate resources privately, rather than potentially diverting organizational missions based on government grant guidelines. Private-sector direction also ensures that providers' programs are designed for success rather than in accordance with the approach currently in political favor.

Instead of focusing exclusively on measures such as the length of time people have spent experiencing homelessness, the percentage of participants transferred to permanent supportive housing, or the percentage who returned to homelessness, a program should adopt performance measures focused on improving individuals' quality of life and ability to reach full success. We recommend adopting the following performance measures:

- numbers and percentages of clients who complete the service plan or shelter program within 30 months of entry,
- increases in clients' earned incomes,
- clients' abilities to maintain their jobs for 6 months or more,
- increases in clients' educational attainments,
- clients' abilities to remain in safe, permanent housing 12 months after exit,
- numbers and percentages of clients referred to mental health or substance abuse programs who completed those programs within 12 and 24 months, and
- percentages of clients satisfied with the programs and services they received.

Target the Housing First approach to those most likely to benefit from it.
Housing First began as a program aimed primarily at people suffering from chronic homelessness, particularly single men and others presenting severe substance abuse, mental illness, or physical disability issues, and included the promised supportive services. The approach has since been expanded to become a one-size-fits-all solution for the entire homeless population, despite a dearth of evidence that it is effective for everyone. Although Housing First may serve some subpopulations well, alternative approaches will serve other subpopulations better.

Moreover, serious concerns have been raised that Housing First's low-barrier, harm reduction approach perpetuates the issues that led or contributed to individuals' homelessness in the first place. Furthermore, as explained in the "Our Definition of Success" text box in Chapter 1, Housing First too often gives up on a certain segment of the population once people have a roof over their heads and does not address their needs sufficiently to allow them to live more independent, fulfilling lives. In addition, largely because of the extraordinary costs of providing new affordable housing for such programs, Housing First simply cannot scale to a level that would be necessary to house everyone in need. Thus, if Housing First is to be used as a strategy to address homelessness, it should be more modestly scaled and targeted to the subset of individuals experiencing homelessness who would benefit from it the most.

Encourage one-stop shop models such as Haven for Hope.

The successes of housing readiness programs such as Haven for Hope in San Antonio, Texas (see Chapter 7), can—and should—be replicated in many other cities across the nation where homelessness remains a persistent problem. This one-stop shop model allows an organization to serve a large number of people and more efficiently and cost-effectively connect each person with the housing and support services tailored to their needs at each stage of recovery.

Providing security is a key component. As has been the case at Haven for Hope, hiring some off-duty local police officers can serve the dual purposes of (1) better protecting clients, staff, and residents in the surrounding neighborhoods (which may also assuage nearby residents' concerns and help to blunt potential local opposition to such projects) and (2) offering the police officers greater insight and training on how to deal with the homeless population, particularly those who are more volatile due to struggles with substance abuse or mental health issues.

The government need not take the primary role in establishing such a campus; indeed, as noted previously, such an effort is far more likely to succeed if it is operated privately and government does not interfere with program structure or operation or tie operators' hands with needless regulations and the political strings that come along with public funding. There are some things that state and local governments can do, however, to encourage—or at least not *discourage*—such facilities. For starters, since facility siting is likely to be a significant issue in many places, governments may make available unused public properties. Governments should also streamline zoning, plan review, permitting, and other bureaucratic requirements ("red tape") and ensure that these requirements are not overly restrictive.

Improve tracking of participants after they graduate from or leave programs.

When resources are tied to results, service providers have stronger incentives to track and report on participants' outcomes. Devoting more effort to tracking individuals and families who are experiencing (or formerly experienced) homelessness, for longer periods of time, could make it easier to evaluate program performance and determine whether particular approaches are working. Retrospective studies also could help to flag and address problems before they worsen so much that people are forced to return to homelessness. Although such efforts could consist simply of more follow-up interviews, they also could involve taking better advantage of technology. Pathways Vermont, for example, discovered that purchasing computers and communicating electronically with its former participants ended up saving money on follow-up consultations.[2] Other viable technological solutions include providing program graduates with smartphones on which reporting apps have been preinstalled. In exchange for making regular reports, participants could receive small payments electronically. As with the first recommendation on our list, retrospective tracking of program graduates should include quality-of-life performance measures. The same outcome metrics should be used to direct resources to successful programs. Apps allowing participants to keep records of the programs and services they have accessed previously, as well as apps that allow them to set and track progress against personal goals, such as Poverty Stoplight, also hold tremendous promise. Participants' ability to gain access to new service providers and provide them with more accurate histories of past services utilized—and the results—would help providers and participants make better decisions about how best to build on past care.

Educate the public about actual outcomes of various approaches and policies.

Accurate information, delivered effectively, can build support for programs that actually assist individuals experiencing homelessness, rather than programs that exacerbate underlying issues. Although we must be empathetic with and compassionate toward people experiencing homelessness, and understanding of the traumas they have suffered, there is nothing compassionate about allowing people to live in conditions that put them and the wider community in danger. Homelessness policies and approaches that worsen public drug dealing and use, encampments and street living, aggressive panhandling, and disposal of used drug needles, bodily waste, and other debris in public spaces degrade the quality of life both for individuals experiencing homelessness and others in the general community. Ultimately, life on the streets leads to premature death, which is not a compassionate outcome.

Although the public generally understands that the aforementioned and visible consequences of homelessness are not acceptable options, until recently most people have not been aware of viable alternatives. Armed with facts, people in the community likely would support programs and services that provide superior outcomes to unsheltered street living. Given the massive amounts of funding currently spent in the fight to "end homelessness," resources easily could be redirected to expand service capacities across an array of better alternatives, both governmental and private. Similarly, although a harm reduction approach can have positive effects in certain circumstances, we must ensure that such services and treatments are not merely perpetuating addictive behaviors that could be remedied more effectively by addressing the underlying traumas and offering personally tailored recovery services, allowing individuals to achieve full success.

Adopt pretrial diversion programs for those suspected of committing crimes.

It is unfortunate when a person experiencing homelessness violates the law, but it can also be an opportunity for individuals to obtain the help they need to improve their lives and exit homelessness. A number of local communities have adopted programs that give people experiencing homelessness who have been arrested on suspicion of committing low-level offenses the option to avoid jail by being connected with housing and support services and completing treatment programs. Once the program has been successfully completed, the charges are dropped. This choice between support services and the prospect of jail is often the extra nudge service-resistant people experiencing homelessness need so that they agree to accept help. A March 2024 report from the Cicero Institute noted that diversion programs in places such as San Francisco; Harris County, Texas; and Vermont had resulted in significant reductions in recidivism, cost savings due to less reliance on public services, and increases in employment, and thus recommended implementing diversion programs specifically targeted at offenders who are experiencing homelessness.[3]

A successful pretrial diversion program requires conducting more detailed screening than the standard police intake screening process in order to best determine an individual's needs and the appropriate treatment program. In addition, the police or sheriff's department should seek an agreement with the district attorney that information provided during such evaluations that may potentially incriminate the accused in other matters unrelated to their arrest cannot be used against them. This agreement is important to build trust, solicit honest responses, and better evaluate how to help diversion program participants. Contracting out case management to a third-party provider can also improve trust—and, therefore, results—because participants are likely to feel less intimidated than they would if they were dealing with uniformed officers. Outsourcing case management may also offer the added benefit of cost savings.

Securing the buy-in of administrators and rank-and-file officers is critical to the success of pretrial diversion programs. Doing so might even involve changing the culture at some law enforcement agencies to embrace the value of such an approach. In some cases, this may be a lengthy and difficult process, but it is necessary to develop an effective program that better serves people experiencing homelessness, local residents, and taxpayers alike.

Reexamine conservatorship laws.

People should be free to live their lives as they please, provided that they don't encroach on the rights of others—even if the way someone lives their life is offensive or seems foolish to others or makes them uncomfortable. But when an individual violates the rights of others by threatening their health or safety, the person may forfeit that freedom. Thus, in such extreme cases, with due process and the ruling of a judge, for specified periods of time and with regular reevaluations, the use of court-ordered conservatorship to compel involuntary treatment might be a last resort.

With the aforementioned provisos in mind, it may be worth reexamining conservatorship laws. California lawmakers did just that in recent years. Senate Bill 1045 in 2018 (along with SB 40 in 2019, which made some modifications to SB 1045) allowed the counties of Los Angeles, San Diego, and San Francisco to establish pilot programs that would make it easier to be granted conservatorship over people deemed unable to care for themselves. The laws' qualifications were so strict that they applied to almost no one, however, rendering them ineffective.

Senate Bill 1338 in 2022 and SB 43 in 2023 offer slightly more promise. SB 1338, the Community Assistance, Recovery, and Empowerment (CARE) Act, established CARE Court, a civil process that allows individuals, families, clinicians, and first responders to seek court-ordered treatment plans for people struggling with schizophrenia spectrum or other psychotic disorders. The process is intended to provide early intervention to avoid more restrictive conservatorships, institutionalization, or incarceration. SB 43 expanded eligibility requirements for involuntary commitment and treatment under the Lanterman-Petris-Short Act of 1967, which prohibits the indefinite and involuntary commitment of people suffering from mental health issues. Now people with substance use disorders or co-occurring mental health issues may be eligible for conservatorship.

It is too soon to determine whether CARE Court and expanded conservatorship eligibility are effective strategies, but it stands to reason that conservatorship should be an option for individuals who have severely diminished capacities to reason or to understand the consequences of their actions on their personal health and safety or that of others. Once again, however, such an approach should be reserved for extreme cases, and all efforts should be made to protect the civil liberties of potential conservatees as much as reasonably possible.

Housing Policy Recommendations

Many state and local policies restrict the supply of developable land and otherwise make the building of housing units more expensive and less profitable than it would be in a freer market. The result is dramatically higher prices and housing shortages, especially at the lower end of the market, which causes the greatest harm to those who can least afford it. As noted in Chapter 4, even "affordable housing" in California now costs close to $1 million per unit—or more—to build, especially in the San Francisco Bay Area. A 2021 National Association of Home Builders (NAHB) study found that federal, state, and local government regulations were responsible for 24 percent of the price of a new single-family home;[4] a similar 2018 study for the NAHB and the National Multifamily Housing Council concluded that regulations accounted for more than 32 percent of the cost of an average multifamily development.[5] Such government regulations add hundreds of thousands of dollars to the price of a home, particularly in California. Other estimates find that government regulations increase housing prices to roughly double what prices would be in a truly free market.[6]

The provision of more housing would help prevent people from falling into homelessness and provide needed opportunities for individuals recovering from homelessness to obtain stable housing. Prices can decline meaningfully, and affordability can improve substantially, only if the supply of housing at all price levels is increased.

The following recommendations offer ways to make housing cheaper by increasing the supply and mix of housing options, reducing the cost of construction, freeing up markets, and protecting property rights. (For more details on California's housing crisis and additional housing reform recommendations, see the Independent Institute's January 2020 California Golden Fleece® Awards report, *How to Restore the California Dream: Removing Obstacles to Fast and Affordable Housing Development*, by Lawrence J. McQuillan.)[7]

Relax zoning restrictions, eliminate urban growth boundaries, and enhance property rights.

Separation-of-use zoning laws restrict development to particular kinds of construction in specific areas of a community. Such top-down planning may be imposed for aesthetic reasons, in an attempt to improve the efficiency of infrastructure, or as a way to prevent negative impacts on quality of life resulting from the mixing of incompatible land uses (although the common law of nuisance already resolves those types of disputes between property owners by, for example, prohibiting a chemical plant or a chicken ranch from being built in the middle of a residential neighborhood). Zoning laws can be quite strict, limiting the type and number of units that may be built on a parcel of land in a given part of a city. But such zoning also infringes on property rights by limiting what property owners can build where. After all, if a person has acquired property legally (whether as an individual homeowner or as a developer), should that owner not be able to do what they want with the property, so long as they do not create a nuisance for others?

For people who prefer more rules and restrictions on housing development and improvements within their neighborhoods, a large number and variety of master-planned communities and homeowners' associations exist that are intended to enforce more uniformity and preserve the character of their communities. Such private arrangements are quite popular—and would continue to be so with or without additional governmental zoning laws. The big difference is that such arrangements are entirely voluntary (with homeowners and renters in these communities agreeing to abide by covenants, conditions, and restrictions, including the imposition of fines for failing to abide by the rules) and still offer others the freedom to live in less restrictive communities, rather than forcing restrictions on the population at large.[8] Although zoning laws are not going away anytime soon (though Houston, the fourth-largest city in the nation, has shown that even big cities can thrive without zoning laws), they easily could be relaxed to allow for the development of more housing units on a property owner's land, whether by allowing duplexes to be built on properties formerly zoned only for single-family houses, permitting more high-density developments, or opening up more land for housing development generally. Such actions would increase the supply of housing while strengthening property rights.

This goes double for urban growth boundaries, which seek to concentrate development within arbitrary lines drawn on a map around a city's core. Growth boundaries limit the amount of developable land, encouraging higher-density development and driving up housing prices in city centers. In addition, the boundaries violate the property rights of people who would like to build beyond them and reduce the quality of life of many consumers by denying them their preferences for more affordable homes with larger houses and lot sizes, as well as other potential amenities, such as better schools and lower crime rates. These forms of zoning should be eliminated in favor of market-based solutions that allow developers and consumers to determine the values and best uses for land through natural forces of supply and demand. Note, however, that the term "consumers" need not be restricted to homeowners or renters, but also may include nonprofit organizations or private land trusts dedicated to purchasing land for the purpose of preserving open spaces. Conservation easements are another form of voluntary environmental agreement, whereby the land remains in private hands but the owner agrees to limit land uses or adopt certain measures to maintain its environmental value. These easements also may be donated, and landowners may be able to realize significant tax benefits from the transfer.[9]

Eliminate inclusionary zoning (affordable housing) requirements and rent controls.

Affordable housing mandates, or "inclusionary zoning" requirements, should likewise be eliminated in favor of private property rights. Those laws require developers to offer a specified fraction of the units in a new development at below-market prices—or else pay expensive "in lieu" fees to the government, which are meant to fund affordable housing programs. Although at first blush it might sound like a good idea to require some units to be "affordable" (and, often, to reserve them for owners or tenants below a predetermined income threshold), we also must consider the secondary effects, or unintended consequences, of such a policy. Such mandates may force the developer to incur losses on the affordable units, prompting the developer to raise prices even higher on the remaining units (basically an "inclusionary zoning tax"). These mandates may even reduce the development's value so much that it is no longer profitable to build at all, leaving the city and state without any additional housing units—"affordable" or otherwise. Moreover, such laws violate the developer's property rights by dictating pricing and other business practices, thereby reducing the value of the property without compensation.

Rent control laws similarly may end up making housing less affordable by reducing the profitability of building and maintaining apartments—or even turning them into entirely unprofitable investments. Rent control reduces the supply of housing, degrades its quality by providing incentives for landlords to skimp on maintenance, and encourages the conversion of rent-controlled apartments to higher-end condos, which are not subject to such laws, putting upward pressure on the prices of the remaining units. A lucky few tenants, who may not even be poor, will be able to secure rent-controlled units, thus benefiting from the price ceiling, but many other prospective renters will be shut out of the housing market entirely. Even people who do live in rent-controlled units may be harmed by the policy, as it may prompt them to stay in their apartments longer than they otherwise would, causing them to forgo exploring new job opportunities, moving to be closer to family members, or building up equity in a house or condo out of fear of losing their below-market rents. Moreover, rent control tends to result in lower-quality housing, as the excess demand and competition for rent-controlled units reduce landlords' incentives to invest in building and facility maintenance or amenities to entice tenants. Rent control may also prompt landlords to try to make up lost revenue elsewhere by imposing new or increased fees for such things as rental applications, parking spaces, pets, key replacement, lock changes, or access to amenities such as gyms, conference rooms, or laundry facilities.

Abolish prevailing wage laws.

Prevailing wage requirements force developers to pay construction workers union wage scales—and generally force them to hire unionized workers—which are significantly more costly than nonunion (market-rate) labor. Prevailing wages may be mandated by law or included in project labor agreements. A March 2020 study by UC Berkeley's Terner Center for Housing Innovation reported that prevailing wage requirements increased the cost of affordable housing developments in California by an average of more than $53,000 per unit, or 13 percent.[10] Similarly, a May 2017 report from the California Center for Jobs and the Economy and the California Business Roundtable found that prevailing wages increased average construction costs for affordable housing projects by 10–25 percent; moreover, the prevailing wage rule could raise total project costs for market-rate housing in areas such as Los Angeles by as much as 46 percent, which translates into tens of thousands of dollars or even more than $100,000 per unit.[11] The report furthermore concluded that imposing a statewide prevailing wage requirement would push up rents so much that it would drive 481,000 people into poverty.[12] Repealing this law across numerous local jurisdictions would go a long way toward enhancing housing affordability and preventing Californians (and others) from falling into poverty because of their inability to bear the state's very high housing costs.

Streamline or eliminate CEQA and other unnecessarily burdensome environmental regulations.

Many Californians have long taken pride in their concern for protecting the environment, but as often happens, good intentions led to the passage of an overly broad law that has had many deleterious effects. "One clear culprit in the housing crisis is the lengthy and costly environmental review process required under the California Environmental Quality Act (CEQA), even for housing that complies with local general plans and zoning codes, and the hundreds of applicable environmental, health, safety, and labor laws and regulations," declared a 2019 study from the Chapman University Center for Demographics and Policy.[13] CEQA is the strictest environmental impact law in the nation, and has become so burdensome that it frequently is wielded as a cudgel to extract concessions from developers or kill projects for reasons that have nothing to do with the environment—be it labor unions threatening CEQA lawsuits to require prevailing wages or the hiring of union labor, local residents seeking additional amenities, NIMBY (not in my backyard) homeowners exploiting the law to prevent growth and keep new people out altogether, or businesses trying to prevent competitors from moving in. Such practices are so prevalent that they have come to be known as "greenmail."

Unfortunately, greenmail is quite effective. CEQA lawsuits can hold up developments for many years, at great cost, so that developers often find it more practical to give in to such demands and to consider compliance as just another cost of doing business in California. Other developers simply abandon their homebuilding plans. As a testament to the need for reform, governors from both sides of the political aisle have called for significant fixes but have little to show for their efforts. In 2012, then-Governor Jerry Brown described CEQA reform as "the Lord's work."[14] And in a 2013 column in the *Sacramento Bee*, former Republican Governors George Deukmejian and Pete Wilson and former Democratic Governor Gray Davis decried what the law had become, writing, "Today, CEQA is too often abused by those seeking to gain a competitive edge, to leverage concessions from a project or by neighbors who simply don't want any new growth in their community—no matter how worthy or environmentally beneficial a project may be."[15] Moreover, 98 percent of the potential housing units targeted by CEQA lawsuits are located in "infill" areas surrounded by existing developments, not in open spaces or on rural lands, which are much more likely to be environmentally sensitive.[16]

In a tacit admission that CEQA is unnecessarily burdensome, in September 2019 the California legislature and Governor Newsom passed Assembly Bill 1197, which exempts shelters and housing for people experiencing homelessness in Los Angeles from environmental review. Newsom touted the bill in his February 2020 State of the State address and called for expanding it "to all homeless shelters and supportive housing statewide."[17] (Another bill, AB 1907, introduced in January 2020, would have done just that, but the bill died in committee that year.) Similarly, the state has exempted from CEQA review its purchases of hotels, motels, and other properties for the purpose of housing people experiencing homelessness, using federal coronavirus relief funds that had to be spent by the end of 2020, through its Project Homekey (formerly Project Roomkey) program. Lawmakers occasionally have exempted certain developments from CEQA when it has been politically beneficial to do so—such as for the renovation of the Capitol annex building or the construction of professional basketball arenas for the Sacramento Kings and Golden State Warriors—yet legislators cannot seem to reform policy requirements for the rest of us when the law is preventing the development of much-needed housing.

CEQA is hardly the only environmental law inhibiting housing affordability, however. At the same time that lawmakers were wringing their hands over California's housing crisis, they imposed a solar roof mandate that went into effect on January 1, 2020. The California Energy Commission estimated that the solar panels would cost about $9,500 on average,[18] but this estimate likely understates the actual costs considerably. Solar panels currently average approximately $15,000 in California,[19] though including the costs of installation and the mandate's additional standards for energy-efficient appliances, windows, lighting, and insulation can bring the total cost to $30,000 per home.[20] In addition, affordable housing projects that adhere to stricter environmental standards, such as energy conservation measures, cost an average of $17,000 more per apartment.[21] "To have the best chance at winning tax credit funding, low-income housing developers also must build their projects to environmental standards that exceed even what the state requires of developers of new luxury condominiums," the *Los Angeles Times* reported in April 2020. "That includes using solar power for most of their electricity or certifying their energy efficiency with LEED [Leadership in Energy and Environmental Design] or other third parties."[22] The *Times*'s analysis extends to building standards generally, which now often greatly exceed basic health and safety needs.

Housing that might be considered substandard by today's lofty requirements may not be ideal, but it can still be safe, and it certainly is better than no housing at all.[23] Such high standards may be admirable, but policymakers must keep in mind that the drive toward mandated perfection prices some people out of homes. Imagine how many more people would be able to afford housing if homes were tens of thousands of dollars cheaper because such unnecessary environmental regulations and other cost-elevating building standards were eliminated.

Minimize development impact fees.

Development impact fees represent another significant driver of housing costs. Although they may be reasonably tailored to compensate local governments for additional infrastructure that may be needed to support the larger populations and vehicle traffic that accompany new housing developments, some municipalities apply the principle more broadly by charging fees for additional amenities and things that may not be closely related to a development's impacts, from parks to public art, even in cases in which the funding had been previously rejected by voters or local governments. As with seemingly every other aspect of home building, California's costs are among the highest in the nation. A March 2015 Legislative Analyst's Office report found that local development fees averaged more than $22,000 per single-family home—about three and a half times the national average of $6,000.[24] Even worse, these fees can be substantially larger in some municipalities, reaching more than $62,000 in Oakland, more than $146,000 in Irvine, and nearly $157,000 in Fremont.[25] If communities wish to expand housing affordability, they can save prospective buyers thousands—or even tens of thousands—of dollars by minimizing development impact fees and tailoring them narrowly to the direct impacts of the developments to be built. Alternatively, parks, sports facilities, and other community amenities could be built and operated by developers or other private entities and funded through user fees or membership fees, so that only those who use those facilities pay for them.

Conclusion

Homelessness has become a pervasive and intractable problem in California and many other parts of the country. Although due, in large part, to the traumas and life choices among people experiencing homelessness, the problem is also exacerbated by public policies that have needlessly driven up the cost of housing; ignored, tolerated, or even encouraged the negative effects of street living; and failed to address the underlying causes of homelessness. In addition, California's failure to track how tens of billions of dollars of taxpayers' money have been spent on homelessness programs—much less what outcomes all this spending may have achieved—has resulted in vast resources being directed to ineffective and counterproductive uses with little accountability when programs fail.

In these pages, we have harshly criticized the Housing First approach, the favored tool of the federal government and many state and local governments, for its myopic, one-size-fits-all strategy and its failure to improve the situation. It is not "success" to warehouse people under a roof and leave them with untreated traumas, drug and alcohol addictions, or mental illnesses. If the theoretical arguments are not convincing enough, there is no denying the fact that years and years of doubling down on Housing First policies and throwing billions and billions of dollars at the problem in California and elsewhere have led only to *increasing* homelessness and worsening street conditions. This is not fair to people experiencing homelessness, and it is not fair to the local residents, business owners, and workers who must deal with watching their neighborhoods deteriorate; tiptoeing around used drug needles, trash, and human waste; seeing public spaces intended for all residents taken over by encampments; fearing being accosted by people with untreated mental illness; worrying over the safety of their children who must walk to and from school through such squalor; and becoming trapped in increasingly dirty and dangerous communities because street conditions have eroded the value of their homes and businesses so much that they cannot afford to leave.

It is clear that continuing to do the same things is not a recipe for success and that accepting the current "one step forward, four steps back" outcomes will never solve the homelessness problem. We should seek instead to reward organizations and programs based on results, not politically determined approaches. Politics warps the incentives of providers and leads to the enshrinement of ineffective policies and the spawning of self-perpetuating interest groups that become more concerned with maximizing their taxpayer funding than solving the problems at hand—just as politics has done in the defense, banking, health care, and higher education industries, among others. In other words, it has created a homelessness-industrial complex that is myopic and beholden to political influence and favors. Any real solution must, therefore, be driven by the private/nonprofit sector and respect individual liberties, property rights, and public-health and safety laws.

As daunting as the problem may seem, many people and organizations are working tirelessly and helping to turn lives around every day. Examples such as Haven for Hope in San Antonio, Texas; Union Rescue Mission in Los Angeles; Solutions for Change in San Diego County, California; Step Denver; and The Salvation Army provide cause for optimism and demonstrate a successful path forward. Reforming harmful housing policies and restoring a free market unencumbered by unnecessary government red tape, though a tall order politically in California, would significantly improve the housing market, leading to more affordable housing and helping to prevent people on the margins from falling into homelessness in the first place or helping people to get back on their feet after recovery. The solutions are out there, and in many cases they are already being implemented even in spite of governmental hurdles, but policymakers must stop tying the hands of those who are ready and willing to help if we are to improve the lives of people experiencing homelessness and others in communities hit hard by the damaging effects of street living.

Acknowledgments

A BOOK IS never the product of a single author or even, in the case of this book, of seven authors. We want to thank those who offered their time, expertise, and wisdom to improve the content.

Dr. Drew Pinsky, board-certified physician, addiction medicine specialist, and television, radio, and podcast host, wrote an exceptional foreword explaining how activists and government officials have subverted the mental health delivery system, especially as it relates to people experiencing homelessness. We thank Drew for the foreword and generously providing interviews.

Scott Ackerson, a licensed master social worker with WestEast Design Group and Haven for Hope's former vice president of strategic relationships, drew on his three decades in social work to write an inspirational foreword about how to best address homelessness. In addition, he was always available to answer our questions in emails and interviews. Many thanks, Scott.

Thanks go to those with decades of experience working to improve the lives of people experiencing homelessness who generously provided interviews: David Huete, vice president of transformational services at Haven for Hope; Chris Megison, chief executive officer and cofounder of Solutions for Change; Major Mark Nelson, commander of The Salvation Army's Adult Rehabilitation Centers Command Western Territory; Paul Scudo, chief executive officer of Step Denver; and Paul C. Webster, executive director of the Los Angeles Alliance for Human Rights and founder and director of the Hope Street Coalition, which has a special focus on homelessness, mental illness, and addiction. The book benefited greatly from their insights and expertise.

William F. Shughart II, distinguished research advisor and senior fellow of the Independent Institute and J. Fish Smith Professor in Public Choice at Utah State University, peer-reviewed the manuscript. We are grateful for Bill's keen eye for detail and sharp mind for sound scholarship. Also, Jonathan Caulkins, Stever University Professor of Operations Research and Public Policy with the Heinz College of Information Systems and Public Policy at Carnegie Mellon University, peer-reviewed Chapter 5 on harm reduction. We thank him for sharing his wisdom and helping to refine the chapter.

Finally, we thank Cathy Cambron for her masterful editing of the manuscript.

Mary L. G. Theroux
Lawrence J. McQuillan
Jonathan Hofer
Christopher J. Calton
Adam B. Summers
Hovannes Abramyan
Scott Beyer

Appendix: Homelessness Terms and Definitions

Cabin Community
Also known as community cabins, this is a type of emergency housing in Oakland, San Francisco, and other locations. It typically consists of small "villages" of cabins, offered by a city, that provide temporary transitional housing and basic needs. These sites are intended to serve as an alternative to encampments and help get people off the streets and into more stable housing.[1]

Continuum of Care (CoC) Program
The Continuum of Care Program created a standardized federal framework for assisting people experiencing homelessness. It focuses on ensuring that homeless individuals have support from a variety of city- and community-based programs and that these programs are designed to function in conjunction with one another. The program aims to "promote access to and effect utilization of mainstream programs by homeless individuals and families; and optimize self-sufficiency among individuals and families experiencing homelessness."[2] This program also provides grants for various local initiatives.

Emergency Shelter
This term "typically refers to any facility which provides temporary shelter for the homeless without requiring occupants to sign leases or occupancy agreements."[3] These locations, almost exclusively operated by municipal governments, provide short-term housing for adults experiencing homelessness. In San Francisco, these shelters limit adults to ninety-day stays, after which they must find a more permanent housing solution.

Harm Reduction

As practiced, harm reduction is a series of policies and procedures that seeks to minimize harm from drug use, such as overdoses or disease from used needles, rather than offering recovery services. Proponents tout it as a fairer and more realistic way of meeting people "where they are" in their lives without judgment,[4] while critics contend that it perpetuates substance abuse. As defined, however, harm reduction includes abstinence, and most recovery specialists are advocates of the approach so long as it is a means to recovery.

Housing First

The "Housing First" approach seeks to immediately place people experiencing homelessness in long-term housing, the idea being that once their housing is taken care of, it will be easier for them to work on any other issues underlying their homelessness. In theory, this approach offers effective wraparound services to address related issues, but unlike the transitional housing model (see the definition of **Transitional Housing** below), participation is entirely voluntary, and treatment is based on a harm reduction approach, which may not necessarily emphasize recovery.

Long-Term Intervention

This term refers to policies intended to permanently reduce the number of individuals experiencing homelessness in a given city. Examples include housing subsidies, vouchers, and the development of more affordable housing.[5]

McKinney-Vento Homeless Assistance Act

This 2009 federal law established the Continuum of Care (CoC) Program, consolidating three preexisting homeless assistance programs: the Supportive Housing Program, the Shelter Plus Care Program, and the Moderate Rehabilitation/ Single Room Occupancy (SRO) Program.[6]

Navigation Centers

This term refers to specialized homelessness facilities, in operation in San Francisco since 2015, that are low barrier and utilize intensive services to serve some of the most vulnerable people experiencing homelessness and those who have been unhoused long-term. These places are unlike emergency shelters in that they operate twenty-four hours a day (so people are not kicked out in the morning), and they welcome people's partners, pets, and belongings. In addition, participants are selected by the San Francisco Homeless Outreach Team or a centralized referral system; the centers do not accept walk-ins.[7] Stays range from 30 to 90 days, and the goal is to find guests permanent housing by the end of this time.[8]

Online Navigation and Entry (ONE) System

This is an information technology system launched in June 2017 in San Francisco, intended to track the health, housing, jail, and counseling history of every person experiencing homelessness in the city. The new system consolidates fifteen previous systems, spanning multiple agencies.[9] As an April 2019 report from the Bay Area Council Economic Institute explains, "This information allows caseworkers to calibrate health and housing interventions based on individuals' histories and to effectively place those most in need into housing."[10] It is hoped that the new system will also prevent people experiencing homelessness from slipping through the cracks between multiple agencies and service providers.

Permanent Supportive Housing (PSH)

Permanent supportive housing is community-based housing for individuals and families who formerly experienced homelessness in which tenants have a lease for a minimum of one year. There is no designated length of stay, and leases may be terminated only for cause. PSH is predicated on the Housing First approach (see the definition of **Housing First** above), in which, in theory, effective wraparound services are made available, but individuals are not required to use them. This type of program utilizes a harm reduction approach that may not necessarily emphasize recovery.

Potential Intervention

This term identifies specific and isolated opportunities when officials have the capacity either to prevent an individual from becoming homeless or to help that person onto a pathway out of homelessness. Unlike long-term interventions, potential interventions are often based on whether they will be applied at the "entering homelessness," "experiencing homelessness," or "exiting homelessness" phase.[11]

Rapid Rehousing

This model seeks to help people experiencing homelessness by providing time-limited rental assistance and support services to rapidly connect families and individuals to permanent housing. Assistance may be available for up to two years. Like permanent supportive housing, it takes a "low-barrier," Housing First / harm reduction approach to offering supportive services (see the definitions of **Harm Reduction** and **Permanent Supportive Housing [PSH]** above).

Residential Rehabilitation Facilities

Colloquially known as "rehab," these centers provide patients a temporary living space while they are treated for addiction.

Residential Treatment Centers

See the definition of **Residential Rehabilitation Facilities** above.

Resource Centers

Resource centers offer specialized services for individuals or families who need immediate support. In San Francisco, these usually take the form of family resource centers, which offer child care, counseling, parent education, mentoring, and case management for struggling families.[12]

Sheltered

This term is used by the US Department of Housing and Urban Development to qualify a specific subset of individuals experiencing homelessness who are residing "in an emergency shelter" or "in transitional housing or supportive housing for homeless persons who originally came from the streets or emergency shelters."[13] These individuals are differentiated from individuals experiencing homelessness who are unsheltered (see the definition of **Unsheltered** below).

Stabilization Rooms

Stabilization rooms are short-term subsidized housing, located in single-room occupancy (SRO) hotels, for those experiencing homelessness. Stabilization rooms are utilized to transition people from the streets to permanent housing.[14]

Temporary Shelter
See the definition of **Emergency Shelter** above.

Transformational Housing or Recovery Housing or Housing Readiness
This approach is similar to that of transitional housing (see the definition of **Transitional Housing** below) in that there is a strong focus on providing services to address the underlying conditions that have caused participants to experience homelessness. In practice, however, this approach is more flexible and tolerant of the challenges faced by participants and more willing to work with them to create plans to get back on track when they are falling short of goals and expectations. For those who determine that they are truly not yet ready for a transformational program, arrangements will be made to provide a soft landing to a lower-barrier facility.

Transitional Housing
This approach seeks to help people experiencing homelessness by pairing housing with various wraparound services, such as mental health treatment, substance abuse counseling, and job training, to help participants resolve the underlying issues and causes of their homelessness and reach their full success. In contrast to permanent supportive housing, the services offered in transitional housing programs tend to be "high barrier," as they may require participation in certain services and adherence to certain rules, such as maintaining sobriety, employment, or both in order to remain in the program. These programs may last up to about three years, after which participants are expected to graduate and obtain permanent housing.

Unsheltered
This term is used by the US Department of Housing and Urban Development to qualify a specific subset of individuals experiencing homelessness who are residing "in a place not meant for human habitation, such as cars, parks, sidewalks, abandoned buildings (on the street)."[15] These individuals are differentiated from individuals experiencing homelessness who are sheltered (see the definition of **Sheltered** above).

About the Authors

Dr. Drew Pinsky is a board-certified physician; addiction medicine specialist; and television, radio, and podcast host.

Scott Ackerson is a licensed master social worker with WestEast Design Group and Haven for Hope's former vice president of strategic relationships.

Mary L. G. Theroux is chairman and CEO of the Independent Institute. She received her AB in economics from Stanford University. Theroux also serves as managing director of Lightning Ventures, a San Francisco Bay Area investment firm, and vice president of the C. S. Lewis Society of California. She is former chair and a current member of the Advisory Boards for the San Francisco Salvation Army and the Alameda County Salvation Army, and served on the National Advisory Board of The Salvation Army from 2003 to 2022. Articles by Theroux have appeared in *Forbes*, the *San Francisco Chronicle*, the *San Francisco Examiner*, *Visión Hispana*, the *Washington Examiner*, and other publications. She previously served as chair of Garvey International and president and CEO of San Francisco Grocery Express.

Lawrence J. McQuillan is a senior fellow and director of the Center on Entrepreneurial Innovation at the Independent Institute. Dr. McQuillan earned an MA and PhD in economics from George Mason University, and a BA with a double major in economics and business administration from Trinity University. He has served as chief economist at the Illinois Policy Institute, director of business and economic studies at the Pacific Research Institute, research fellow at the Hoover Institution, and founding publisher and contributing editor at *Economic Issues*. Dr. McQuillan's books and major studies include *California Dreaming: Lessons on How to Resolve America's Public Pension Crisis*; *A Brighter Future: Solutions to Policy Issues Affecting America's Children*; *California Prosperity: Roadmap to Recovery 2011—Ten Steps to Return California to Prosperity*; *Jackpot Justice: The True Cost of America's Tort System*; *US Tort Liability Index*; *The Facts about Medical Malpractice Liability Costs*; *US Economic Freedom Index*; *An Empire Disaster: Why New York's Tort System Is Broken and How to Fix It*; *Tort Law Tally: How State Tort Reforms Affect Tort Losses and Tort Insurance Premiums*; *Bringing More Sunshine to California: How to Expand Open Government in the Golden State*; and *The International Monetary Fund: Financial Medic to the World?* In addition, he is the author of scholarly journal articles and hundreds of commentaries in such leading outlets as the *Wall Street Journal*, the *New York Times*, the *Chicago Tribune*, the *Los Angeles Times*, the *San Francisco Chronicle*, *Investor's Business Daily*, *Forbes*, *USA Today*, the *New York Post*, *Public Choice*, *The Independent Review*, and *Encyclopaedia Britannica*, among others. He founded and directed the California Golden Fleece® Awards to highlight state or local spending programs, regulations, and taxes that fleece California taxpayers, consumers, or businesses. He has been an adviser for the California State Assembly Judiciary Committee, the Socioeconomic Council of Madrid, Colorado Governor Bill Owens, the Heritage Foundation / Wall Street Journal Index of Economic Freedom, Governor Arnold Schwarzenegger's task force on a constitutional spending limit for California, California state Senator Tom McClintock, the Tax and Fiscal Policy Task Force of the American Legislative Exchange Council, the Civil Justice Reform Policy Task Force of the American Legislative Exchange Council, the Law and Judiciary

Policy Committee of the Georgia Chamber of Commerce, the Swedish Office of Science and Technology, and the Adriatic Institute for Public Policy. McQuillan has appeared on NPR, Fox Business Network, CNBC, C-SPAN, CNN, and radio stations and podcasts across the United States.

Jonathan Hofer is a research associate at the Independent Institute. A political science graduate of the University of California, Berkeley, his interests include housing and homelessness, information privacy law, municipal surveillance, and the impact of emerging technologies on civil liberties.

Christopher J. Calton is the research fellow in housing and homelessness at the Independent Institute. He earned a PhD in history at the University of Florida, where his research focused on the history of the corporation. Before joining the Independent Institute, Dr. Calton hosted the *Historical Controversies* podcast for the Ludwig von Mises Institute, where he also contributed commentaries on a wide array of topics, including the criminal justice system, liberal and economic thought, higher education, economic policy, and entrepreneurship. His opinion editorials on housing and homelessness have been published in such media outlets as the *San Francisco Chronicle*, the *Miami Herald*, the *Orange County Register*, *The Hill*, the *Washington Times*, the *Arizona Daily Star*, the *Orlando Sentinel*, and *Inside Sources*. His scholarly writings can be found in journals such as *The Virginia Magazine of History and Biography*, *Libertarian Papers*, and *The Florida Historical Quarterly*.

Adam B. Summers is a writer, economist, editor, and public policy analyst and a former research fellow with the Independent Institute. He previously worked as an editorial writer and columnist at the *Orange County Register* and its ten sister newspapers in the Southern California News Group and as a senior policy analyst at the Reason Foundation. Summers has written extensively about California and national politics, individual liberty, property rights, law and economics, public pension reform, occupational licensing, privatization, privacy / Fourth Amendment and civil liberties issues, government reform, and various other political and economic topics. In addition to his numerous *Orange County Register* articles, Summers's columns have been published by the *Wall Street Journal*, the *Los Angeles Times*, the *San Francisco Chronicle*, the *San Diego Union-Tribune*, the *Atlanta Journal-Constitution*, the *Washington Times*, the *Baltimore Sun*, the *Contra Costa Times*, *The Freeman*, *Reason*, and many other publications. Summers has testified before state legislative committees in Arizona, California, Louisiana, and Michigan on topics such as public pension reform and occupational licensing regulations. Summers holds an MA in economics from George Mason University and a BA with a double major in economics and political science from the University of California, Los Angeles.

Hovannes Abramyan is a former research fellow with the Independent Institute. He previously served as director of the Center for the Study of Ideological Diversity at Reason Foundation and policy fellow at the Pacific Research Institute. Dr. Abramyan earned his PhD in political science at the University of California, Los Angeles, and his BA in political science at the University of California, Berkeley. His commentaries have appeared in the *Wall Street Journal*, *Forbes*, and *Investor's Business Daily*, among other leading outlets.

Scott Beyer is the owner of the Market Urbanism Report, a media company that advances free-market city policy. He is also an urban affairs journalist who writes regular columns for *Forbes*, *Governing Magazine*, HousingOnline.com, and *Catalyst*.

Notes

1. Introduction

1. Trish Thadani and Joaquin Palomino, "San Francisco's Deadly Failure on the Drug Crisis Is Unfolding Inside Its Own Housing Program," *San Francisco Chronicle*, December 15, 2022, https://www.sfchronicle.com/projects/2022/san-francisco-sros-overdoses.
2. Ken Rodriguez, "Transformed: The Journey of a Homeless Addict into Sobriety," *San Antonio Report*, July 12, 2016, https://sanantonioreport.org/transformed-the-journey-of-a-homeless-addict-into-sobriety.
3. Marisa Kendall, "A Tent City in Cupertino: Wealthy Tech Capital Grapples with New Homeless Camp," *Mercury News*, June 1, 2020, https://www.mercurynews.com/2020/06/01/a-tent-city-in-cupertino-wealthy-tech-capitol-struggles-with-new-homeless-camp.
4. See, for example, Erika I. Ritchie, "San Clemente Clears Homeless Camp Site and Requires Proof of Ties to the City for Reentry," *Orange County Register*, August 30, 2019, https://www.ocregister.com/2019/08/30/san-clemente-clears-homeless-camp-site-and-requires-proof-of-ties-to-the-city-for-reentry, and Theresa Walker, "Thousands of Pounds of Human Waste, Close to 14,000 Hypodermic Needles Cleaned Out from Santa Ana River Homeless Encampments," *Orange County Register*, March 8, 2018, https://www.ocregister.com/2018/03/08/thousands-of-pounds-of-human-waste-close-to-14000-hypodermic-needles-cleaned-out-from-santa-ana-river-homeless-encampments.
5. Gavin Newsom, "State of the State Address," available at Office of Governor Gavin Newsom, "Governor Newsom Delivers State of the State Address," February 12, 2019, https://www.gov.ca.gov/2019/02/12/state-of-the-state-address.
6. Anna Gorman and Kaiser Health News, "Medieval Diseases Are Infecting California's Homeless," *Atlantic*, March 8, 2019, https://www.theatlantic.com/health/archive/2019/03/typhus-tuberculosis-medieval-diseases-spreading-homeless/584380.
7. Dennis Romero and Andrew Blankstein, "'Typhus Zone': Rats and Trash Infest Los Angeles' Skid Row, Fueling Disease," NBCNews.com, October 14, 2018, https://www.nbcnews.com/news/us-news/typhus-zone-rats-trash-infest-los-angeles-skid-row-fueling-n919856.

8. "San Diego Hepatitis A Outbreak Ends After 2 Years," Associated Press, October 30, 2018, https://apnews.com/cc40b8c476ef469ebd-c2228772176b03.
9. Heather Knight, "It's No Laughing Matter—SF Forming Poop Patrol to Keep Sidewalks Clean," *San Francisco Chronicle*, August 14, 2018, https://www.sfchronicle.com/bayarea/heatherknight/article/It-s-no-laughing-matter-SF-forming-Poop-13153517.php.
10. Ben Christopher, "Californians Cite Homelessness as Top Concern for First Time Ever, Survey Finds," *Mercury News*, October 7, 2019, https://www.mercurynews.com/2019/10/07/rising-homelessness-remains-a-concerns-survey-finds.
11. Deja Thomas, "Californians See a Rise in Homelessness in Their Communities," Public Policy Institute of California blog, April 14, 2023, https://www.ppic.org/blog/californians-see-a-rise-in-homelessness-in-their-communities.
12. Heather Knight, "A Decade of Homelessness: Thousands in S.F. Remain in Crisis," *San Francisco Chronicle*, June 27, 2014, https://www.sfgate.com/bayarea/article/A-decade-of-homelessness-Thousands-in-S-F-5585773.php.
13. Gavin Newsom, "State of the State Address," available at Office of Governor Gavin Newsom, "Governor Newsom Delivers State of the State Address on Homelessness," February 19, 2020, https://www.gov.ca.gov/2020/02/19/governor-newsom-delivers-state-of-the-state-address-on-homelessness.
14. US Department of Housing and Urban Development, Office of Community Planning and Development, *The 2022 Annual Homeless Assessment Report to Congress*, December 2022, pp. 10, 16–17, https://www.huduser.gov/portal/sites/default/files/pdf/2019-AHAR-Part-1.pdf.
15. US Department of Housing and Urban Development, Office of Community Planning and Development, *The 2022 Annual Homeless Assessment Report to Congress*, p. 17.
16. US Census Bureau, "Annual Estimates of the Resident Population for the United States, Regions, States, and Puerto Rico: April 1, 2010 to July 1, 2019," last revised December 30, 2019, https://www.census.gov/data/datasets/time-series/demo/popest/2010s-national-total.html, and US Census Bureau, "QuickFacts: California," accessed June 2, 2020, https://www.census.gov/quickfacts/CA.
17. US Department of Housing and Urban Development, Office of Community Planning and Development, *The 2022 Annual Homeless Assessment Report to Congress*, December 2022, pp. 12, 16, 72, 74, https://www.huduser.gov/portal/sites/default/files/pdf/2019-AHAR-Part-1.pdf.
18. US Department of Housing and Urban Development, Office of Community Planning and Development, *The 2022 Annual Homeless Assessment Report to Congress*, p. 16.
19. US Department of Housing and Urban Development, Office of Community Planning and Development, *The 2022 Annual Homeless Assessment Report to Congress*, p. 16.
20. US Department of Housing and Urban Development, Office of Community Planning and Development, *The 2022 Annual Homeless Assessment Report to Congress*, p. 17.
21. US Department of Housing and Urban Development, Office of Community Planning and Development, *The 2022 Annual Homeless Assessment Report to Congress*, p. 21.
22. US Department of Housing and Urban Development, Office of Community Planning and Development, *The 2022 Annual Homeless Assessment Report to Congress*, p. 22.

23. California State Auditor, *Homelessness in California: The State Must Do More to Assess the Cost-Effectiveness of Its Homelessness Programs*, Report 2023-102.1, April 9, 2024, p. 4, https://information.auditor.ca.gov/pdfs/reports/2023-102.1.pdf.
24. California State Auditor, *Homelessness in California: The State Must Do More to Assess the Cost-Effectiveness of Its Homelessness Programs*, p. iii.
25. California State Auditor, *Homelessness in California: The State Must Do More to Assess the Cost-Effectiveness of Its Homelessness Programs*, pp. iii, 11.
26. California State Auditor, *Homelessness in California: The State Must Do More to Assess the Cost-Effectiveness of Its Homelessness Programs*, p. 16.

2. The Tragedy of Homelessness: By the Numbers

1. US Department of Housing and Urban Development, Office of Community Planning and Development, *The 2022 Annual Homelessness Assessment Report to Congress*, December 2022, dataset "2007–2022 Point-in-Time Estimates by State," https://www.huduser.gov/portal/datasets/ahar/2022-ahar-part-1-pit-estimates-of-homelessness-in-the-us.html.
2. US Department of Housing and Urban Development, Office of Community Planning and Development, *The 2022 Annual Homelessness Assessment Report to Congress*, December 2022, p. 16, https://www.huduser.gov/portal/sites/default/files/pdf/2022-AHAR-Part-1.pdf.
3. US Department of Housing and Urban Development, Office of Community Planning and Development, *The 2022 Annual Homelessness Assessment Report to Congress*, December 2022, dataset "2007–2022 Point-in-Time Estimates by State," https://www.huduser.gov/portal/datasets/ahar/2022-ahar-part-1-pit-estimates-of-homelessness-in-the-us.html.
4. State of California, Department of Finance, "Population Estimates for Cities, Counties, and the State, 2021–2024 with 2020 Census Benchmark," May 2024, https://dof.ca.gov/forecasting/demographics/estimates/e-4-population-estimates-for-cities-counties-and-the-state-2021-2024-with-2020-census-benchmark.
5. "Cities in California 2024," PopulationU.com, 2020 data from the US Census Bureau, February 23, 2024, https://www.populationu.com/gen/cities-in-california.
6. US Department of Housing and Urban Development, Office of Community Planning and Development, *The 2022 Annual Homelessness Assessment Report to Congress*, December 2022, p. 16, https://www.huduser.gov/portal/sites/default/files/pdf/2022-AHAR-Part-1.pdf.
7. US Department of Housing and Urban Development, Office of Community Planning and Development, *The 2022 Annual Homelessness Assessment Report to Congress*, pp. 52, 64.
8. National Law Center on Homelessness and Poverty, *Don't Count On It: How the HUD Point-in-Time Count Underestimates the Homelessness Crisis in America*, 2017, https://homelesslaw.org/wp-content/uploads/2018/10/HUD-PIT-report2017.pdf; and Alastair Boone, "Is There a Better Way to Count the Homeless?," *Bloomberg*, March 4, 2019, https://www.bloomberg.com/news/articles/2019-03-04/the-problem-with-hud-s-point-in-time-homeless-count.

9. Stephen Metraux, Dennis P. Culhane, Stacy Raphael, Matthew White, Carol Pearson, Eric Hirsch, Patricia Ferrell, Steve Rice, Barbara Ritter, and J. Stephen Cleghorn, "Assessing Homeless Population Size Through the Use of Emergency and Transitional Shelter Services in 1998: Results from the Analysis of Administrative Data from Nine US Jurisdictions," *Public Health Reports* 116, no. 4 (July–August 2001): 344–52, https://www.researchgate.net/publication/11335917_Assessing_Homeless_Population_Size_Through_the_Use_of_Emergency_and_Transitional_Shelter_Services_in_1998_Results_from_the_Analysis_of_Administrative_Data_from_Nine_US_Jurisdictions.
10. Applied Survey Research, *San Francisco Homeless Count and Survey: 2022 Comprehensive Report*, San Francisco Department of Homelessness and Supportive Housing, August 19, 2022, p. 14, https://hsh.sfgov.org/wp-content/uploads/2022/08/2022-PIT-Count-Report-San-Francisco-Updated-8.19.22.pdf.
11. Calculations by Lawrence J. McQuillan using data from Kate Eby, "History of How Many People Are Homeless in the Bay Area," ABC7News.com, August 13, 2019, https://abc7news.com/homeless-homelessness-bay-area-number-of-people/5260657, and data in Figure 5.
12. US Department of Housing and Urban Development, Office of Community Planning and Development, *The 2022 Annual Homelessness Assessment Report to Congress*, December 2022, p. 17, https://www.huduser.gov/portal/sites/default/files/pdf/2022-AHAR-Part-1.pdf.
13. US Department of Housing and Urban Development, Office of Community Planning and Development, *The 2022 Annual Homelessness Assessment Report to Congress*, p. 12.
14. Amy Graff, "67 Percent of Bay Area Homeless Are Unsheltered. In New York, It's 5 Percent," *San Francisco Chronicle*, April 11, 2019, https://www.sfgate.com/bayarea/article//Bay-Area-homeless-unsheltered-67-percent-NYC-13757259.php.
15. Applied Survey Research, *San Francisco Homeless Count and Survey: 2022 Comprehensive Report*, San Francisco Department of Homelessness and Supportive Housing, August 19, 2022, p. 14, https://hsh.sfgov.org/wp-content/uploads/2022/08/2022-PIT-Count-Report-San-Francisco-Updated-8.19.22.pdf.
16. Applied Survey Research, *2022 Alameda County Homeless Count and Survey Comprehensive Report*, EveryOne Home, September 22, 2022, p. 23, https://homelessness.acgov.org/homelessness-assets/docs/reports/2022-Alameda-County-PIT-Report_9.22.22-FINAL-3.pdf.
17. Applied Survey Research, *2022 County of Santa Clara Point-in-Time Report on Homelessness: Census and Survey Results*, Santa Clara County, 2022, p. 11, https://osh.sccgov.org/sites/g/files/exjcpb671/files/documents/2022%20PIT%20Report%20Santa%20Clara%20County.pdf.
18. Robert Johnson, "Welcome to 'The Jungle': The Largest Homeless Camp in Mainland USA Is Right in the Heart of Silicon Valley," *Business Insider*, September 7, 2013, https://www.businessinsider.com/the-jungle-largest-homeless-camp-in-us-2013-8; and Mark Emmons, "The Jungle: San Jose Shuts Notorious Homeless Encampment," *Mercury News*, December 4, 2014, https://www.mercurynews.com/2014/12/04/the-jungle-san-jose-shuts-notorious-homeless-encampment.

19. Los Angeles Homeless Services Authority, *2022 Greater Los Angeles Homeless Count—City of Los Angeles*, updated February 2022, https://www.lahsa.org/documents?id=6516-city-of-la-hc22-data-summary.
20. Chicago Department of Family and Support Services, "Snapshot of Homelessness in Chicago," 2022, https://www.chicago.gov/city/en/depts/fss/provdrs/emerg/svcs/PITcount.html; Metro Denver Homeless Initiative, "Point in Time Count 2022: Denver County Data," accessed September 20, 2024, https://static1.squarespace.com/static/5fea50c73853910bc4679c13/t/6335d639225c631d96b1d818/1664472635714/Denver+County+PIT+2022+Report.pdf; Mayor's Office of Housing, "City of Boston 42nd Annual Homeless Census," June 9, 2022, https://docs.google.com/document/d/1Lqmu7mHeFR1AP8LPENneuQfL9EpgaY0yVAeLdvPwWH0/edit; Chelsia Rose Marcius, Andy Newman, and Ana Ley, "New York City Estimates More Unsheltered People, but Comparisons Are Tricky," *New York Times*, June 17, 2022, https://www.nytimes.com/2022/06/17/nyregion/new-york-city-homeless-count.html; and US Department of Housing and Urban Development, Office of Community Planning and Development, *The 2022 Annual Homelessness Assessment Report to Congress*, December 2022, p. 21, https://www.huduser.gov/portal/sites/default/files/pdf/2022-AHAR-Part-1.pdf.
21. See Lawrence J. McQuillan, "How San Francisco Can Solve Its Homelessness Problem," *American Conservative*, October 3, 2022, https://www.theamericanconservative.com/how-san-francisco-can-solve-its-homelessness-problem; and Lawrence J. McQuillan, "The Phantom National Homelessness Crisis," *American Spectator*, March 30, 2023, https://spectator.org/the-phantom-national-homelessness-crisis.
22. Anna Gorman and Kaiser Health News, "Medieval Diseases Are Infecting California's Homeless," *Atlantic*, March 8, 2019, https://www.theatlantic.com/health/archive/2019/03/typhus-tuberculosis-medieval-diseases-spreading-homeless/584380.
23. Los Angeles Almanac, "Homelessness in Los Angeles County 2024," accessed September 20, 2024, https://www.laalmanac.com/social/so14.php.
24. Division of Social Work and the Center for Health Practice, Policy, and Research at the California State University, Sacramento, *Homelessness in Sacramento County: Results from the 2022 Point-in-Time Count*, Sacramento Steps Forward and Sacramento Continuum of Care, July 2022, pp. 16, 23, https://sacramentostepsforward.org/wp-content/uploads/2022/06/PIT-Report-2022.pdf.
25. Lawrence J. McQuillan, "The Phantom National Homelessness Crisis," *American Spectator*, March 30, 2023, https://spectator.org/the-phantom-national-homelessness-crisis.
26. Kevin Fagan, "Bay Area Homeless Crisis: 97 Answers to Your Questions," *San Francisco Chronicle*, July 28, 2019 (updated July 11, 2020), https://projects.sfchronicle.com/sf-homeless/homeless-questions; Marisa Kendall, "Oakland's Homeless Population Grows 47 Percent in Two Years," *Mercury News*, July 23, 2019, https://www.mercurynews.com/2019/07/23/oakland-saw-a-47-percent-spike-in-homelessness-this-year; and Kevin Fagan and Mallory Moench, "New Data Shows 20,000 People Will Be Homeless in San Francisco This Year," *San Francisco Chronicle*, August 18, 2022, https://www.sfchronicle.com/sf/article/san-francisco-homeless-population-17380942.php.

3. Factors Contributing to Homelessness

1. In 2022, the median household income for the San Francisco Bay Area was $128,151, versus $74,580 for the entire United States. (The disparity is even greater just in San Francisco, where the median household income was $136,692.) See Megan Rose Dickey, Alex Fitzpatrick, and Kavya Beheraj, "San Francisco Bay Area Median Income Dipped from Pre-Pandemic," Axios.com, September 18, 2023, https://www.axios.com/local/san-francisco/2023/09/18/median-income-decrease-census; Gloria Guzman and Melissa Kollar, *Income in the United States: 2022*, US Census Bureau, September 2023, p. 2, https://www.census.gov/content/dam/Census/library/publications/2023/demo/p60-279.pdf; and US Census Bureau, *2022 American Community Survey 1-Year Estimates*, data table S1901: Income in the Past 12 Months (in 2022 Inflation-Adjusted Dollars), accessed October 22, 2023, https://data.census.gov/table/ACSST1Y2022.S1901?g=050XX00US06075.
2. Taken as a whole, the San Francisco Bay Area homeless population is less than that of only Los Angeles County and New York City. See Alexis Krivkovich, Kunal Modi, Eufern Pan, Ramya Parthasarathy, and Robert Schiff, "The Ongoing Crisis of Homelessness in the Bay Area: What's Working, What's Not," McKinsey & Company, March 23, 2023, https://www.mckinsey.com/industries/public-and-social-sector/our-insights/the-ongoing-crisis-of-homelessness-in-the-bay-area-whats-working-whats-not; and US Department of Housing and Urban Development, Office of Community Planning and Development, *The 2022 Annual Homeless Assessment Report to Congress*, December 2022, p. 21, https://www.huduser.gov/portal/sites/default/files/pdf/2019-AHAR-Part-1.pdf.
3. Applied Survey Research, *San Francisco Homeless Count and Survey: 2022 Comprehensive Report*, San Francisco Department of Homelessness and Supportive Housing, August 19, 2022, https://hsh.sfgov.org/wp-content/uploads/2022/08/2022-PIT-Count-Report-San-Francisco-Updated-8.19.22.pdf.
4. Applied Survey Research, *San Francisco Homeless Count and Survey: 2022 Comprehensive Report*, p. 14.
5. Applied Survey Research, *San Francisco Homeless Count and Survey: 2022 Comprehensive Report*, p. 25.
6. Ana B. Ibarra, "The Fastest-Growing Homeless Population? Seniors," *CalMatters*, February 10, 2023, https://calmatters.org/health/2023/02/california-homeless-seniors.
7. Rebecca T. Brown, Jennifer L. Evans, Karen Valle, David Guzman, Yea-Hung Chen, and Margot B. Kushel, "Factors Associated with Mortality Among Homeless Older Adults in California," *JAMA Internal Medicine* 182, no. 10 (2022): 1052–60, https://jamanetwork.com/journals/jamainternalmedicine/fullarticle/2795475.
8. Kevin Fagan, "Aging onto the Street," *San Francisco Chronicle*, March 8, 2019, https://www.sfchronicle.com/bayarea/article/Aging-onto-the-street-Nearly-half-of-older-13668900.php.
9. Applied Survey Research, *San Francisco Homeless Count and Survey: 2022 Comprehensive Report*, San Francisco Department of Homelessness and Supportive Housing,

August 19, 2022, p. 26, https://hsh.sfgov.org/wp-content/uploads/2022/08/2022-PIT-Count-Report-San-Francisco-Updated-8.19.22.pdf.
10. Applied Survey Research, *San Francisco Homeless Count and Survey: 2022 Comprehensive Report*, p. 28.
11. Roger Tourangeau and Ting Yan, "Sensitive Questions in Surveys," *Psychology Bulletin* 133, no. 5 (2007): 859–83, https://psycnet.apa.org/record/2007-12463-007.
12. Applied Survey Research, *San Francisco Homeless Count and Survey: 2022 Comprehensive Report*, San Francisco Department of Homelessness and Supportive Housing, August 19, 2022, p. 35, https://hsh.sfgov.org/wp-content/uploads/2022/08/2022-PIT-Count-Report-San-Francisco-Updated-8.19.22.pdf.
13. Applied Survey Research, *San Francisco Homeless Count and Survey: 2022 Comprehensive Report*, p. 45.
14. Phil Matier, "San Francisco—Where Drug Addicts Outnumber High School Students," *San Francisco Chronicle*, January 30, 2019, https:// www.sfchronicle.com/bayarea/philmatier/article/San-Francisco-where-street-addicts-outnumber-13571702.php.
15. Applied Survey Research, *San Francisco Homeless Count and Survey: 2022 Comprehensive Report*, San Francisco Department of Homelessness and Supportive Housing, August 19, 2022, p. 41, https://hsh.sfgov.org/wp-content/uploads/2022/08/2022-PIT-Count-Report-San-Francisco-Updated-8.19.22.pdf.
16. See, for example, Jane Fountain, Samantha Howes, John Marsden, Colin Taylor, and John Strang, "Drug and Alcohol Use and the Link with Homelessness: Results from a Survey of Homeless People in London," *Addiction Research and Theory* 11, no. 4 (2003): 245–56, https://doi.org/10.1080/1606635031000135631; US Substance Abuse and Mental Health Services Administration, *Current Statistics on the Prevalence and Characteristics of People Experiencing Homelessness in the United States*, last updated July 2011, p. 4, citing Martha Burt, Laudan Y. Aron, Edgar Lee, and Jesse Valente, *Helping America's Homeless: Emergency Shelter or Affordable Housing?* (Washington, DC: Urban Institute Press, 2001); and Ramona Russell, "The Only Plan to End Homelessness," *California Globe*, January 28, 2020, https://californiaglobe.com/section-2/the-only-plan-to-end-homelessness.
17. See, for example, Jim Dalrymple II and Blake Montgomery, "Open Drug Use Has Exploded in San Francisco, Pushing the City's Liberal Image to the Limit," *BuzzFeed News*, May 9, 2018, https://www.buzzfeednews.com/article/jimdalrympleii/public-drug-use-san-francisco; Randy Shaw, "SF's Drug Containment Zone," *BeyondChron*, October 10, 2017, https://beyondchron.org/sfs-drug-containment-zone; and Nick Givas, "Homelessness in San Francisco: Here Are the Statistics," FoxNews.com, February 13, 2020, https://www.foxnews.com/us/homelessness-san-francisco-statistics.
18. Applied Survey Research, *San Francisco Homeless Count and Survey: 2022 Comprehensive Report*, San Francisco Department of Homelessness and Supportive Housing, August 19, 2022, p. 41, https://hsh.sfgov.org/wp-content/uploads/2022/08/2022-PIT-Count-Report-San-Francisco-Updated-8.19.22.pdf.
19. Applied Survey Research, *San Francisco Homeless Count and Survey: 2022 Comprehensive Report*, p. 35.

20. Applied Survey Research, *San Francisco Homeless Count and Survey: 2022 Comprehensive Report*, p. 41.
21. Superior Court of California, County of Los Angeles, "What Is the Lanterman-Petris-Short Act?," accessed September 20, 2024, https://www.lacourt.org/division/mentalhealth/MH0017.aspx.
22. Jessica Placzek, "Did the Emptying of Mental Hospitals Contribute to Homelessness?," KQED.org, December 8, 2016, https://www.kqed.org/news/11209729/did-the-emptying-of-mental-hospitals-contribute-to-homelessness-here.
23. Applied Survey Research, *San Francisco Homeless Count and Survey: 2022 Comprehensive Report*, San Francisco Department of Homelessness and Supportive Housing, August 19, 2022, p. 35, https://hsh.sfgov.org/wp-content/uploads/2022/08/2022-PIT-Count-Report-San-Francisco-Updated-8.19.22.pdf.
24. Jared Walczak, "State and Local Sales Tax Rates, Midyear 2023," Tax Foundation, July 17, 2023, https://taxfoundation.org/data/all/state/2023-sales-tax-rates-midyear.
25. California Department of Tax and Fee Administration, *California City and County Sales and Use Tax Rates (Effective 07/01/2023 Through 12/31/2023)*, https://www.cdtfa.ca.gov/taxes-and-fees/Archive-Rates-07-01-23-12-31-23.pdf.
26. Erica York and Jared Walczak, *State and Local Tax Burdens, Calendar Year 2022*, 2022, p. 2, https://files.taxfoundation.org/20220407173521/State-and-Local-Tax-Burdens-2022.pdf.
27. Adam Hoffer and Jessica Dobrinsky-Harris, "How High Are Gas Taxes in Your State?," Tax Foundation, August 15, 2023, https://taxfoundation.org/data/all/state/state-gas-tax-rates-2023.
28. Zumper, "Zumper National Rent Report," October 25, 2023, https://www.zumper.com/blog/rental-price-data.
29. US Census Bureau, *2022 American Community Survey 1-Year Estimates*, data table S1901: Income in the Past 12 Months (in 2022 Inflation-Adjusted Dollars), accessed October 22, 2023, https://data.census.gov/table/ACSST1Y2022.S1901?g=050XX00US06075.
30. Chris Glynn and Alexander Casey, "Homelessness Rises Faster Where Rent Exceeds a Third of Income," Zillow, December 11, 2018, https://www.zillow.com/research/homelessness-rent-affordability-22247.
31. Kevin Corinth, *Ending Homelessness: More Housing or Fewer Shelters?*, American Enterprise Institute, Economic Policy Working Paper 2015-12, November 4, 2015, p. 22, https://www.aei.org/wp-content/uploads/2015/11/Corinth-Ending-Homelessness.pdf.
32. Bay Area Council Economic Institute, *Bay Area Homelessness: A Regional View of a Regional Crisis*, April 2019, pp. 22–24, http://www.bayareaeconomy.org/files/pdf/Homelessness_Report_2019_web.pdf.
33. Marco della Cava, "San Francisco Is Losing Residents Because It's Too Expensive for Nearly Everyone," *USA Today*, October 19, 2019, https://www.usatoday.com/story/news/nation/2019/10/19/california-housing-crisis-residents-flee-san-francisco-because-costs/3985196002.

34. Bay Area Council Economic Institute, *Bay Area Homelessness: A Regional View of a Regional Crisis*, April 2019, p. 24, http://www.bayareaeconomy.org/files/pdf/Homelessness_Report_2019_web.pdf.
35. Miranda Leitsinger and Peter Jon Shuler, "Bay Area Has 3rd-Largest Homeless Population in Country; Nearly 70% Have No Shelter," KQED.org, April 12, 2019, https://www.kqed.org/news/11739894/bay-area-has-3rd-largest-homeless-population-in-country-nearly-70-have-no-shelter.
36. Central City SRO Collaborative, "History of S.R.O. Residential Hotels in San Francisco," accessed October 22, 2023, https://www.ccsroc.net/s-r-o-hotels-in-san-francisco.
37. For more on how urban renewal, zoning, and other regulations have destroyed low-cost housing, as well as economic opportunity and upward mobility, see Howard Husock, *The Poor Side of Town: And Why We Need It* (New York: Encounter Books, 2021).
38. Calculated based on average annual employment from California Employment Development Department, "San Francisco County, California: Local Area Unemployment Statistics (LAUS)—San Francisco County," accessed July 31, 2023, https://labormarketinfo.edd.ca.gov/geography/sanfrancisco-county.html.
39. Calculated based on housing stock figures from San Francisco Planning Department, *2022 San Francisco Housing Inventory*, April 2023, p. 5, https://sfplanning.s3.amazonaws.com/default/files/publications_reports/2022_Housing_Inventory.pdf, and San Francisco Planning Department, *2012 San Francisco Housing Inventory*, April 2014, p. 4, https://sfplanning.s3.amazonaws.com/archives/documents/9252-Housing_Inventory_2012.pdf.
40. Mac Taylor, *California's High Housing Costs: Causes and Consequences,* California Legislative Analyst's Office, March 17, 2015, p. 10, https://lao.ca.gov/reports/2015/finance/housing-costs/housing-costs.pdf.
41. Executive Office of the President of the United States, Council of Economic Advisers, *The State of Homelessness in America*, September 2019, pp. 1–2, https://www.nhipdata.org/local/upload/file/The-State-of-Homelessness-in-America.pdf.
42. Applied Survey Research, *San Francisco Homeless Count and Survey: 2022 Comprehensive Report*, San Francisco Department of Homelessness and Supportive Housing, August 19, 2022, p. 36, https://hsh.sfgov.org/wp-content/uploads/2022/08/2022-PIT-Count-Report-San-Francisco-Updated-8.19.22.pdf.
43. For a more in-depth look at the negative effects of government land-use, urban-planning, "smart growth," and other housing regulations, including rent control, inclusionary zoning, eminent domain, and excessive building codes and development impact fees—and the benefits of voluntary, market-based arrangements—see Randall G. Holcombe and Benjamin Powell, eds., *Housing America: Building Out of a Crisis* (Oakland, CA: Independent Institute, 2009).
44. Randal O'Toole, "The Planning Penalty: How Smart Growth Makes Housing Unaffordable," Independent Institute, Policy Briefing, May 12, 2006, executive summary and pp. 2, 21–23, https://www.independent.org/publications/article.asp?id=9262.

45. Benjamin Powell and Edward Stringham, *Housing Supply and Affordability: Do Affordable Housing Mandates Work?*, Reason Foundation, Policy Study No. 318, April 2004, pp. 17–18, 20, https://reason.org/wp-content/uploads/files/020624933d4c04a615569374fdbeef41.pdf.
46. Powell and Stringham, *Housing Supply and Affordability*, p. 20.
47. Edward J. López, Edward Stringham, and Thomas Means, "Below-Market Housing Mandates as Takings: Measuring Their Impact," in *Property Rights: Eminent Domain and Regulatory Takings Re-examined*, ed. Bruce L. Benson (New York: Palgrave Macmillan, 2010), p. 240 (also available as a stand-alone report at https://www.independent.org/publications/article.asp?id=9268).
48. Jacob Krimmel and Betty X. Wang, "Upzoning with Strings Attached: Evidence from Seattle's Affordable Housing Mandate," August 2023, p. 15, https://papers.ssrn.com/sol3/papers.cfm?abstract_id=4578637.
49. Krimmel and Wang, "Upzoning with Strings Attached," p. 21.
50. Krimmel and Wang, "Upzoning with Strings Attached," p. 26.
51. California Legislature, California Legislative Information, "AB-1229 Land Use: Zoning Regulations," accessed August 26, 2020, https://leginfo.legislature.ca.gov/faces/billStatusClient.xhtml?bill_id=201320140AB1229.
52. See, for example, Joel Kotkin and Alan M. Berger, "The Urban Revival Is an Urban Myth, and the Suburbs Are Surging," *Daily Beast*, December 3, 2017, https://www.thedailybeast.com/the-urban-revival-is-an-urban-myth-and-the-suburbs-are-surging.
53. Samuel R. Staley, Jefferson G. Edgens, and Gerard C. S. Mildner, *A Line in the Land: Urban-Growth Boundaries, Smart Growth, and Housing Affordability*, Reason Foundation, Policy Study No. 263, October 1999, p. 49, https://reason.org/wp-content/uploads/files/c5ba9be86e1bda65352dcf0e87a46c5a.pdf.
54. Staley et al., *A Line in the Land*, p. 51.
55. Teri Shore, "What Are Urban Growth Boundaries and Why Do We Need Them?," Greenbelt Alliance blog, February 18, 2020, https://www.greenbelt.org/blog/what-are-urban-growth-boundaries-need.
56. Paul Rogers, "New Report Shows Huge Gains in Bay Area Open Space, but Nearly 300,000 Acres Still at Risk," *Mercury News*, January 31, 2017, https://www.mercurynews.com/2017/01/31/new-report-shows-huge-gains-in-bay-area-open-space-but-nearly-300000-acres-still-at-risk.
57. Samuel R. Staley and Gerard C. S. Mildner, *Urban-Growth Boundaries and Housing Affordability: Lessons from Portland*, Reason Foundation, Policy Brief No. 11, October 1999, p. 1, https://reason.org/wp-content/uploads/files/65590101cc82afbe097e264f97deb13b.pdf.
58. Jenny Schuetz and Cecile Murray, "California Needs to Build More Apartments," *Commentary* (blog), Brookings, July 11, 2019, https://www.brookings.edu/blog/the-avenue/2019/07/10/california-needs-to-build-more-apartments.
59. Wendell Cox, "San Francisco's Abundant Developable Land Supply," NewGeography.com, October 20, 2017, https://www.newgeography.com/content/005773-san-franciscos-abundant-developable-land-supply.

60. Metropolitan Transportation Commission and Association of Bay Area Governments, *Plan Bay Area 2040: Draft EIR*, April 2017, pp. 1.2-1, 2.3-10, http://2040.planbayarea.org/files/2020-02/PBA%202040%20DEIR_0.pdf.
61. Metropolitan Transportation Commission and Association of Bay Area Governments, *Plan Bay Area 2040: Final*, July 26, 2017, p. 33, http://2040.planbayarea.org/files/2020-02/Final_Plan_Bay_Area_2040.pdf.
62. Wendell Cox, "San Francisco's Abundant Developable Land Supply," NewGeography.com, October 20, 2017, https://www.newgeography.com/content/005773-san-franciscos-abundant-developable-land-supply.
63. Urban Reform Institute and Frontier Centre for Public Policy, *Demographia International Housing Affordability: 2022 Edition*, p. 15, http://www.demographia.com/dhi2022.pdf.
64. Wendell Cox and Hugh Pavletich, *16th Annual Demographia International Housing Affordability Survey: 2020*, Demographia and Performance Urban Planning, p. 29, http://www.demographia.com/dhi2020.pdf.
65. Wendell Cox, "San Francisco's Abundant Developable Land Supply," NewGeography.com, October 20, 2017, https://www.newgeography.com/content/005773-san-franciscos-abundant-developable-land-supply.
66. Mac Taylor, *California's High Housing Costs: Causes and Consequences,* California Legislative Analyst's Office, March 17, 2015, p. 15, https://lao.ca.gov/reports/2015/finance/housing-costs/housing-costs.pdf.
67. See, for example, Paul Emrath and Caitlin Walter, *Regulation: Over 30 Percent of the Cost of a Multifamily Development*, National Association of Homebuilders and National Multifamily Housing Council, June 2018, https://www.nmhc.org/contentassets/60365effa073432a8a168619e0f30895/nmhc-nahb-cost-of-regulations.pdf.
68. See, for example, Eilidh Geddes and Nicole Holz, "Rational Eviction: How Landlords Use Evictions in Response to Rent Control," Cato Research Briefs in Economic Policy No. 339, July 5, 2023, https://www.cato.org/sites/cato.org/files/2023-06/research-brief-339.pdf.
69. Liam Dillon, Ben Poston, and Julia Barajas, "Affordable Housing Can Cost $1 Million in California. Coronavirus Could Make It Worse," *Los Angeles Times*, April 9, 2020, https://www.latimes.com/homeless-housing/story/2020-04-09/california-low-income-housing-expensive-apartment-coronavirus.
70. See, for example, Rone Tempest, "San Francisco Rethinks Cash Aid to Homeless," *Los Angeles Times*, August 26, 2002, https://www.latimes.com/archives/la-xpm-2002-aug-26-me-homeless26-story.html, and Dakota Smith, "Gavin Newsom's Approach to Fixing Homelessness in San Francisco Outraged Activists. And He's Proud of It," *Los Angeles Times*, October 23, 2018, https://www.latimes.com/politics/la-pol-ca-gavin-newsom-homelessness-san-francisco-20181023-story.html.
71. Heather Mac Donald, "San Francisco, Hostage to the Homeless," *City Journal*, Autumn 2019, https://www.city-journal.org/san-francisco-homelessness.
72. Amy Graff, "SF Confirms It's Giving Drugs to Homeless in Hotels in 'Limited Quantities,'" *San Francisco Chronicle*, May 7, 2020, https://www.sfgate.com/bayarea/article/San-Francisco-homeless-hotels-drugs-alcohol-15253297.php.

73. Applied Survey Research, *San Francisco Homeless Count and Survey: 2022 Comprehensive Report*, San Francisco Department of Homelessness and Supportive Housing, August 19, 2022, p. 30, https://hsh.sfgov.org/wp-content/uploads/2022/08/2022-PIT-Count-Report-San-Francisco-Updated-8.19.22.pdf.
74. Applied Survey Research, *San Francisco Homeless Count and Survey: 2022 Comprehensive Report*, p. 15.
75. "6,686: A Civic Disgrace," editorial, *San Francisco Chronicle*, July 3, 2016, https://projects.sfchronicle.com/sf-homeless/civic-disgrace.
76. Applied Survey Research, *San Francisco Homeless Count and Survey: 2022 Comprehensive Report*, San Francisco Department of Homelessness and Supportive Housing, August 19, 2022, p. 30, https://hsh.sfgov.org/wp-content/uploads/2022/08/2022-PIT-Count-Report-San-Francisco-Updated-8.19.22.pdf. Note that the data are self-reported and that many of the people who respond to such surveys are suffering from a variety of serious mental and behavioral issues, so it may not be entirely accurate.

4. Housing First Puts People's Most Critical Needs Last

1. National Alliance to End Homelessness, "What Is a Continuum of Care?," January 14, 2010, https://endhomelessness.org/resource/what-is-a-continuum-of-care. On its website, HUD states, "The Continuum of Care (CoC) Program is designed to promote communitywide commitment to the goal of ending homelessness; provide funding for efforts by nonprofit providers, and state and local governments to quickly rehouse homeless individuals and families while minimizing the trauma and dislocation caused to homeless individuals, families, and communities by homelessness; promote access to and effect utilization of mainstream programs by homeless individuals and families; and optimize self-sufficiency among individuals and families experiencing homelessness." See US Department of Housing and Urban Development, HUD Exchange, "Continuum of Care (CoC) Program," accessed April 16, 2021, https://www.hudexchange.info/programs/coc.
2. Libby Perl, "The HUD Homeless Assistance Grants: Programs Authorized by the HEARTH Act," Congressional Research Service, August 30, 2017, p. 7, https://fas.org/sgp/crs/misc/RL33764.pdf.
3. California Legislature, California Legislative Information, "SB-1380 Homeless Coordinating and Financing Council," accessed April 16, 2021, https://leginfo.legislature.ca.gov/faces/billTextClient.xhtml?bill_id=201520160SB1380.
4. Ana Stefancic, Benjamin F. Henwood, Hilary Melton, Soo-Min Shin, Rebeka Lawrence-Gomez, and Sam Tsemberis, "Implementing Housing First in Rural Areas: Pathways Vermont," *American Journal of Public Health*, December 2013, https://ajph.aphapublications.org/doi/abs/10.2105/AJPH.2013.301606.
5. Molly M. Brown, Leonard A. Jason, Daniel K. Malone, Debra Srebnik, and Laurie Sylla, "Housing First as an Effective Model for Community Stabilization Among Vulnerable Individuals with Chronic and Nonchronic Homelessness Histories," *Journal of Community Psychology* 44, no. 3 (April 2016), https://onlinelibrary.wiley.com/doi/abs/10.1002/jcop.21763.

6. Julian M. Somers, Akm Moniruzzaman, Michelle Patterson, Lauren Currie, Stefanie N. Rezansoff, Anita Palepu, and Karen Fryer, "A Randomized Trial Examining Housing First in Congregate and Scattered Site Formats," *PLOS ONE* 12, no. 1 (January 2017), https://journals.plos.org/plosone/article/file?id=10.1371/journal.pone.0168745&type=printable.
7. See, for example, Stefan G. Kertesz, Kimberly Crouch, Jesse B. Milby, Robert E. Cusimano, and Joseph E. Schumacher, "Housing First for Homeless Persons with Active Addiction: Are We Overreaching?," *Milbank Quarterly* 87, no. 2 (2009): 495–534, https://homelesshub.ca/sites/default/files/jyyv1i11.pdf, and Guy Johnson, Sharon Parkinson, and Cameron Parsell, *Policy Shift or Program Drift? Implementing Housing First in Australia*, Australian Housing and Urban Research Institute, Final Report No. 184, March 2012, https://www.ahuri.edu.au/sites/default/files/migration/documents/AHURI_Final_Report_No184_Policy_shift_or_program_drift_Implementing_Housing_First_in_Australia.pdf.
8. Guy Johnson, Sharon Parkinson, and Cameron Parsell, *Policy Shift or Program Drift? Implementing Housing First in Australia*, Australian Housing and Urban Research Institute, Final Report No. 184, March 2012, p. 17, https://www.ahuri.edu.au/sites/default/files/migration/documents/AHURI_Final_Report_No184_Policy_shift_or_program_drift_Implementing_Housing_First_in_Australia.pdf.
9. Danielle Groton, "Are Housing First Programs Effective? A Research Note," *Journal of Sociology and Social Welfare* 40, no. 1 (March 2013): 61, https://scholarworks.wmich.edu/cgi/viewcontent.cgi?article=3714&context=jssw.
10. David Trilling, "Chronic Homelessness and the Housing First Program: Research Review of How Programs Have Worked," *Journalist's Resource*, August 26, 2016, https://journalistsresource.org/studies/society/housing/chronic-homeless-housing-first-research.
11. Jill S. Roncarati, Henning Tiemeier, Rebecca Tachick, Tyler J. VanderWeele, and James J. O'Connell, "Housing Boston's Chronically Homeless Unsheltered Population: 14 Years Later," *Medical Care* 59, no. 4, Suppl. 2 (April 2021): S170–74, https://journals.lww.com/lww-medicalcare/fulltext/2021/04001/housing_boston_s_chronically_homeless_unsheltered.15.aspx.
12. Roncarati et al., "Housing Boston's Chronically Homeless."
13. Roncarati et al., "Housing Boston's Chronically Homeless."
14. Roncarati et al., "Housing Boston's Chronically Homeless."
15. National Academies of Sciences, *Permanent Supportive Housing: Evaluating the Evidence for Improving Health Outcomes Among People Experiencing Chronic Homelessness* (Washington, DC: National Academies Press, 2018), p. 4, https://www.ncbi.nlm.nih.gov/books/NBK519594/pdf/Bookshelf_NBK519594.pdf.
16. Stefan G. Kertesz and Guy Johnson, "Housing First: Lessons from the United States and Challenges for Australia," *Australian Economic Review* 50, no. 2 (June 2017), https://onlinelibrary.wiley.com/doi/abs/10.1111/1467-8462.12217.
17. Angela Ly and Eric Latimer, "Housing First Impact on Costs and Associated Costs Offsets: A Review of the Literature," *Canadian Journal of Psychiatry* 60, no. 11 (November 2015): 475–87, https://www.ncbi.nlm.nih.gov/pmc/articles/PMC4679128.

18. Max Tipping, *Set Up to Fail: Rapid Re-Housing in the District of Columbia*, Washington Legal Clinic for the Homeless, May 2017, p. 1, https://www.legalclinic.org/wp-content/uploads/2018/03/Set-up-to-fail-2nd-edition.pdf.
19. Kevin Corinth, *Ending Homelessness: More Housing or Fewer Shelters?*, American Enterprise Institute Economic Policy Working Paper 2015-12, November 4, 2015, p. 3, https://www.aei.org/wp-content/uploads/2015/11/Corinth-Ending-Homelessness.pdf.
20. Corinth, *Ending Homelessness*, p. 14.
21. Corinth, *Ending Homelessness*, p. 18.
22. Corinth, *Ending Homelessness*, p. 23.
23. Major Mark Nelson, interview with the authors, October 21, 2020.
24. Kevin Fagan, "Trump's New Tough-Love Homelessness Czar Might Surprise Skeptics," *San Francisco Chronicle*, February 24, 2020, https://www.sfchronicle.com/bayarea/article/Trump-s-new-tough-love-homelessness-czar-might-15078533.php.
25. John Fund, "It's Not 'Compassionate' to Allow Addicts and the Mentally Ill to Live on the Streets," *National Review*, August 17, 2015, https://www.nationalreview.com/2015/08/homeless-sleeping-streets-doj-cruel-unusual-punishment.
26. Paul Webster, interview with the authors, October 15, 2019.
27. Webster, interview with the authors, October 15, 2019.
28. Alexandra Pamias, "Who Gets Left Behind by the 'Housing First' Model?," *Street Sense Media*, October 8, 2015, https://www.streetsensemedia.org/article/dc-homeless-mental-health-care-anosognosia-housing-first-coordinated-entry-vi-spdat-vulnerability-index, and National Alliance on Mental Illness, "Anasognosia," updated March 2015, https://www.nami.org/NAMI/media/NAMI-Media/Images/FactSheets/Anosognosia-FS.pdf.
29. Drew Pinsky, MD, interview with the authors, July 7, 2020.
30. Pinsky, interview with the authors, July 7, 2020.
31. Liam Dillon, Ben Poston, and Julia Barajas, "Affordable Housing Can Cost $1 Million in California. Coronavirus Could Make It Worse," *Los Angeles Times*, April 9, 2020, https://www.latimes.com/homeless-housing/story/2020-04-09/california-low-income-housing-expensive-apartment-coronavirus.
32. Liam Dillon and Ben Poston, "Affordable Housing in California Now Routinely Tops $1 Million per Apartment to Build," *Los Angeles Times*, June 20, 2022, https://www.latimes.com/homeless-housing/story/2022-06-20/california-affordable-housing-cost-1-million-apartment.
33. Ron Galperin, *High Cost of Homeless Housing: Review of Proposition HHH*, Los Angeles Controller, October 8, 2019, pp. 4–5, https://firebasestorage.googleapis.com/v0/b/lacontroller-2b7de.appspot.com/o/audits%2F2020%2FThe-High-Cost-of-Homeless-Housing_Review-of-Prop-HHH_10.8.19.pdf?alt=media&token=19e1a0d9-0a16-46ae-bffc-27dbe8625b92.
34. Ron Galperin, *The Problems and Progress of Prop. HHH*, Los Angeles Controller, February 23, 2022, pp. 3–4, https://firebasestorage.googleapis.com/v0/b/lacontroller-2b7de.appspot.com/o/audits%2F2022%2F2.22.23_The-Problems-and-Progress-of-Prop-HHH_Final.pdf?alt=media&token=8ebb4887-6208-4166-aa91-7e2c305d3c87.
35. Galperin, *The Problems and Progress of Prop. HHH*, p. 3.

36. Galperin, *The Problems and Progress of Prop. HHH*, p. 5.
37. Galperin, *The Problems and Progress of Prop. HHH*, p. 7.
38. Jason Henry, "Prop. HHH Projects in LA Cost up to $700,000 a Unit to House the Homeless. Here's Why," *Los Angeles Daily News*, February 21, 2020, https://www.dailynews.com/2020/02/21/prop-hhh-projects-in-la-cost-up-to-700000-a-unit-to-house-homeless-heres-why.
39. Office of Governor Gavin Newsom, "At Newly Converted Motel, Governor Newsom Launches Project Roomkey: A First-in-the-Nation Initiative to Secure Hotel and Motel Rooms to Protect Homeless Individuals from COVID-19," April 3, 2020, https://www.gov.ca.gov/2020/04/03/at-newly-converted-motel-governor-newsom-launches-project-roomkey-a-first-in-the-nation-initiative-to-secure-hotel-motel-rooms-to-protect-homeless-individuals-from-covid-19.
40. Governor Gavin Newsom press conference, May 29, 2020, video available at "California Coronavirus Latest: Gov. Newsom Briefing (May 29, 2020)," ABC10.com, https://www.youtube.com/watch?v=GkA9xvNttAg (Project Roomkey discussion begins at 30:20).
41. Tristi Rodriguez, "FEMA Will Permanently Fund CA's Project Roomkey," KRON4.com, December 18, 2020, https://www.kron4.com/news/california/fema-will-permanently-fund-cas-project-roomkey.
42. Dominic Fracassa and Kevin Fagan, "SF Gives Methadone, Alcohol, Cannabis to Some Addicts and Homeless Isolating from Coronavirus in Hotels," *San Francisco Chronicle*, May 6, 2020, https://www.sfchronicle.com/bayarea/article/SF-providing-medications-alcohol-cannabis-to-15251350.php.
43. Erica Sandberg, "Accommodating Dysfunction," *City Journal*, June 24, 2020, https://www.city-journal.org/san-francisco-hotel-motel-plan-for-homeless.
44. Yael Halon, "San Francisco Reporter Details 'Disaster' of City's 'Hotels for Homeless' Program: 'It Is Pandemonium,'" Foxnews.com, July 15, 2020, https://www.foxnews.com/media/san-francisco-hotels-for-homeless-absolute-disaster.
45. Amy Graff, "Police Shut Down Alleged Meth Lab in SF Hotel Being Used as COVID-19 Shelter," *San Francisco Chronicle*, August 5, 2020, https://www.sfgate.com/crime/article/Police-shut-down-meth-lab-in-SF-hotel-reported-ly-15461397.php.
46. Erin Baldassari and Molly Solomon, "Thousands of Homeless People Were Placed in Hotels During COVID-19. Now, Many Are Homeless Again," KQED.org, November 20, 2020, https://www.kqed.org/news/11847782/thousands-of-homeless-people-were-placed-in-hotels-due-to-covid-19-now-many-are-homeless-again.
47. Mallory Moench, "S.F. Mayor London Breed and Board of Supervisors Reach Deal on $13 Billion Budget," *San Francisco Chronicle*, June 29, 2021 (updated July 22, 2021), https://www.sfchronicle.com/sf/article/S-F-Mayor-London-Breed-and-Board-of-Supervisors-16283388.php.
48. Nicole Hayden, "Project Roomkey Funding Ends Soon. Over 11,000 Californians Could Become Homeless, Again," *Palm Springs Desert Sun*, October 30, 2020, https://www.desertsun.com/in-depth/news/health/2020/10/30/over-11-000-californians-could-become-homeless-again/5875241002.
49. Cody Dulaney and Jill Castellano, "Emails Show County Knew of Mental Health Care Gaps in COVID-19 Motels Before Suicide Occurred at One," KPBS, May 2,

2020, https://www.kpbs.org/news/2020/may/02/emails-show-county-knew-mental-health-care-gaps-co.

50. Courtney Gross, "Close to 20 Percent of NYC Hotels Are Housing the Homeless," Spectrum News / NY1, June 25, 2020, https://ny1.com/nyc/all-boroughs/homelessness/2020/06/25/close-to-20-percent-of-nyc-hotels-are-housing-the-homeless.

51. Emily Zanotti, "De Blasio Tosses Homeless Out of Hotels After Complaints of Crime, Funding," *Daily Wire*, August 18, 2020, https://www.dailywire.com/news/deblasio-tosses-homeless-out-of-hotels-after-complaints-of-crime-funding.

52. Erica Sandberg, "Accommodating Dysfunction," *City Journal*, June 24, 2020, https://www.city-journal.org/san-francisco-hotel-motel-plan-for-homeless.

53. Kathleen Clanon, MD, "Housing and Homelessness Zoominar," webinar hosted by Assemblyman Bill Quirk, May 8, 2020.

54. California Legislative Analyst's Office, *The 2021–22 Budget: Analysis of Housing and Homelessness Proposals*, February 5, 2021, p. 11, https://lao.ca.gov/handouts/localgov/2021/2021-22-Budget-Analysis-Housing-and-Homelessness-Proposals-020521.pdf.

55. Office of Governor Gavin Newsom, "Governor Newsom Signs Historic Housing and Homelessness Funding Package as Part of $100 Billion California Comeback Plan," July 19, 2021, https://www.gov.ca.gov/2021/07/19/governor-newsom-signs-historic-housing-and-homelessness-funding-package-as-part-of-100-billion-california-comeback-plan.

56. Office of Governor Gavin Newsom, "Governor Newsom Visits Project Roomkey Site in Bay Area to Announce 'Homekey,' the Next Phase in State's COVID-19 Response to Protect Homeless Californians," June 30, 2020, https://www.gov.ca.gov/2020/06/30/governor-newsom-visits-project-roomkey-site-in-bay-area-to-announce-homekey-the-next-phase-in-states-covid-19-response-to-protect-homeless-californians.

57. California State Auditor, *Homelessness in California: The State Must Do More to Assess the Cost-Effectiveness of Its Homelessness Programs*, Report 2023-102.1, April 9, 2024, p. 17, http://www.auditor.ca.gov/pdfs/reports/2023-102.1.pdf.

58. California State Auditor, *Homelessness in California: The State Must Do More to Assess the Cost-Effectiveness of Its Homelessness Programs*, pp. 17–18.

59. Daniel Gligich, "Calif. Spent $18.5bil on Affordable Housing. It's Only Built 57,000 Units," *San Joaquin Valley Sun*, March 11, 2024, https://sjvsun.com/california/calif-spent-18-5bil-on-affordable-housing-its-only-built-57000-units.

60. Evan Symon, "Project Roomkey Housing: Homeless Say It Wasn't a Benefit," *California Globe*, December 2, 2022, https://californiaglobe.com/fr/project-roomkey-housing-homeless-say-it-wasnt-a-benefit.

61. Symon, "Project Roomkey Housing."

62. Zarina Khairzada, "Homeless Residents Say Project Roomkey Restrictions Feel Like 'Jail,'" Spectrum News 1, May 20, 2021, https://spectrumnews1.com/ca/la-east/homelessness/2021/05/20/unhoused-residents-say-project-roomkey-restrictions-feel-like--jail-.

63. Evan Symon, "Gov. Newsom Announces $156.4 Million Project Homekey Expansion," *California Globe*, November 9, 2023, https://californiaglobe.com/fr/gov-newsom-announces-156-4-million-project-homekey-expansion.

5. The Promise and Pitfalls of Harm Reduction for Reducing Homelessness

1. Bernadette Pauly, Dan Reist, Lynne Belle-Isle, and Chuck Schactman, "Housing and Harm Reduction: What Is the Role of Harm Reduction in Addressing Homelessness?," *International Journal of Drug Policy* 24, no. 4 (July 2013), 284–90, https://doi.org/10.1016/j.drugpo.2013.03.008.
2. National Harm Reduction Coalition, "Principles of Harm Reduction," accessed February 16, 2021, https://harmreduction.org/about-us/principles-of-harm-reduction.
3. Seena Fazel, Vivek Khosla, Helen Doll, and John Geddes, "The Prevalence of Mental Disorders Among the Homeless in Western Countries: Systematic Review and Meta-Regression Analysis," *PLOS Medicine* 5, no. 12 (December 2, 2008): e225, https://doi.org/10.1371/journal.pmed.0050225.
4. Applied Survey Research, *San Francisco Homeless Count and Survey: 2022 Comprehensive Report*, San Francisco Department of Homelessness and Supportive Housing, August 19, 2022, p. 36, https://hsh.sfgov.org/wp-content/uploads/2022/08/2022-PIT-Count-Report-San-Francisco-Updated-8.19.22.pdf.
5. Thomas Fuller, "San Francisco Contends with a Different Sort of Epidemic: Drug Deaths," *New York Times*, April 23, 2021, https://www.nytimes.com/2021/04/23/us/fentanyl-overdoses-san-francisco.html.
6. Jack Tsai and Robert A. Rosenheck, "Risk Factors for Homelessness Among US Veterans," *Epidemiologic Reviews* 37, no. 1 (January 16, 2015): 177–95, https://doi.org/10.1093/epirev/mxu004.
7. Guy Johnson and Chris Chamberlain, "Homelessness and Substance Abuse: Which Comes First?," *Australian Social Work* 61, no. 4 (November 20, 2008): 342–56, https://doi.org/10.1080/03124070802428191.
8. Robert E. Booth, Carol F. Kwiatkowski, and Dale D. Chitwood, "Sex Related HIV Risk Behaviors: Differential Risks Among Injection Drug Users, Crack Smokers, and Injection Drug Users Who Smoke Crack," *Drug and Alcohol Dependence* 58, no. 3 (March 1, 2000): 219–26, https://doi.org/10.1016/s0376-8716(99)00094-0.
9. Drug Policy Alliance, "Harm Reduction," accessed June 7, 2020, https://www.drugpolicy.org/issues/harm-reduction.
10. Drug Policy Alliance, "Harm Reduction," accessed June 7, 2020, https://www.drugpolicy.org/issues/harm-reduction.
11. Nora D. Volkow and Carlos Blanco, "The Changing Opioid Crisis: Development, Challenges and Opportunities," *Molecular Psychiatry* 26, no. 1 (January 2021): 218–33, https://doi.org/10.1038/s41380-020-0661-4.
12. US Centers for Disease Control and Prevention, "Understanding the Opioid Overdose Epidemic," accessed December 1, 2023, https://www.cdc.gov/overdose-prevention/about/understanding-the-opioid-overdose-epidemic.html?CDC_AAref_Val=https://www.cdc.gov/opioids/basics/epidemic.html.

13. Gery P. Guy Jr., Kun Zhang, Michele K. Bohm, Jan Losby, Brian Lewis, Randall Young, Louise B. Murphy, and Deborah Dowell, "Vital Signs: Changes in Opioid Prescribing in the United States, 2006–2015," *Morbidity and Mortality Weekly Report* 66, no. 26 (July 7, 2017): 697–704, http://dx.doi.org/10.15585/mmwr.mm6626a4.
14. US Food and Drug Administration, "FDA Approves First Over-the-Counter Naloxone Nasal Spray," https://www.fda.gov/news-events/press-announcements/fda-approves-first-over-counter-naloxone-nasal-spray.
15. California Civil Code § 1714.22, https://leginfo.legislature.ca.gov/faces/codes_displaySection.xhtml?sectionNum=1714.22.&lawCode=CIV.
16. Raymond J. March, "FDA's Rare Positive Move," *The Beacon* (blog), Independent Institute, April 4, 2023, https://blog.independent.org/2023/04/04/fdas-rare-positive-move.
17. Ayae Yamamoto, Jack Needleman, Lillian Gelberg, Gerald Kominski, Steven Shoptaw, and Yusuke Tsugawa, "Association Between Homelessness and Opioid Overdose and Opioid-Related Hospital Admissions / Emergency Department Visits," *Social Science and Medicine* 242, no. 112585 (December 2019), https://doi.org/10.1016/j.socscimed.2019.112585.
18. National Institute on Drug Abuse, "Drug Overdose Death Rates," June 30, 2023, https://nida.nih.gov/research-topics/trends-statistics/overdose-death-rates.
19. Thomas Fuller, "San Francisco Contends with a Different Sort of Epidemic: Drug Deaths," *New York Times*, April 23, 2021, https://www.nytimes.com/2021/04/23/us/fentanyl-overdoses-san-francisco.html.
20. Phillip O. Coffin, Kyna Long, and Vanessa McMahan, "Substance Use Trends in San Francisco Through 2021," Department of Public Health, City and County of San Francisco, October 6, 2022, https://web.archive.org/web/20230705123154/https://www.sf.gov/sites/default/files/2022-10/Substance_Use_Report_SF_2021_FINAL.pdf.
21. Maggie Angst and Christian Leonard, "S.F. Surpasses Deadliest Year for Drug Overdoses. This Is the Grim Toll," *San Francisco Chronicle*, December 14, 2023, https://www.sfchronicle.com/sf/article/sf-drug-deaths-18553010.php. See also City and County of San Francisco, Office of the Chief Medical Examiner, "Accidental Overdose Reports," accessed March 19, 2024, https://www.sf.gov/resource/2020/ocme-accidental-overdose-reports.
22. City and County of San Francisco, "COVID-19 Deaths," accessed December 1, 2023, https://sf.gov/data/covid-19-cases-and-deaths.
23. Thomas Fuller, "San Francisco Contends with a Different Sort of Epidemic: Drug Deaths," *New York Times*, April 23, 2021, https://www.nytimes.com/2021/04/23/us/fentanyl-overdoses-san-francisco.html.
24. Erica Sandberg, "San Francisco's Substance Abuse Crisis," *City Journal*, April 26, 2021, https://www.city-journal.org/san-francisco-substance-abuse-crisis; Holly McDede, "Staff at a San Francisco Hotel Battle an Overdose Crisis," KQED.org, May 5, 2022, https://www.kqed.org/news/11910405/staff-at-a-san-francisco-hotel-battle-an-overdose-crisis.
25. Moonseong Heo, Taylor Beachler, Laksika B. Sivaraj, Hui-Lin Tsai, Ashlyn Chea, Avish Patel, Alain H. Litwin, and T. Aaron Zeller, "Harm Reduction and Recovery

Services Support (HRRSS) to Mitigate the Opioid Overdose Epidemic in a Rural Community," *Substance Abuse Treatment, Prevention, and Policy* 18, no. 23 (April 19, 2023), https://doi.org/10.1186/s13011-023-00532-3; Allison M. Salmon, Ingrid Van Beek, Janaki Amin, Andrew Grulich, and Lisa Maher, "High HIV Testing and Low HIV Prevalence Among Injecting Drug Users Attending the Sydney Medically Supervised Injecting Centre," *Australian and New Zealand Journal of Public Health* 33, no. 3 (June 2009): 280–83, https://doi.org/10.1111/j.1753-6405.2009.00389.x.

26. Evan Wood, Thomas Kerr, Will Small, Kathy Li, David C. Marsh, Julio S. G. Montaner, and Mark W. Tyndall, "Changes in Public Order After the Opening of a Medically Supervised Safer Injecting Facility for Illicit Injection Drug Users," *Canadian Medical Association Journal* 171, no. 7 (September 28, 2004): 731–34, https://www.ncbi.nlm.nih.gov/pmc/articles/PMC517857.

27. Sharon Larson, Norma Padron, Jennifer Mason, and Tyler Bogaczyk, "Supervised Consumption Facilities—Review of the Evidence," Main Line Health Center for Population Health Research at Lankenau Institute for Medical Research, December 2017, https://dbhids.org/wp-content/uploads/2018/01/OTF_LarsonS_PHLReportOnSCF_Dec2017.pdf.

28. Kier Junos, "City of Vancouver Says It Won't Renew Yaletown Overdose Prevention Site Lease," *CityNews Vancouver*, July 24, 2023, https://vancouver.citynews.ca/2023/07/24/vancouver-yaletown-overdose-prevention-site.

29. Aaron Chalfin, Brandon del Pozo, and David Mitre-Becerril, "Overdose Prevention Centers, Crime, and Disorder in New York City," *JAMA Network Open* 6, no. 11 (November 13, 2023), https://jamanetwork.com/journals/jamanetworkopen/fullarticle/2811766.

30. Heather Knight, "Jeffrey's Journey: An Addict's Trail from Street to Cell," *San Francisco Chronicle*, May 24, 2019, https://www.sfchronicle.com/bayarea/heatherknight/article/Hard-journey-happy-kid-to-homeless-SF-drug-13877402.php.

31. British Columbia Centre for Disease Control, "Unregulated Drug Poisoning Emergency Dashboard," August 30, 2022, https://public.tableau.com/app/profile/bccdc/viz/UnregulatedDrugPoisoningEmergencyDashboard/Introduction.

32. City and County of San Francisco, Office of the Chief Medical Examiner, "OCME Accidental Overdose Reports," accessed December 1, 2023, https://sf.gov/resource/2020/ocme-accidental-overdose-reports.

33. Julian M. Somers, Akm Moniruzzaman, and Stefanie N. Rezansoff, "Migration to the Downtown Eastside Neighborhood of Vancouver and Changes in Service Use in a Cohort of Mentally Ill Homeless Adults: A 10-Year Retrospective Study," *BMJ Open* 6, no. 1 (January 2016), https://bmjopen.bmj.com/content/6/1/e009043.

34. Sarah Larney, Amy Peacock, Bradley M. Mathers, Matthew Hickman, and Louisa Degenhardt, "A Systematic Review of Injecting-Related Injury and Disease Among People Who Inject Drugs," *Drug and Alcohol Dependence* 171 (February 1, 2017): 39–49, https://doi.org/10.1016/j.drugalcdep.2016.11.029.

35. Louisa Degenhardt, Wayne Hall, and Matthew Warner-Smith, "Using Cohort Studies to Estimate Mortality Among Injecting Drug Users That Is Not Attributable to AIDS," *Sexually Transmitted Infections* 82, Suppl. 3 (2006): iii56–iii63, https://doi.org/10.1136/sti.2005.019273.

36. Hansel Tookes, Chanelle Diaz, Hua Li, Rafi Khalid, and Susanne Doblecki-Lewis, "A Cost Analysis of Hospitalizations for Infections Related to Injection Drug Use at a County Safety-Net Hospital in Miami, Florida," *PLOS ONE* 10, no. 6 (June 15, 2015): e0129360, https://doi.org/10.1371/journal.pone.0129360.
37. Sabriya L. Linton, David D. Celentano, Gregory D. Kirk, and Shruti H. Mehta, "The Longitudinal Association Between Homelessness, Injection Drug Use, and Injection-Related Risk Behavior Among Persons with a History of Injection Drug Use in Baltimore, MD," *Drug and Alcohol Dependence* 132, no. 3 (October 2013): 457–65, https://doi.org/10.1016/j.drugalcdep.2013.03.009.
38. Elisa Lloyd-Smith, Evan Wood, Ruth Zhang, Mark W. Tyndall, Sam Sheps, Julio S. G. Montaner, and Thomas Kerr, "Determinants of Hospitalization for Cutaneous Injection-Related Infection Among Injection Drug Users: A Cohort Study," *BMC Public Health* 10, no. 327 (June 9, 2010), https://bmcpublichealth.biomedcentral.com/articles/10.1186/1471-2458-10-327.
39. Daniela P. Sanchez, Hansel Tookes, Irena Pastar, and Hadar Lev-Tov, "Wounds and Skin and Soft Tissue Infections in People Who Inject Drugs and the Utility of Syringe Service Programs in Their Management," *Advances in Wound Care* 10, no. 10 (July 23, 2021): 571–82, https://doi.org/10.1089/wound.2020.1243.
40. San Francisco AIDS Foundation, "History of Health: Needle Exchange in San Francisco," accessed June 7, 2020, https://www.sfaf.org/resource-library/needle-exchange-in-san-francisco.
41. San Francisco AIDS Foundation, "Syringe Disposal Services," accessed June 7, 2020, https://www.sfaf.org/services/syringe-access-disposal/syringe-pick-up-crew.
42. National Research Council and Institute of Medicine Panel on Needle Exchange and Bleach Distribution Programs, *Preventing HIV Transmission: The Role of Sterile Needles and Bleach*, ed. Jacques Normand, David Vlahov, and Lincoln E. Moses (Washington, DC: National Academies Press, 1995), chapter 7, "The Effects of Needle Exchange Programs," https://www.ncbi.nlm.nih.gov/books/NBK232343.
43. Lucy Platt, Silvia Minozzi, Jennifer Reed, Peter Vickerman, Holly Hagan, Clare French, Ashly Jordan, Louisa Degenhardt, Vivian Hope, Sharon Hutchinson, Lisa Maher, Norah Palmateer, Avril Taylor, Julie Bruneau, and Matthew Hickman, "Needle Syringe Programs and Opioid Substitution Therapy for Preventing Hepatitis C Transmission in People Who Inject Drugs," *Cochrane Database Systematic Review* 2017, no. 9 (September 2017), https://www.ncbi.nlm.nih.gov/pmc/articles/PMC5621373.
44. Heather Knight, "Jeffrey's Journey: An Addict's Trail from Street to Cell," *San Francisco Chronicle*, May 24, 2019, https://www.sfchronicle.com/bayarea/heatherknight/article/Hard-journey-happy-kid-to-homeless-SF-drug-13877402.php.
45. Joshua Sabatini, "City Increases Efforts to Collect Used Needles as Part of Needle Exchange Program," *San Francisco Examiner*, April 7, 2019, https://www.sfexaminer.com/the-city/city-increases-efforts-to-collect-used-needles-as-part-of-needle-exchange-program.
46. Sabatini, "City Increases Efforts to Collect Used Needles as Part of Needle Exchange Program."

47. Samantha Raphelson, "San Francisco Squalor: City Streets Strewn with Trash, Needles, and Human Feces," NPR.org, August 1, 2018, https://www.npr.org/2018/08/01/634626538/san-francisco-squalor-city-streets-strewn-with-trash-needles-and-human-feces.
48. San Diego County Office of the Public Defender, "Proposition 47 FAQ," accessed September 20, 2024, https://www.sandiegocounty.gov/content/sdc/public_defender/prop_47_faq.html; and Lawrence J. McQuillan, "California Property Crime Surge Is Unintended Consequence of Proposition 47," Independent Institute, *Policy Briefing*, 2018, https://www.independent.org/publications/article.asp?id=9417.
49. David B. Wilson, Ojmarrh Mitchel, and Doris L. MacKenzie, "PROTOCOL: Effects of Drug Courts on Criminal Offending and Drug Use," *Campbell Systematic Reviews* 3, no. 1 (August 31, 2007): 1–27, https://doi.org/10.1002/CL2.35.
50. Aaron Arnold, Precious Benally, and Michael Friedrich, "Drug Courts in the Age of Sentencing Reform," Center for Court Innovation, 2020, https://www.innovatingjustice.org/sites/default/files/media/documents/2020-03/report_sentencingreform_03262020.pdf.
51. Sarah B. Hunter, Lois M. Davis, Rosanna Smart, and Susan Turner, *Impact of Proposition 47 on Los Angeles County Operations and Budget*, RAND, 2017, https://www.rand.org/pubs/research_reports/RR1754.html.
52. Ramona Russell, "The Only Plan to End Homelessness," *California Globe*, January 28, 2020, https://californiaglobe.com/section-2/the-only-plan-to-end-homelessness.
53. City and County of San Francisco, Department of Public Health, "Housing Conservatorship," accessed December 1, 2023, https://sf.gov/information/housing-conservatorship.
54. Superior Court of California, County of Santa Clara, "LPS (Mental Health) Conservatorship," accessed March 24, 2025, https://santaclara.courts.ca.gov/self-help/self-help-probate/probate-conservatorship/lps-mental-health-conservatorship.
55. City and County of San Francisco, Department of Public Health, "Housing Conservatorship," accessed December 1, 2023, https://sf.gov/information/housing-conservatorship.
56. Harder+Company Community Research, *San Francisco Housing Conservatorship: Annual Evaluation Report*, January 2023, https://sf.gov/sites/default/files/2023-02/SF%20Housing%20Conservatorship_Local%20Report%202023.pdf.
57. Harder+Company Community Research, *San Francisco Housing Conservatorship*.
58. Harder+Company Community Research, *San Francisco Housing Conservatorship*.
59. Joshua Sabatini, "Conservatorship Off to a Slow Start with Just One Person in Court-Ordered Treatment," *San Francisco Examiner*, March 11, 2021, https://www.sfexaminer.com/news/conservatorship-off-to-a-slow-start-with-just-one-person-in-court-ordered-treatment. See also Trisha Thadani, "Why SF's New Laws to Force More Mentally Ill, Addicted People into Treatment Haven't Been Used Yet," *San Francisco Chronicle*, June 5, 2020, https://www.sfchronicle.com/politics/article/Why-SF-s-new-laws-to-force-more-mentally-ill-15318574.php.
60. Office of Governor Gavin Newsom, "Governor Newsom Signs CARE Court Into Law, Providing a New Path Forward for Californians Struggling with Serious Mental Illness," press release, September 14, 2022, https://www.gov.ca.gov/2022/09/14/

governor-newsom-signs-care-court-into-law-providing-a-new-path-forward-for-californians-struggling-with-serious-mental-illness.

61. Jerel Ezell, "California's New Plan to Treat the Mentally Ill May End Up Violating Their Rights," *Time*, November 29, 2023, https://time.com/6340526/california-care-courts-homeless-mentally-ill.

62. Laura DuQue, "16.22 Process," Bexar County, accessed December 1, 2023, https://www.bexar.org/DocumentCenter/View/30049/2021-Nuts--Bolts---1622-Presentation.

63. Peggy O'Hare, "Haven for Hope Jail Release Program Wins Support," *San Antonio Express*, April 21, 2015, https://www.expressnews.com/news/healthcare/article/Haven-for-Hope-s-jail-release-program-wins-6215205.php.

64. Haven for Hope, "Haven for Hope Fact Sheet," January 31, 2020, https://www.havenforhope.org/wp-content/uploads/2020/02/H4H-Fact-Sheet-January-2020.pdf.

65. Haven for Hope, "Haven for Hope Fact Sheet."

66. Haven for Hope, "Haven for Hope Fact Sheet."

67. Scott Ackerson, interview with the authors, February 12, 2021.

68. Sam Tsemberis, Leyla Gulcur, and Maria Nakae, "Housing First, Consumer Choice, and Harm Reduction for Homeless Individuals with a Dual Diagnosis," *American Journal of Public Health* 94, no. 4 (April 1, 2004): 651–56, https://www.doi.org/10.2105/ajph.94.4.651.

69. Tim Aubry, Paula Goering, Scott Veldhuizen, Carol E. Adair, Jimmy Bourke, Jino Distasio, Eric Latimer, Vicky Stergiopoulos, Julian Somers, David L. Streiner, and Sam Tsemberis, "A Multiple-City RCT of Housing First with Assertive Community Treatment for Homeless Canadians with Serious Mental Illness," *Psychiatric Services* 67, no. 3 (March 1, 2016): 275–81, https://www.doi.org/10.1176/appi.ps.201400587.

70. Stephen W. Hwang, Russell Wilkins, Michael Tjepkema, Patricia J. O'Campo, and James R. Dunn, "Mortality Among Residents of Shelters, Rooming Houses, and Hotels in Canada: 11 Year Follow-Up Study," *BMJ* 339 (October 27, 2009): b4036, https://www.doi.org/10.1136/bmj.b4036.

71. Donna Fitzpatrick-Lewis, Rebecca Ganann, Shari Krishnaratne, Donna Ciliska, Fiona Kouyoumdjian, and Stephen W. Hwang, "Effectiveness of Interventions to Improve the Health and Housing Status of Homeless People: A Rapid Systematic Review," *BMC Public Health* 11, no. 638 (August 10, 2011), https://www.doi.org/10.1186/1471-2458-11-638.

72. Drew Pinksy, MD, interview with the authors, July 6, 2020.

73. Ramona Russell, "The Only Plan to End Homelessness," *California Globe*, January 28, 2020, https://californiaglobe.com/section-2/the-only-plan-to-end-homelessness.

74. Russell, "The Only Plan to End Homelessness."

75. Samina T. Syed, Ben S. Gerber, and Lisa K. Sharp, "Traveling Towards Disease: Transportation Barriers to Health Care Access," *Journal of Community Health* 38 (March 31, 2013): 976–93, https://doi.org/10.1007/s10900-013-9681-1.

76. "Moving Toward a Recovery-Oriented System of Care: A Resource for Service Providers and Decision Makers," Canadian Centre on Substance Use and Addiction, 2017, https://www.ccsa.ca/moving-toward-recovery-oriented-system-care-resource-service-providers-and-decision-makers.

6. The Homelessness-Industrial Complex: Spending More but Falling Further Behind

1. Hannah Wiley and Sophia Bollag, "How Much Does California Really Spend on Homelessness? Democrat Wants a Final Answer," *Sacramento Bee*, February 18, 2020, https://www.sacbee.com/news/politics-government/capitol-alert/article240314016.html.
2. Department of Homelessness and Supportive Housing, *HSH Budget*, "Adopted Budget Overview," accessed October 21, 2023, https://hsh.sfgov.org/about/budget. San Francisco's fiscal year runs from July 1 through June 30.
3. Severin Campbell, *Performance Audit of the Department of Homelessness and Supportive Housing*, prepared for the Board of Supervisors of the City and County of San Francisco by the San Francisco Budget and Legislative Analyst, August 6, 2020, p. v, https://sfbos.org/sites/default/files/BLA_Performance_Audit_Homelessness_%26_Supportive_Housing_080620.pdf. The staff vacancy rate has averaged about 18 percent since HSH was created, leading the audit report to conclude, "With ongoing staffing shortages, the Department cannot perform to its maximum capacity" (p. v).
4. City and County of San Francisco, Office of the Mayor, "Mayor Appoints Nationally Recognized Leader to Help Ambitious Goal of Ending Homelessness for 8,000 People in Next Four Years," news release, May 11, 2016, https://sfmayor.org/article/mayor-lee-announces-city%E2%80%99s-new-department-homelessness-supportive-housing-appoints-jeff. In addition, the city's Department of Housing and Supportive Services states, on the "About HSH" page of its website, "The department combines key homeless serving programs and contracts from the Department of Public Health (DPH), the Human Services Agency (HSA), the Mayor's Office of Housing and Community Development (MOHCD), and the Department of Children, Youth, and Their Families (DCYF). This consolidated department has a singular focus on preventing and ending homelessness for people in San Francisco." Department of Homelessness and Supportive Housing website, accessed April 16, 2021, http://hsh.sfgov.org.
5. The *San Francisco Standard* reported that HSH payments to nonprofit suppliers were $268 million in fiscal year 2021–22, when the department's budget was $668 million (or 40 percent). See David Sjostedt and Maryann Jones Thompson, "The Standard Top 25: The Nonprofits Getting the Most from SF's $668M Homelessness Budget," *San Francisco Standard*, April 27, 2022, https://sfstandard.com/public-health/the-standard-top-25-san-franciscos-top-paid-homeless-nonprofits.
6. Mary L. G. Theroux, Adam B. Summers, Lawrence J. McQuillan, Jonathan Hofer, Hovannes Abramyan, and Scott Beyer, *Beyond Homeless: Good Intentions, Bad Outcomes, Transformative Solutions*, white paper report (Oakland, CA: Independent Institute, 2021), p. 31.
7. Nami Sumida, "S.F. Spent $5.8 Billion on City Contracts Last Year. Here's Where that Money Goes," *San Francisco Chronicle*, March 20, 2023, https://www.sfchronicle.com/projects/2023/san-francisco-contracts.

8. Josh Koehn and Noah Baustin, "SF Paid $25 Million to Revoked, Suspended, Delinquent Nonprofits," *San Francisco Standard*, January 12, 2023, https://sfstandard.com/politics/san-francisco-nonprofits-revoked-suspended-delinquent-millions.
9. Severin Campbell, *Performance Audit of the Department of Homelessness and Supportive Housing*, prepared for the Board of Supervisors of the City and County of San Francisco by the San Francisco Budget and Legislative Analyst, August 6, 2020, pp. iii–iv, https://sfbos.org/sites/default/files/BLA_Performance_Audit_Homelessness_%26_Supportive_Housing_080620.pdf.
10. Mallory Moench, "5 Patients Cost $4 Million in Ambulance Rides: S.F.'s Struggling Behavioral Health System Exposed in Hearing," *San Francisco Chronicle*, July 28, 2022, https://www.sfchronicle.com/sf/article/5-patients-cost-S-F-4-million-in-ambulance-17336870.php. For more on the San Francisco Behavioral Health Plan, see the San Francisco Department of Public Health website: https://sf.gov/departments/department-public-health.
11. CAAP is funded by the county. The website of the City and County of San Francisco states, "CAAP is the primary safety net program that provides support and services to individuals who are not eligible for other public assistance programs. CAAP consists of four sub-programs": General Assistance (GA), Personal Assisted Employment Services (PAES), Cash Assistance Linked to Medi-Cal (CALM), and Supplemental Security Income Pending (SSIP). See City and County of San Francisco, "CAAP Active Caseload," accessed September 23, 2024, https://sf-gov.org/scorecards/safety-net/county-adult-assistance-programs-caap-active-caseload, and San Francisco Human Services Agency, "County Adult Assistance Programs (CAAP)," accessed September 23, 2024, https://www.sfhsa.org/services/financial-assistance/county-adult-assistance-programs-caap.
12. City and County of San Francisco, *OCOH Fund Annual Report FY21–22: Executive Summary*, accessed September 23, 2024, https://sf.gov/data/ocoh-fund-annual-report-fy21-22-executive-summary.
13. Department of Homelessness and Supportive Housing, "Adopted Budget Overview," *HSH Budget*, https://hsh.sfgov.org/about/budget.
14. Susan Dyer Reynolds, "Sobriety First, Housing Plus," *Marina Times*, September 2018, https://www.marinatimes.com/wp-content/issue/2018.09.pdf.
15. Christopher Rufo, "How San Francisco's Progressive Policies Made the Homelessness Crisis Worse," *Daily Signal*, August 21, 2020, https://www.dailysignal.com/2020/08/21/how-san-franciscos-progressive-policies-made-the-homelessness-crisis-worse.
16. "SF Homeless Project: How You Can Help," *San Francisco Chronicle*, accessed July 14, 2020, https://projects.sfchronicle.com/sf-homeless/how-to-help.
17. Heather Knight, "Progress Slow for Philanthropist with $100 Million Vision for Cutting SF Homelessness," *San Francisco Chronicle*, May 31, 2019, https://www.sfchronicle.com/bayarea/heatherknight/article/Philanthropist-with-100-million-vision-for-13911194.php.

18. Adele Peters, "This Tech Company Is Giving Half a Million to Fight Homelessness," *Fast Company*, February 5, 2019, https://www.fastcompany.com/90302358/this-tech-company-is-giving-half-a-million-to-fight-homelessness.
19. "Mayor London Breed, Airbnb, Twilio Announce $2.7 Million Commitment to Address Youth Homelessness," press release, Twilio, January 28, 2019, https://web.archive.org/web/20200927103742/https://www.twilio.com/press/releases/mayor-london-breed-airbnb-twilio-announce-27-million-commitment-address-youth-homelessness.
20. Larkin Street Youth Services, *Celebrating 35 Years of Empowering Young People to Reach Their Potential, 2018–2019 Annual Impact Report*, 2019, p. 15, https://larkinstreetyouth.org/wp-content/uploads/2019/09/Larkin-Street-Annual-Impact-Report-2018-2019-Released.pdf.
21. Lyanne Melendez, "YouTube CEO, Google Donate $1.35 Million to San Francisco Nonprofit Helping Homeless Families," ABC7, November 21, 2019, https://www.hamiltonfamilies.org/newsroom/abc7news/society/youtube-ceo-google-donate-135-million-to-sf-nonprofit-helping-homeless-families/5712105.
22. To view a map of California's 44 CoCs, visit https://homelessstrategy.com/wp-content/uploads/2022/09/California_ContinuumsOfCare-Map.pdf.
23. For more information on the San Francisco CoC's Local Homeless Coordinating Board, visit https://hsh.sfgov.org/committees/lhcb.
24. US Department of Housing and Urban Development, "HUD Awards and Allocations," *HUD Exchange*, https://www.hudexchange.info/grantees/allocations-awards.
25. US Department of Housing and Urban Development, HUD Public Affairs, "HUD Announces $2.8 Billion in Annual Funding to Help People Experiencing Homelessness," press release, HUD No. 23-062, March 28, 2023, https://www.hud.gov/press/press_releases_media_advisories/hud_no_23_062.
26. US Department of Housing and Urban Development, *Fiscal Year 2022 Continuum of Care Competition Homeless Assistance Award Report*, California, March 27, 2023, https://www.hud.gov/sites/dfiles/CPD/documents/CoC/2022/CA_Press_Report.pdf.
27. US Interagency Council on Homelessness, *Federal Programs That Support Individuals Experiencing Homelessness*, April 2020, pp. 9–26, https://web.archive.org/web/20210122014703/https://www.phe.gov/emergency/events/COVID19/atrisk/Documents/Federal-Homelessness-Programs-krb508.pdf. According to its website, the US Interagency Council on Homelessness (USICH) is the "only federal agency with the sole mission of preventing and ending homelessness in America. We coordinate with our 19 federal member agencies, state and local governments, and the private sector to create partnerships, use resources in the most efficient and effective ways, and implement evidence-based best practices." For more information on the USICH, visit its website, https://www.usich.gov (accessed April 16, 2021).
28. Participants are required to reapply for benefits occasionally. The full cost of SNAP benefits is paid by the federal government, and administration costs are split between the federal government and state government, which supervises county operation of the program in California.

29. Center on Budget and Policy Priorities, "A Quick Guide to SNAP Eligibility and Benefits," March 3, 2023, https://www.cbpp.org/research/food-assistance/a-quick-guide-to-snap-eligibility-and-benefits.
30. Center on Budget and Policy Priorities, "Policy Basics: Special Supplemental Nutrition Program for Women, Infants, and Children," October 5, 2022, https://www.cbpp.org/research/food-assistance/special-supplemental-nutrition-program-for-women-infants-and-children.
31. Center on Budget and Policy Priorities, "Policy Basics: Supplemental Security Income," March 20, 2024, https://www.cbpp.org/research/social-security/supplemental-security-income.
32. Center on Budget and Policy Priorities, "Policy Basics: Social Security Disability Insurance," August 6, 2024, https://www.cbpp.org/research/social-security/social-security-disability-insurance.
33. California Interagency Council on Homelessness, *Statewide Homelessness Assessment (July 1, 2018–June 30, 2021): Report to the Legislature*, February 2023, p. 27, https://bcsh.ca.gov/calich/documents/homelessness_assessment.pdf. Pages 27–28 of the report list the thirty-five state programs.
34. California Interagency Council on Homelessness, *Statewide Homelessness Assessment (July 1, 2018–June 30, 2021)*, p. 35.
35. Office of Governor Gavin Newsom, "Building Off Historic Investment and Action to Help Cities and Counties Tackle Homelessness, Governor Newsom Signs Series of Bills Addressing Homelessness," September 26, 2019, https://www.gov.ca.gov/2019/09/26/building-off-historic-investment-action-to-help-cities-and-counties-tackle-homelessness-governor-newsom-signs-series-of-bills-addressing-homelessness.
36. Benjamin Oreskes, "Even If California Spends Millions More on Homelessness, Here's Why Few Will Notice," *Los Angeles Times*, May 24, 2019, https://www.latimes.com/local/lanow/la-me-ln-state-homeless-count-newsom-housing-funding-grants-20190524-story.html.
37. Office of Governor Gavin Newsom, "Governor Newsom Announces Regional Leaders and Statewide Experts Who Will Advise on Solutions to Combat Homelessness," July 16, 2019, https://www.gov.ca.gov/2019/07/16/governor-newsom-announces-regional-leaders-statewide-experts-who-will-advise-on-solutions-to-combat-homelessness.
38. Office of Governor Gavin Newsom, "Governor Newsom Signs 2020 Budget Act," June 29, 2020, https://www.gov.ca.gov/2020/06/29/governor-newsom-signs-2020-budget-act.
39. California Legislative Analyst's Office, *The 2021–22 Budget: Analysis of Housing and Homelessness Proposals*, February 5, 2021, p. 11, https://lao.ca.gov/handouts/localgov/2021/2021-22-Budget-Analysis-Housing-and-Homelessness-Proposals-020521.pdf.
40. Kevin Yamamura, "California Has a Staggering $75.7B Budget Surplus," *Politico*, May 10, 2021, https://www.politico.com/states/california/story/2021/05/10/california-has-a-staggering-757b-budget-surplus-1381195.

41. Office of Governor Gavin Newsom, "Governor Newsom Signs Historic Housing and Homelessness Funding Package as Part of $100 Billion California Comeback Plan," July 19, 2021, https://www.gov.ca.gov/2021/07/19/governor-newsom-signs-historic-housing-and-homelessness-funding-package-as-part-of-100-billion-california-comeback-plan/.
42. California Interagency Council on Homelessness, *Statewide Homelessness Assessment (July 1, 2018–June 30, 2021): Report to the Legislature*, February 2023, p. 37, https://bcsh.ca.gov/calich/documents/homelessness_assessment.pdf.
43. Benjamin Oreskes, "Even If California Spends Millions More on Homelessness, Here's Why Few Will Notice," *Los Angeles Times*, May 24, 2019, https://www.latimes.com/local/lanow/la-me-ln-state-homeless-count-newsom-housing-funding-grants-20190524-story.html.
44. City and County of San Francisco, Department of Housing and Supportive Services, *New State Funding to Address Homelessness: Homeless Emergency Assistance Program and California Emergency Solutions and Housing Program*, Local Homeless Coordinating Board Funding Committee Meeting, September 24, 2018, p. 3, http://hsh.sfgov.org/wp-content/uploads/2018/09/HEAP.pdf.
45. California Business, Consumer Services, and Housing Agency and California Homeless Coordinating and Financing Council, *Homeless Emergency Aid Program (HEAP) Grant Program Guidance*, August 2018, p. H2, https://www.bcsh.ca.gov/hcfc/documents/heap_overview.pdf.
46. City and County of San Francisco, Department of Housing and Supportive Services, *New State Funding to Address Homelessness: Homeless Emergency Assistance Program and California Emergency Solutions and Housing Program*, Local Homeless Coordinating Board Funding Committee Meeting, September 24, 2018, p. 6, http://hsh.sfgov.org/wp-content/uploads/2018/09/HEAP.pdf.
47. California Interagency Council on Homelessness, *Statewide Homelessness Assessment (July 1, 2018–June 30, 2021): Report to the Legislature*, February 2023, p. 180, https://bcsh.ca.gov/calich/documents/homelessness_assessment.pdf.
48. California Department of Social Services, *Reference Documents for the 2023–24 Governor's Budget: SSI/SSP Payment Standards*, p. 34, https://cdss.ca.gov/Portals/9/Additional-Resources/Fiscal-and-Financial-Information/LOcal-Assistance-Estimates/2023-24/reference-documents.pdf, and Daniel Macht, "Inflation Relief? California SSP Grant Boost for Aged, Blind, and Disabled Is Split Over 2 Years," KCRA 3, January 12, 2023, https://www.kcra.com/article/inflation-relief-california-ssp-grant-boost-for-aged-blind-and-disabled-is-split-over-2-years/42479165#.
49. Center on Budget and Policy Priorities, "Policy Basics: Temporary Assistance for Needy Families," March 1, 2022, https://www.cbpp.org/research/family-income-support/temporary-assistance-for-needy-families.
50. Liam Dillon, "Billions of Dollars to Help California's Homeless Population Are Piling Up—and Going Unspent," *Los Angeles Times*, March 25, 2018, https://www.latimes.com/politics/la-pol-ca-slow-homelessness-spending-20180325-story.html.
51. Employment Development Department, State of California, "Calculator—Unemployment Benefits," accessed September 23, 2024, https://edd.ca.gov/en/Unemployment/UI-Calculator.

52. Note that, as with standard payroll taxes for Social Security, employers may reduce wage offers to workers to offset their UI program costs.
53. Maggie Angst, "$2 Billion a Year to Solve Homelessness? That's What California Mayors Now Say They Need," *Sacramento Bee*, May 17, 2023, https://www.sacbee.com/news/politics-government/capitol-alert/article275515151.html.
54. California State Auditor, *Homelessness in California: The State Must Do More to Assess the Cost-Effectiveness of Its Homelessness Programs*, Report 2023-102.1, April 9, 2024, p. 4, http://www.auditor.ca.gov/pdfs/reports/2023-102.1.pdf; US Department of Housing and Urban Development, "2023 AHAR: Part 1—PIT Estimates of Homelessness in the US," December 2023, https://www.huduser.gov/portal/datasets/ahar/2023-ahar-part-1-pit-estimates-of-homelessness-in-the-us.html.
55. City and County of San Francisco, Department of Homelessness and Supportive Housing, *Five-Year Strategic Framework Update and Implementation Plan 2019*, July 2019, p. 2, https://hsh.sfgov.org/wp-content/uploads/2019/08/2019-HSH-Implementation-Plan-7.31.19.pdf. A new strategic plan was released on April 14, 2023. See City and County of San Francisco, Department of Homelessness and Supportive Housing, *Home By the Bay: An Equity-Driven Plan to Prevent and End Homelessness in San Francisco 2023–2028*, April 14, 2023, https://hsh.sfgov.org/wp-content/uploads/2023/02/Home-by-the-Bay-Single_Page-Layout.pdf.
56. California State Auditor, *Homelessness in California: The State's Uncoordinated Approach to Addressing Homelessness Has Hampered the Effectiveness of Its Efforts*, Report 2020-112, February 2021, p. 1, http://www.auditor.ca.gov/pdfs/reports/2020-112.pdf.
57. California State Auditor, *Homelessness in California: The State Must Do More to Assess the Cost-Effectiveness of Its Homelessness Programs*, Report 2023-102.1, April 9, 2024, http://www.auditor.ca.gov/pdfs/reports/2023-102.1.pdf.
58. Susan Dyer Reynolds, "Sobriety First, Housing Plus," *Marina Times*, September 2018, https://www.marinatimes.com/wp-content/issue/2018.09.pdf.

7. Alternative Models: Improving Outcomes with Housing Readiness

1. Haven for Hope, "Founder: Bill Greehey," accessed October 22, 2023, https://www.havenforhope.org/about/founder.
2. David Huete, interview with the authors, July 12, 2023.
3. Huete, interview with the authors, July 12, 2023.
4. Huete, interview with the authors, July 12, 2023.
5. Haven for Hope, "Courtyard 2023 1080p," video, August 25, 2023, https://www.youtube.com/watch?v=99cCG2pice8.
6. David Huete, email exchange with the authors, September 17, 2024.
7. Scott Ackerson, interview with the authors, July 12, 2023.
8. Steven R. Nivin, "Cost-Benefit Analysis of Haven for Hope," Kronkosky Charitable Foundation, January 9, 2023, p. 4, https://www.havenforhope.org/wp-content/uploads/2023/06/Haven-Economic-Impact-Report_2023.pdf.
9. Nivin, "Cost-Benefit Analysis of Haven for Hope," pp. 9–10.
10. Nivin, "Cost-Benefit Analysis of Haven for Hope," p. 8.

11. Katherine R. Dillard Gonzalez, "Systemic Strategies to Address Homelessness: A Situation Analysis of the Response in San Antonio, Texas," PhD diss., Milano School of International Affairs, Management, and Urban Policy, 2022, p. 90, https://www.dropbox.com/s/1qjhstqab7jl36q/Systemic%20Strategies%20%28Final%205.5.22%29.pdf?dl=0.
12. Quoted in Gonzalez, "Systemic Strategies to Address Homelessness," p. 118.
13. Gonzalez, "Systemic Strategies to Address Homelessness," p. 119.
14. BronxWorks and Center for Urban Community Services, *Improving Care Coordination for Homeless Individuals with Severe Mental Illness in NYC*, February 2022, https://bronxworks.org/wp-content/uploads/2022/02/Improving-Care-Coordination-for-Homeless-Individuals-with-Severe-Mental-Illness-in-NYC-2.8.2022.pdf.
15. See, for example, Joaquin Palomino and Trisha Thadani, "Broken Homes," *San Francisco Chronicle*, April 26, 2022, https://www.sfchronicle.com/projects/2022/san-francisco-sros/; Liam Dillon, Doug Smith, and Benjamin Oreskes, "Inside the World's Largest AIDS Charity's Troubled Move into Homeless Housing," *Los Angeles Times*, November 16, 2023, https://www.latimes.com/homeless-housing/story/2023-11-16/aids-healthcare-foundation-low-income-housing-landlords; and Liam Dillon and Doug Smith, "How Problems at Two of Skid Row's Largest Landlords Could Make L.A.'s Homelessness Crisis Worse," *Los Angeles Times*, December 28, 2023, https://www.latimes.com/homeless-housing/story/2023-12-28/aids-healthcare-skid-row-housing-trust-problems-homelessness.
16. Robert Wilonsky, "Salvation Army's 20-Acre NW Dallas Campus for Homeless Wins Council's Approval—and Cheers," *Dallas Morning News*, May 8, 2019, https://www.dallasnews.com/news/politics/2019/05/09/salvation-army-s-20-acre-nw-dallas-campus-for-homeless-wins-council-s-approval-and-cheers.
17. Step Denver, "This Is Step: Our History," accessed April 16, 2021, https://stepdenver.org/our-history.
18. Eric Dexheimer, "Bob Coté," *Westword*, January 29, 1998, https://www.westword.com/news/bob-cot-5058276.
19. Step Denver, "Four Pillars for Success," accessed June 7, 2020, https://stepdenver.org/our-4-pillars.
20. Paul Scudo, interview with the authors, May 11, 2020.
21. Scudo, interview with the authors, May 11, 2020.
22. Union Rescue Mission, "Our History," accessed October 22, 2023, https://urm.org/about/history.
23. Andrew J. Bales, "Housing First Push," *Rev Andy's Blog*, Union Rescue Mission, June 4, 2009, https://urm.org/2009/06/housing-first-push.
24. Bales, "Housing First Push."
25. Union Rescue Mission, "Gateway Project," accessed October 22, 2023, https://urm.org/services/gateway-project.
26. LA CityView 35, "LA Currents: Union Rescue Mission (Full Interview)," video, July 4, 2023, https://www.youtube.com/watch?v=-A73BhM56_I; see comments beginning at 28:28.

27. LA CityView 35, "LA Currents: Union Rescue Mission (Full Interview)," video, July 4, 2023, https://www.youtube.com/watch?v=-A73BhM56_I; see comments beginning at 28:20.
28. The Salvation Army, "How the Salvation Army's Adult Rehabilitation Centers Work," *Caring Magazine*, September 23, 2019, https://caringmagazine.org/how-the-salvation-armys-adult-rehabilitation-centers-work.
29. Byron Johnson and William H. Wubbenhorst, *Assessing the Faith-Based Response to Homelessness in America: Findings from Eleven Cities*, Baylor Institute for Studies of Religion, May 2017, pp. 7, 20, https://www.researchgate.net/publication/316692033_Assessing_the_Faith-Based_Response_to_Homelessness_in_America_Findings_from_Eleven_Cities.
30. Johnson and Wubbenhorst, *Assessing the Faith-Based Response to Homelessness in America*, pp. 24–25.
31. Chris Megison, interview with the authors, May 14, 2020.
32. Megison, interview with the authors, May 14, 2020.
33. Megison, interview with the authors, May 14, 2020.
34. Harvest Prude, "When a Home Isn't Enough," *World*, January 31, 2019, https://wng.org/articles/when-a-home-isnt-enough-1617299647.
35. Chris Megison, interview with the authors, May 14, 2020.
36. Gary Warth, "Solutions for Change Ends Drug Testing, Programs at Some Housing Projects," *San Diego Union-Tribune*, October 25, 2020, https://www.sandiegouniontribune.com/news/homelessness/story/2020-10-25/solutions-for-change-severs-from-county-program.
37. Warth, "Solutions for Change Ends Drug Testing, Programs at Some Housing Projects."
38. Chris Megison, interview with the authors, July 1, 2021.
39. Megison, interview with the authors, May 14, 2020.
40. Megison, interview with the authors, July 1, 2021.
41. Megison, interview with the authors, May 14, 2020.
42. Megison, interview with the authors, May 14, 2020.
43. Megison, interview with the authors, July 1, 2021.

8. Recommendations and Conclusions

1. Heather Knight, "A Decade of Homelessness: Thousands in S.F. Remain in Crisis," *San Francisco Chronicle*, June 27, 2014, https://www.sfgate.com/bayarea/article/A-decade-of-homelessness-Thousands-in-S-F-5585773.php.
2. Ana Stefancic, Benjamin F. Henwood, Hilary Melton, Soo-Min Shin, Rebeka Lawrence-Gomez, and Sam Tsemberis, "Implementing Housing First in Rural Areas: Pathways Vermont," *American Journal of Public Health*, December 2013, https://ajph.aphapublications.org/doi/abs/10.2105/AJPH.2013.301606.
3. Devon Kurtz, Eli Oaks, and Ryan Quandt, "Homelessness Diversion Programs: Mandating Treatment While Reducing Incarceration," Cicero Institute, March 1, 2024, https://ciceroinstitute.org/research/homelessness-diversion-programs-mandating-treatment-while-reducing-incarceration.

4. Paul Emrath, *Government Regulation in the Price of a New Home: 2021*, National Association of Home Builders, May 5, 2021, p. 2, https://www.nahb.org/-/media/NAHB/news-and-economics/docs/housing-economics-plus/special-studies/2021/special-study-government-regulation-in-the-price-of-a-new-home-may-2021.pdf.
5. Paul Emrath and Caitlin Walter, *Multifamily Cost of Regulation*, National Association of Home Builders and National Multifamily Housing Council, June 12, 2018, p. 1.
6. See, for example, Bryan Caplan, *Build, Baby, Build: The Science and Ethics of Housing Regulation* (Washington, DC: Cato Institute, 2024), and Caplan's interview on the *Gold Exchange* podcast, "Bryan Caplan: Why Housing Costs DOUBLED," June 11, 2004 (at 2:13), https://monetary-metals.com/bryan-caplan-housing.
7. Lawrence J. McQuillan, *How to Restore the California Dream: Removing Obstacles to Fast and Affordable Housing Development*, Independent Institute, California Golden Fleece Awards, January 8, 2020, https://www.independent.org/pdf/briefings/2020_01_08_cagf_winter_2020.pdf.
8. For more on how voluntary "proprietary communities" such as homeowners' associations, cooperatives, land trusts, marinas, hotels, and shopping centers provide services more efficiently and preserve neighborhood character and sense of community better than coercive government zoning regimes, see David T. Beito, Peter Gordon, and Alexander Tabarrok, eds., *The Voluntary City: Choice, Community, and Civil Society* (Oakland, CA: Independent Institute, 2002).
9. National Conservation Easement Database, "What Is a Conservation Easement?," accessed April 16, 2021, https://www.conservationeasement.us/what-is-a-conservation-easement.
10. Carolina Reid, *The Costs of Affordable Housing Production: Insights from California's 9 Percent Low-Income Housing Tax Credit Program*, UC Berkeley Terner Center for Housing Innovation, March 2020, pp. 21–22, http://ternercenter.berkeley.edu/uploads/LIHTC_Construction_Costs_March_2020.pdf.
11. California Center for Jobs and the Economy and California Business Roundtable, *Regulation and Housing: Effects on Housing Supply, Costs, and Poverty*, May 2017, pp. 9–13, 17–18, https://centerforjobs.org/wp-content/uploads/center_for_jobs_regulation_and_housing_study_may_2017.pdf.
12. California Center for Jobs and the Economy and California Business Roundtable, *Regulation and Housing*, p. 29.
13. Jennifer Hernandez, *California Getting in Its Own Way: In 2018, Housing Was Targeted in 60 Percent of Anti-Development Lawsuits*, Chapman University Center for Demographics and Policy, December 2019, p. 6, https://www.hklaw.com/-/media/files/insights/publications/2019/12/coureport.pdf?la=en.
14. Susan Lovenburg, "CEQA Reform Placed on Backburner Until Next Session," California Forward, August 24, 2012, https://cafwd.org/news/ceqa-reform-placed-on-backburner-until-next-session.
15. George Deukmejian, Pete Wilson, and Gray Davis, "Preserve CEQA's Goals, End Its Abuses," *Sacramento Bee*, February 3, 2013, archived version available online at https://web.archive.org/web/20130212080145/https://www.sacbee.com/2013/02/03/5159564/preserve-ceqas-goals-end-its-abuses.html.

16. Jennifer Hernandez, *California Getting in Its Own Way: In 2018, Housing Was Targeted in 60 Percent of Anti-Development Lawsuits*, Chapman University Center for Demographics and Policy, December 2019, p. 6, https://www.hklaw.com/-/media/files/insights/publications/2019/12/coureport.pdf?la=en.
17. Gavin Newsom, "State of the State Address," available at Office of Governor Gavin Newsom, "Governor Newsom Delivers State of the State Address on Homelessness," February 19, 2020, https://www.gov.ca.gov/2020/02/19/governor-newsom-delivers-state-of-the-state-address-on-homelessness.
18. California Energy Commission, "2019 Building Energy Efficiency Standards: Frequently Asked Questions," March 2018, https://www.energy.ca.gov/sites/default/files/2020-06/Title24_2019_Standards_detailed_faq_ada.pdf.
19. Timothy Dale, "Breaking Down Solar Panel Cost: California-Specific Factors and Considerations," BobVila.com, December 19, 2023, https://www.bobvila.com/articles/solar-panel-cost-california.
20. Lee Ohanian, "California's Solar Power Madness," Hoover Institution, June 8, 2018, https://www.hoover.org/research/californias-solar-power-madness.
21. Carolina Reid, *The Costs of Affordable Housing Production: Insights from California's 9 Percent Low-Income Housing Tax Credit Program*, UC Berkeley Terner Center for Housing Innovation, March 2020, pp. 21–22, http://ternercenter.berkeley.edu/uploads/LIHTC_Construction_Costs_March_2020.pdf.
22. Liam Dillon, Ben Poston, and Julia Barajas, "Affordable Housing Can Cost $1 Million in California. Coronavirus Could Make It Worse," *Los Angeles Times*, April 9, 2020, https://www.latimes.com/homeless-housing/story/2020-04-09/california-low-income-housing-expensive-apartment-coronavirus.
23. Lawrence J. McQuillan, "California Would Have Low-Cost Housing If Government Allowed It: The Mortenson Experiment," *The Beacon* (blog), Independent Institute, March 19, 2020, https://blog.independent.org/2020/03/19/california-would-have-low-cost-housing-if-government-allowed-it-the-mortenson-experiment/.
24. Mac Taylor, *California's High Housing Costs: Causes and Consequences,* California Legislative Analyst's Office, March 17, 2015, p. 14, https://lao.ca.gov/reports/2015/finance/housing-costs/housing-costs.pdf.
25. Sarah Mawhorter, David Garcia, and Hayley Raetz, *It All Adds Up: The Cost of Housing Development Fees in Seven California Cities*, UC Berkeley Terner Center for Housing Innovation, March 2018, p. 20, http://ternercenter.berkeley.edu/uploads/Development_Fees_Report_Final_2.pdf.

Appendix: Homelessness Terms and Definitions

1. Housing Innovation Collaborative, "Oakland Community Cabins: Transitional Shelter in Lake Merritt, Northgate, 6th/Castro, and Beyond," accessed April 16, 2021, https://housinginnovation.co/deal/oakland-community-cabins.
2. US Department of Housing and Urban Development, HUD Exchange, "Continuum of Care (CoC) Program," accessed April 16, 2021, https://web.archive.org/web/20210420234333/https://www.hudexchange.info/programs/coc.

3. Bay Area Council Economic Institute, *Bay Area Homelessness: A Regional View of a Regional Crisis,* April 2019, p. 11, http://www.bayareaeconomy.org/files/pdf/Homelessness_Report_2019_web.pdf.
4. Harm Reduction International, "What Is Harm Reduction?," accessed June 7, 2020, https://www.hri.global/what-is-harm-reduction.
5. Bay Area Council Economic Institute, *Bay Area Homelessness: A Regional View of a Regional Crisis,* April 2019, p. 13, http://www.bayareaeconomy.org/files/pdf/Homelessness_Report_2019_web.pdf.
6. US Department of Housing and Urban Development, HUD Exchange, "The McKinney-Vento Homeless Assistance Act, as Amended by S. 896 Homeless Emergency Assistance and Rapid Transition to Housing (HEARTH) Act of 2009," May 2009, https://www.hudexchange.info/resource/1715/mckinney-vento-homeless-assistance-act-amended-by-hearth-act-of-2009.
7. City and County of San Francisco, Department of Homelessness and Supportive Housing, "Navigation Centers," accessed April 16, 2021, https://web.archive.org/web/20210424192722/https://hsh.sfgov.org/services/the-homelessness-response-system/shelter/navigation-centers.
8. Jonathan Bloom, "Inside a Navigation Center: An Up-Close Look at San Francisco's New Kind of Homeless Shelter," NBCBayArea.com, May 2, 2019, https://www.nbcbayarea.com/news/local/inside-a-navigation-center-an-up-close-look-at-san-franciscos-new-kind-of-homeless-shelter/188643.
9. Aria Bendix, "San Francisco's Out-of-Control Homelessness Crisis Could Be Combated by a New Tracking Tool," *Business Insider,* September 4, 2018, https://www.businessinsider.com/san-francisco-system-to-track-homeless-person-2018-9; "About the ONE System," Bitfocus, https://onesf.bitfocus.com/about-one.
10. Bay Area Council Economic Institute, *Bay Area Homelessness: A Regional View of a Regional Crisis,* April 2019, p. 15, http://www.bayareaeconomy.org/files/pdf/Homelessness_Report_2019_web.pdf.
11. Bay Area Council Economic Institute, *Bay Area Homelessness,* p. 10.
12. City and County of San Francisco, Human Services Agency, "Family Resource Centers," accessed June 7, 2020, https://web.archive.org/web/20200531003520/https://www.sfhsa.org/services/child-care-family-services/family-resource-centers.
13. US Department of Housing and Urban Development, Office of Community Planning and Development, *HUD's Homeless Assistance Programs: A Guide to Counting Unsheltered Homeless People,* October 2004, p. 4, https://www.hudexchange.info/onecpd/assets/File/Guide-for-Counting-Unsheltered-Homeless-Persons.pdf.
14. City and County of San Francisco, Budget and Legislative Analyst's Office, *Impact of Supportive Housing on the Costs of Homelessness, Report to Supervisor Farrell,* May 31, 2016, p. 44, https://sfbos.org/sites/default/files/FileCenter/Documents/56020-Cost%20of%20Homelessness.pdf.
15. US Department of Housing and Urban Development, Office of Community Planning and Development, *HUD's Homeless Assistance Programs: A Guide to Counting Unsheltered Homeless People,* October 2004, p. 4, https://www.hudexchange.info/onecpd/assets/File/Guide-for-Counting-Unsheltered-Homeless-Persons.pdf.

Index

Note: Page numbers in *italics* refer to figures; pages in **bold** refer to tables.

abstinence, 128; *see also* sobriety requirements
accountability, 9, 97, 98, 104, 105
Ackerson, Scott, 93, 96
acute care clinics, 93, 95
addiction: as cause of homelessness, 91, 104; causing psychiatric symptomatology, xi; enabling, 97; increase in, ix–x; to opiates, x; overcoming, 96–98, 99, 101; as primary mental illness, xi; recovery from, xi, 93; self-awareness of, 44; treatment of, ix, 44, 130; unaddressed, 7, 8, 68, 122; *see also* drug use and abuse; substance use disorders
Adult Rehabilitation Centers (ARCs), 100–101; *see also* rehabilitation programs
adulterant screening, 57; *see also* drug testing
African Americans, 22
Airbnb, 77
Alameda County (California), 16, 17, *17*; Care Connect, 50; Health Care Services Agency, 50; urban growth boundaries, 30; *see also* Oakland, California
alcohol abuse, 13, 23, 56; public intoxication, 33
alcohol addiction. *See* addiction; substance use disorders
alcohol treatment facilities, 52
American Public Health Association, 39
American Rescue Plan, 51
anger management, 99
animal kennels, 93
anosognosia, xi, 44
Antioch, California, 30
Arizona, 5

Asian Americans, 22
Australia, 40
Australian Housing and Urban Research Institute, 40

Baldassare, Mark, 3
Bales, Andy, 98–100
Bay Area. *See* San Francisco City and County (and the Bay Area)
Bay Area Council Economic Institute, 26, 129
Baylor Institute for Studies of Religion, 101
Bayview Hunters Point Foundation for Community Improvement, 75
behavioral health programs, 75, 81
benefits assistance, 93
Bexar County, Texas: Population Impact Control Unit, 67; *see also* San Antonio, Texas
Bible study, 99
Biden, Joe, **37**
Big City Mayors coalition, 84
biohazardous waste, 59, 63; *see also* human waste; needle debris
Boston, 18; Housing First strategy, 41; Massachusetts General Hospital, 41
Breed, London, 63
Brown, Jerry, 29, **37**, 82, 119
Bush, George H. W., 97
Bush, George W., 36, 103

cabin community, 127
California: access to naloxone, 57–58; affordable housing, 31–32, 45, 115; Assembly Bill 1197, 120; Assembly Bill 1907, 120; Assembly Budget Subcommittee on Accountability and Oversight, 52; available housing, 45; Big

City Mayors coalition, 84; budget surplus, 81–82; CalFresh, 78–79; CalWORKs, 83; CARE Act, 24–25, 65–66, 114; climate, 19; conservatorship laws, 45; Continuum of Care (CoC) Program, 77–78, 82; costs of building new housing, 45; Department of Health Care Services (DHCS), 66, **80**; Department of Housing and Community Development (HCD), **80**; development impact fees, 121; Emergency Solutions and Housing Program, 82; Homeless Emergency Aid Program, 82; Homeless Housing, Assistance, and Prevention program, 81; homelessness aid to local governments, 81–82; homelessness in, 2–6, 7, 11–13, *12*, 19–20, *20*, 122; homelessness programs, 48–54; housing crisis, xiv; and the housing readiness model, 101–103; increase in homelessness in, *12*, **18**, *20*; increase in Housing First beds, 38; Lanterman-Petris-Short Act (1967), x, 24, 64, 114; laws enabling addicts, x; Legislative Analyst's Office (LAO), 27, 121; Medi-Cal, 78; negative quality-of-life consequences of homelessness, 19; number of beds available, *39*; Proposition 47, 32, 64; Proposition 57, 32; Proposition 63, 83–84; Proposition I, 52, 54; Senate Bill 40, 64–65, 114; Senate Bill 43, 66, 114; Senate Bill 1045, 64–65, 114; Senate Bill 1338, 114; Senate Bill 1380, **37**; spending on homelessness, 79–84, **80**; state and local taxes, 25, 47, 76; State Auditor's Office, 6, 52, 88; State Supplementary Payment (SSP), 83; unsheltered homelessness in, 12, 13, 18–19, **18**; *see also* Los Angeles City and County; San Diego City and County; San Francisco City and County (and the Bay Area); *other California cities by name*
California Business Roundtable, 118
California Center for Jobs and the Economy, 118
California Community Colleges Chancellor's Office (CCCCO), **80**
California Department of Corrections and Rehabilitation (CDCR), **80**
California Department of Social Services (CDSS), **80**
California Energy Commission, 120
California Environmental Quality Act (CEQA), 31, 51, 119–121
California Governor's Office of Emergency Services (Cal OES), **80**
California Housing Finance Agency (Cal HFA), **80**
California Interagency Council on Homelessness (Cal ICH), 6, 79–80, **80**, 82, 87
California Supreme Court, 76
California Tax Credit Allocations Committee (TCAC), **80**
Canada, 68
cannabis, 49
Care Connect, 50
CARE Court, 24–25, 65–66, 114
case management, 1, 6, 113, 129, 130
Catholic Charities, 101
Center for Court Innovation, 64
Chapman University Canter for Demographics and Policy, 119
Chatsworth, California, 53
Chicago, Illinois, 18
child care, 130
children: custody of, 44; homeless, 94; single women with, 99, 101–103; youth homelessness, 77, 87
Chiu, David, 73
Christianity, 100
Church of Jesus Christ of Latter-day Saints, 101
Cicero Institute, 113
Cisco Systems, 77
Clanon, Kathleen, 50
cocaine, 64
codeine, 57
colocation, 95–96
common law of nuisance, 115
Community Assistance, Recovery, Empowerment (CARE) Act, 24–25, 65–66, 114
community cabins, 127
Community Mental Health Act (1963), ix
computers, 111
conservation easements, 117
conservatorship, 44–45, 65, 66, 113–114
Continuum of Care (CoC) Program, 36–37, 77–78, 82, 98–99, 127, 128, 148n1; Competition Awards, 78
Contra Costa County (California), 16, *17*; urban growth boundaries, 30; *see also* San Francisco City and County (and the Bay Area)
Corinth, Kevin, 42

coronavirus. *See* COVID-19 pandemic
Coronavirus Relief Fund, 51–52
correctional facilities. *See* jail
Coté, Bob, 43–44, 97
counseling, 130; financial sustainability, 93; substance abuse, 60, 69, 131
COVID-19 pandemic, 13, 32, 48, 50, 51, 59, 76, 81
Cox, Wendell, 31
crime: decriminalization, x, 32, 64; petty crime, x, 32, 64; pretrial diversion programs, 112–113; and Project Roomkey, 50; reduction of, 8, 59; related to substance use disorders, 64
criminal justice system, ix
curfews, 52, 53, 54

Dallas, Texas, 96
Davis, Gray, 119
deinstitutionalization movement, 24
Del Toro, Lemanda, 2, 3
Denver, Colorado, 18; *see also* Step Denver
depression, 23
Deseret Industries, 101
Deukmejian, George, 119
development impact fees, 121, 145n43
disabled people: aid to, 83; "gravely" disabled, x–xi, 24–25, 64, 66
disease: chronic illness, 24, 68–69, 70; COVID-19 pandemic, 48; hepatitis A, 3; hepatitis C, 63, 72; HIV/AIDS, 41, 59, 62, 72; in homeless encampments, 3, 13, 19; infectious, 56, 57; tuberculosis, 19; typhus, 3, 19
drug addiction. *See* addiction; drug use and abuse
drug checking, 57
drug counselors, 60, 69, 131
drug courts, 64
drug dealers, 23
Drug Overdose Prevention and Education Project, 58
drug paraphernalia: provision of, 60, 64, 68; sharing of, 56, 61, 63; *see also* needle debris; needle sharing
Drug Policy Alliance, 56
drug testing, 36, 57, 103, 104
drug tourism, 61
drug use and abuse, 56, 128; cannabis, 49; cocaine, 64; codeine, 57; fentanyl, 23, 57, 58, 59; heroin, 56, 57, 59, 64; hydrocodone, 57; methadone, 49; methamphetamine, ix–x, 49, 56, 64; morphine, 57; needle sharing, 56, 61, 63, 128; OxyContin, 57; penalties for, 64; public drug use, 7, 13, 32; public health, 59; reducing stigma associated with, 57; reporting to emergency services, 57; in the San Francisco Bay Area, 23; *see also* opioids; substance use disorders

emergency room visits, 67
emergency services, 57, 68
Emergency Shelter Grants Program, 36
emergency shelters, 36, 81, 98–100, 99, 127; closing of, xiii; lack of, xiv; short-term, 37; *see also* homeless shelters
Emergency Soilutions Grants Program, 36–37
eminent domain, 145n43
employment. *See* job training and placement
environmental regulations, 119–121
Episcopal Community Services of San Francisco, 75
eviction, 25, 31, 41; *see also* housing

Fairfield, California, 30
faith-based services, 98–101
Father Joe's Villages, 96
Federal Emergency Management Agency (FEMA), 48, 50
fentanyl, 23, 57, 58, 59
financial sustainability counseling, 93
Five Keys Schools and Programs, 75
Florida, 4, 5, **18**, 19
Food Stamp Program, 78–79
Fremont, California, 30, 121
Fund, John, 44
funding: continuum of care, 36–37, 77–78, 82, 98–99, 127, 128; from nonprofits, 9, 43, 71, 98, 107, 123; from private donors and organizations, 9, 43, 62, 71, 76–77, 92–93, 98, 100, 102, 105, 107, 108–109, 110, 116–117, 121, 123, 161n27; state/federal, xiii–xiv, 9, 13, 31–32, 42, 44, 46, 51, 52, 66, 76, **80**, 82–84, 101, 104, 105, 107, 110, 112, 123, 161n27; tax credit, 120

Galperin, Ron, 46
Georgia, 4
Goldstein, Karyn, 53
Gonzalez, Katherine, 94
government assistance. *See* funding, state/federal

"gravely disabled" individuals, x–xi, 24–25, 64, 66
Greater Victoria Coalition to End Homelessness, 55
Greehey, William, 92
Greenbelt Alliance, 30
greenmail, 119

Hamilton Families, 77
harm reduction, 7, **37**, 48, 55, 71–72, 109, 112, 129, 130; better path to recovery, 68–71; definitions of, 55–56, 128; goals and features of, 56–57; vs. homeless reduction, 71; interventions for, 69; legal environment of care, 64–67; naloxone, 56, 57–59; one-stop facilities, 70–71; paired with recovery programs, 71–72; provision of drug paraphernalia, 64, 68; supervised consumption services (SCSs), 56, 59–61; syringe exchanges, 62–63; wound management clinics, 61–62
Harris County, Texas, 113
Harvard, T. H. Chan School of Public Health, 41
Haven for Hope, xiv, 2, 36, 43, 92–96, 110, 123; Courtyard (South Campus), 92–93; jail diversion initiative, 66–67; Jail Release Program (JRP), 67; Transformational Campus, 93
Hawaii, 5; Honolulu, 31
Hayward, California, 30
health care costs, 41
health care programs, 93; behavioral health, 75, 81; Medicare, 78
health clinics and facilities: acute care, 93, 59; hospital admissions, 67, 72; psychiatric facilities and hospitals, ix, 40, 69; wound management, 61–62
health emergencies: as cause of homelessness, 5, 33; chronic health problems, 24, 70; injection-related injuries, 61–62, 72; medical treatment referrals, 60; traumatic brain injury, 24
health practitioners, 66, 69; paramedics, 95
hepatitis A, 3
hepatitis C, 63, 72
heroin, 56, 57, 59, 64
HIV/AIDS, 41, 62, 72; transmission of, 59
Hollywood, California, 45

Homeless Emergency Aid Program, 82
Homeless Emergency Assistance and Rapid Transition to Housing (HEARTH) Act (2009), xiii–xiv, 36
homeless encampments, 3, 11, 32, 87, 89, 122; alternatives to, 127; on public sidewalks, 33
homeless population: age, 21–22; children, 94; compassion for, 111–112; cycle of dependency, 47; distrustful of public officials, 42; education for, 109; families, 99, 101–103; gender, 22; "gravely disabled," x–xi, 24–25, 64, 66; individual rights of, 66; with legal issues, 40; life choices of, 122; men struggling with addiction, 96–98; performance metrics for, 109; race and ethnicity, 22–23; services and resources for, 32–33; sheltered, 130; single, elderly women, 99; single men, 99, 109; single women with children, 99, 101–103; with substance use disorders, 56, 69–70, 109; tracking of, 111, 129; traumatized, 42, 43; unsheltered, 5, 12–13, *12*, 15, *15*, 18–19, **18**, 20, 41, 61, 112, 130, 131; vagabond lifestyle preference, 5; veterans, 56; *see also* mental illness; substance abuse
homeless shelters, xiv, 19, 74, 76; exemption from environmental review, 120; faith-based, 100–101; government-run, 43; for LGBTQ youth, 96; *see also* emergency shelters
homelessness: in California, 3–6, 7, 11–13, *12*, 19–20, *20*; California state spending on, 79–84, **80**, 122; chronic, 4–5, 7, 23, 36, 40, 42, 54, 77, 87; combatting, 81; cultural, 43; cultural permissiveness toward, 19, 32–33; definitions of, 14; as "doorstep" problem, 11; family, 76, 87; federal programs, 77–79; as housing problem, x, 27; increase in 11–20, *12*, *14*, *15*, *16*, *17*, *20*; long-term, 128; number of US beds available, *38*; overall decrease in, 4–5; overlapping programs, 73; point-in-time (PIT) count, 13, 16; policy recommendations, 108–121; preventive programs, 37, 44, 76; reduction of, 71; resigned public attitude toward, 32; return to, 49; in the San Francisco Bay Area, 7, 11, *14*, 16–17, *17*, 19, 21–23, *85*, 86–89, 105, 142n2; subsidizing of, 19; unsheltered, 18–19, **18**; as voter concern, 3–4; youth, 77, 87
homelessness (contributing factors): failure to address, 36, 52; health emergencies, 5,

Index | 175

33; and Housing First, 42; substance abuse and substance use, 5, 23, 40, 43, 56, 88, 110; trauma, 43; underlying causes, xiii, xiv, 5, 7, **37**, 88, 105, 122, 131; *see also* addiction; alcohol abuse; drug use and abuse; mental illness; substance abuse disorders
homelessness-industrial complex, xi–xii, 7, 73–89, 123; spending by City and County of San Francisco, 74–77; spending contributions by the federal government, 77–79; spending contributions by the state of California, 79–84
homeowners' associations, 116, 167n8
Honolulu, Hawaii, 31
hospital admissions, 67, 72
housing: affordability multiples, 31; affordable, xiv, 26–28, 30–31, 45, 88, 102–103, 110, 115, 118, 123, 128; affordable housing construction, 45, 52, 115, 118; affordable housing mandates, 28, 117; apartments for families, 96; in California, 3; on-campus, 104; community treatment--intensive case management approach, 40; conservatorship for, 65; construction, rehabilitation, and preservation of, 81; construction and renovation regulations, 31; deregulation of, 27; financing for affordable housing, 31–32; in hotels and motels, 48–54, 120; interim, 46; long-term, 93; multifamily, 29, 30; one-stop facilities, 70–71, 92, 110–111; permanent, xiii, 6, 27, 74, 76, 93, 99, 109, 130; permanent supportive (PSH), 1, 2, **37**, 38, *38*, 39, 41–42, 44, 48, 91, 104, 129; policy recommendations, 114–121; precarious, 40; public, 19; in public properties, 110; rapid rehousing, 37, **37**, *38*, 39, 41, 130; recovery services, 131; rehabilitation facilities, 130; relocations, 41; residential care facilities, 51; retention rates, 39–40, 41; shortages and limitations, 33, 114–115; short-term rental assistance, **37**; single-family, 115; single-room occupancy (SRO) units, 96, 130–131; sober-living homes, 98; stabilization rooms, 130–131; subsidies and vouchers, 77, 128; supportive, 46; temporary, 48, 131; tent cities, 3; tiny homes, 51; trailers, 48; transformational, 42, 91, 92, 99, 131; transitional, **37**, 38, *38*, *39*, 42, 43, 44, 91, 96, 99, 102, 104, 127, 128, 131; *see also* emergency shelters; eviction; homeless shelters; housing readiness
Housing Choice Voucher Program, 103
Housing First Plus program, 68
Housing First strategy, xiv, 1, 6–9, 35–36, 73, 87, 89, 91, 96, 108; beneficiaries of, 109–110; criticisms of, 39–47, 98, 100, 109–110, 122; defined, 128; as expensive and inefficient, 45–47; federal support for, 36; government preference for, 103, 104–105, 122; and harm reduction strategies, 55, 72; history of, 36–39; neglecting care of the individual, 43–45; and Permanent Supportive Housing (PSH), 129; positive outcomes, 39–40; Project Roomkey, 33, 48–54; and rapid rehousing, 130
housing readiness, 91–105, 110, 131
Houston, Texas, 116; *see also* Texas
How to Restore the California Dream (McQuillan), 115
HSH (San Francisco Department of Homelessness and Supportive Housing), 1, 49, 74–77, 84, *85*, 86, 159n4
HUD (US Department of Housing and Urban Development), 13, 36–37, 39, 43, 44; defining unsheltered, 131; Notice of Funding Availability, **37**; *see also* Continuum of Care (CoC) Program
Huete, David, 92
human waste, 3, 7, 19, 32, 122
hydrocodone, 57
hygiene services, 76

ICNA Relief, 101
Illinois, 4; Chicago, 18
illness: chronic, 24, 68–69, 70; *see also* disease; health emergencies; mental illness
IMPACT (Integrated Mobile Partners Action Care Team), 67
incarceration. *See* jail
individual rights, 9, 66; and conservatorship laws, 45; of drug users, 55
injection-related injuries, 61–62, 72
institutionalization, 114; ending, 24; prevention of, 65; resistance to, ix
interventions: long-term, 128, 129; potential, 129–130; transformational, 7
Irvine, California, 121

jail, 44, 67, 97, 114; prison outreach, 92
jail diversion initiatives, 66–67, 112–113, 114

Jail Diversion Program, 67
Jail Release Program (JRP), 67
Jewish Family Service, 101
job loss, 25
job training and placement, 6–9, 68–70, 77, 93, 97, 131
Jungle, The, 18

Kennedy, John F., ix
Kesey, Ken, ix
Kramer, Logan, 53–54
Kronkosky Charitable Foundation, 94

land trusts, 117, 167n8
land-use regulations, 28
Lanterman-Petris-Short Act (1967), x, 24, 64, 114
Latino/a persons, 22
Lee, Ed, 74
LEED (Leadership in Energy and Environmental Design), 121
legal issues, 40
life-skills training, 6, 7, 43, 93, 101
Local Homeless Coordinating Board (LHCB), 77–78
long-term intervention, 128, 129
Los Angeles City and County: affordable housing shortage, 27, 45; conservatorship initiatives, 114; construction costs in, 118; disease in homeless encampments, 19; drug courts, 64; homelessness in, 5, 53–54, 89, 142n2; Housing First strategy, **37**, 47; overdose deaths in, 59; Proposition HHH, 45–46; Skid Row, 18, 98; unsheltered homelessness in, 18; *see also* Union Rescue Mission
Louisiana, 4

Maine, 4
mandated care, 44
Mandelman, Rafael, 65
Marbut, Robert, 43
Marin County (California), 16–17, *17*, 30
market exchange, 9
Mason, Jackie, 1–2, 3
Mason, Venus, 1–2
master-planned communities, 116
McKinney-Vento Homeless Assistance Act (2009), 128
McQuillan, Lawrence J., 115

Medeiros, Christa, 104
Medicaid (Medi-Cal), 78
Medicare, 9
Megison, Chris, 76, 88, 101, 102, 103, 104–105
Megison, Tammy, 101
mental health facilities and services, 52, 93; counseling, 70; programs, 109; services, 68, 70, 76
Mental Health Services Act (MHSA), 83–84, **84**
mental illness: community-based approach, 24, 65; early interventions, 65, 66; ending institutionalization for, 24; and homelessness, ix–x, 5, 19, 24–25, 33, 36, 40, 44, 56, 61, 68, 69, 88, 91, 109, 110; involuntary commitments, 24, 64, 113–114; last-resort interventions, 66; meth psychosis, x; outpatient treatment, 65; posttraumatic stress disorder, 24; psychotic disorders, 65; recovery from, xi; schizophrenia spectrum, 65, 114; treatment of, 6, 33, 41, 50, 131; untreated, 7, 68, 122; wellness and recovery support, 65; *see also* conservatorship
mentoring, 130
meth psychosis, x
methadone, 49
methamphetamine, ix–x, 56, 64; meth labs, 49
Mission Academy, 104
Mississippi, 5
Moderate Rehabilitation/Single Room Occupancy (SRO) Program, 128
morphine, 57
motivated care, 44

naloxone, 56, 57–59, 72
Napa County (California), 16–17, *17*, 30
Narcan. *See* naloxone
National Academies of Sciences, 41
National Alliance to End Homelessness, 36
National Association of Home Builders (NAHB), 115
National Harm Reduction Coalition, 55
National Law Center on Homelessness and Poverty, 13
National Multifamily Housing Council, 115
navigation centers, 128–129
needle debris, 3, 7, 19, 23, 32, 49, 61, 63, 122
needle exchanges, 57, 60, 62–63
needle sharing, 56, 61, 63, 128
New Jersey, 4

New York (state), 4
New York City: affordable housing shortage, 27; homelessness in, 142n2; housing in hotels, 50; lack of coordination in, 96; overdose deaths in, 59; overdose-prevention centers, 60; rental rates, 25; syringe-service programs, 60; unsheltered homelessness in, 5, 18
Newsom, Gavin: as governor of California, 3, 4, 81–82, 84, 120; as mayor of San Francisco, 4, 32, 108; and Project Roomkey/Homekey, 48, 51–52, 54
nonprofit organizations, 43, 71, 74–77, 98, 107, 117, 123, 159n5; out-of-compliance, 75
nursing homes, ix

Oakland, California, 89, 121; cabin communities in, 127; increase in homelessness in, 15, 19; unsheltered homelessness in, 18; *see also* Alameda County
Obama, Barack, 36
occupational therapy, 69
Olmstead, Zachary, 52
One Flew Over the Cuckoo's Nest (Kesey), ix
one-stop facilities, 70–71, 92, 110–111
Online Navigation and Entry (ONE) System, 129
opioids, 57–58; opiate-prescribing catastrophe, ix; synthetic, 58; overdoses, 56, 57, 58
Our City, Our Home (OCOH) Fund, 76
outreach services, 62; prison outreach, 92
overdose deaths, 1, 49, 57, 58, 128; during the COVID-19 pandemic, 59; decline in, 60–61; reduction of, 60
overdose reversal agents, 72; *see also* naloxone
overdose-prevention centers, 60
OxyContin, 57

Painter, Gary, 47
panhandling, 33
paramedics, 95
parent education, 130
Pathways Vermont, 39, 111
performance metrics, 108–109, 111
personal protective equipment, 50
physical disabilities, 24–25, 33, 36, 109
Pinsky, Drew, 44–45, 69
PLOS ONE, 40
point-in-time (PIT) count, 13, 16
police officers, 110, 113

post-traumatic stress disorder, 24
potential intervention, 129–130
poverty, 25–26, 77, 118
Poverty Stoplight, 111
Prevention Point, 63
prison outreach, 92; *see also* jail
private-sector organizations, 43, 71, 92, 93, 98
probation officers, 97
Project Homekey, 51–52, 81, 82, 84, 120; criticisms of, 52–54
Project Roomkey, 33, 48–54, 81, 82, 120
property rights, 9, 115–117, 123
psychiatric facilities and hospitals, ix, 40, 69
psychiatrists and psychologists, 69
public health, 19, 32, 45, 63, 123; *see also* disease; sanitation issues
public intoxication, 33; *see also* alcohol abuse
public officials, distrust of, 42
Public Policy Institute of California (PPIC), 3
public sector, 47, 93
public services, 32, 61, 113
public spaces, 13, 112, 122
public-private partnerships, 77

Quirk, Bill, 50

rapid rehousing, 37, **37**, *38*, *39*, 41, 130
rats, 3
Reagan, Ronald, 24
recovery programs and services, 69–70, 112; barriers to, 70; coordination of, 70–71; paired with harm-reduction strategies, 71–72; paired with shelter, 72
rehabilitation programs, 1, 64, 69, 81, 100–101, 130
rent controls, 31, 117–118, 145n43
rental assistance, 74, 81, 130; short-term, **37**
residential treatment centers, 7, 130; rehabilitation facilities, 130; residential care facilities, 81
resource centers, 130
responsibility, 91, 99–100; *see also* self-sufficiency
Richmond, California, 30
Rising Up, 77
rule of law, 9

Sacramento and Sacramento County, 5, 26, 89; Housing First strategy, **37**
safety laws, 123

Salvation Army, 36, 43, 60, 96, 100–101, 123; Adult Rehabilitation Centers (ARCs), 100–101

San Antonio, Texas, xiv, 2, 43; Center for Health Care Services, 67; IMPACT (Integrated Mobile Partners Action Care Team), 67; Police Department, 95; *see also* Bexar County, Texas; Haven for Hope; Texas

San Diego City and County: affordable housing shortage, 27; conservatorship initiatives, 114; Father Joe's Villages, 96; Project Roomkey, 50; *see also* Solutions for Change

San Diego Rescue Mission, 104

San Francisco City and County (and the Bay Area): affordable housing shortage, 26–28, 30–31, 45, 115; Behavioral Health Plan, 75; Board of Supervisors, 78; cabin communities in, 127; Cash Assistance Linked to Medi-Cal (CALM), 160n11; CoC funds for, *85*, 86; composition of homeless population in, 21–23; conservatorship initiatives, 65, 114; cost of living in, 25–26; County Adult Assistance Programs (CAAP), 75, 79, 160n11; Department of Children, Youth, and Their Families (DCYF), 159n4; Department of Homelessness and Supportive Housing (HSH), 1, 49, 74–77, 84, *85*, 86, 159n4; Department of Public Health (DPH), 32, 65, 159n4; diversion programs, 113; Drug Overdose Prevention and Education Project, 58; emergency shelters, 127; General Assistance (GA) program, 160n11; harm reduction strategies, 60, 64; HIV/AIDS crisis, 62; *Homeless Count and Survey* (2022), 21, 25; Homeless Outreach Team, 129; homelessness in, 7, 11, 16–17, 19, 21–23, *85*, 86–89; 105, 142n2; Housing Authority, 45; Housing First strategy, **37**, 47; Human Services Agency (HSA), 159n4; increase in homelessness in (2009/2022), *14*, *17*, 82–83, 84, 86, 87; Integrated Soft Tissue Infection Services Clinic, 62; Local Homeless Coordinating Board (LHCB), 77–78; low-income households, 26; Mayor's Office of Housing and Community Development (MOHCD), 159n4; median income, 142n1; mental health issues and physical disabilities in, 24–25; navigation centers, 128–129; needle exchanges, 62, 63; Newsom as mayor of, 4, 32, 108; ONE System, 129; Our City, Our Home (OCOH) Fund, 76; overdose deaths in, 58–59; overdose-prevention centers, 60; permissiveness toward homelessness, 19, 32–33; Personal Assisted Employment Services (PAES), 160n11; Police Department, 49; Proposition C, 76; rental rates, 25–26; resource centers, 130; services for homeless population, 32–33; Shelter-in-Place Hotel Program, 59; specific goals, 87; spending on homelessness, 74–77, 88–89; state homelessness aid to, 82–84, **84**, *85*, 86–87; street-cleaning efforts, 63; substance abuse among homeless population, 23, 56; Supplemental Security Income Pending (SSIP), 160n11undeveloped land in, 30–31; unsheltered homelessness in, 3, 15, 18; urban growth boundaries, 30; zoning and land-use regulations, 28–32; *see also* California

San Francisco Housing Conservatorship Program, 65

San Jose, California: affordability multiples, 31; affordable housing shortage, 27; homeless encampments, 89; increase in homelessness in, 15–16, *16*; unsheltered homelessness in, 18; urban growth boundaries, 30

San Mateo County (California), 30

Sandberg, Erica, 49

sanitation issues, 7, 13, 19; *see also* human waste; needle debris

Santa Ana-Anaheim, California, 27

Santa Clara County (California), 5, 16, *17*

Santa Rosa, California, 30

schizophrenia spectrum, 65, 114; *see also* mental illness

Scudo, Paul, 97–98, 105

Seattle, Washington, 26, 29

Section 8 rent subsidies, 103

self-destructive behaviors, 44

self-empowerment, 99–100

self-reliance, 97, 98

self-sufficiency, 8–9, 44, 98–99, 100

sexual abuse, 2

sexual assault, 49

Shelter Plus Care Program, 128

sheltered individuals, 130; *see also* homeless population

shelters. *See* homeless shelters

Silicon Valley, 77

Simon Fraser University, 61
"smart growth" policies, 28
smartphones, 111
SnapCrap app, 3
sobriety requirements, 1, 9, **37**, 48, 52, 91, 97, 101, 103
social assistance, 68
social entrepreneurship, 101
social justice, 55
Social Security, 9
Social Security Disability Insurance (SSDI), 79
Social Security Disability programs, 43
social workers, xi–xii, xiii, 66, 69, 93
Sol Price Center for Social Innovation (USC), 47
Solano County (California), 16–17, *17*
solar panel mandates, 31, 120
Solutions Academy, 104
Solutions Farms, 102
Solutions for Change, 44, 76, 88, 101–103, 123; funding issues, 103–105
Solutions in the Community, 102–103
Solutions University, 101–102, 103, 104
Sonoma County (California), 16–17, *17*
Southwest Texas Regional Advisory Council (STRAC), 94
Special Supplemental Nutrition Program for Women, Infants, and Children (WIC), 79
speedballing, 56
stabilization, 43
stabilization rooms, 130–131
Step 13 Evolution Process, 43; *see also* Step Denver
Step Denver, 96–98, 101, 102, 105, 123
Stewart-Kahn, Abigail, 49
substance abuse: addressing, 71; complications of, 69; counseling for, 60, 69, 131; government assistance, 48–49; and homelessness, 5, 23, 40, 43, 56, 88, 110; and Housing First, 36, 43; programs for, 109; public, 19, 92; reducing negative consequences of, 55; rehabilitation programs, 60; in the San Francisco Bay Area, 23; treatment of, 6, 25, 33, 41, 52, 67, 96; *see also* addiction
substance use disorders: and the CARE Court, 65–66; chronic, 68; conservatorship for, 65, 114; crimes related to, 64; recovery from, 2, 64, 93; treatment of, 68; untreated, 1–2, 8, 122
success: aspirational goals, 8–9; definition of, 8–9, 43, 47, 110

suicide attempts, 50
supervised consumption services (SCSs), 56, 59, 59–61
supervised injection facilities (SIFs), 56; *see also* supervised consumption services (SCSs)
Supplemental Nutrition Assistance Program (SNAP), 78–79, 161n28
Supplemental Security Income (SSI), 79
Supportive Housing Program, 128
supportive services, xiii, 6, 51, 52, 93, 109; adulterant screening, 57; benefits assistance, 93; case management, 1, 6, 113, 129, 130; child care, 130; emergency services, 57, 68; faith-based, 98–101; hygiene services, 76; mentoring, 130; navigation centers, 128–129; occupational therapy, 69; overdose-prevention centers, 60; parent education, 130; public services, 32, 61, 113; rehabilitation programs, 1, 64, 69, 81; resource centers, 130; transitional services, 99; transportation services, 62, 70; *see also* counseling; job training and placement; life-skills training; outreach services; recovery programs and services; social workers; treatment programs and facilities; wraparound services
syringes. *See* needle debris; needle exchanges; needle sharing

T. H. Chan School of Public Health (Harvard), 41
Temporary Assistance for Needy Families (TANF), 83
temporary shelters, 48, 131
Tenderloin Housing Clinic, 75
Tener Center for Housing Innovation (UC Berkeley), 118
tent cities, 3; *see also* homeless encampments
Texas, 4, 5, **18**; Department of State Health Services, 94; homelessness in, 19; unsheltered homelessness in, 19; *see also* Bexar County; Houston, Texas; San Antonio
Tides Center, 75
Tipping Point Community, 77
traffic congestion, 30
transaction costs, 70
transitional services, 99
transportation services, 62, 70
trash problem. *See* sanitation issues
traumas, 112, 122; childhood, 5; unaddressed, 68

traumatic brain injury, 24
treatment programs and facilities, 45, 112;
    alcohol, 52; drugs, 52, 75; mental health, 52,
    68, 70, 76, 93, 109
treatment requirements, 48
Tribes and Tribally Designated Housing Entities
    (TDHEs), 82
tuberculosis, 19
Twilio, 77
typhus, 3, 19

unemployment benefits, 9
unemployment insurance (UI), 83
Unhoused Tenants Against Carceral Housing,
    53
Union Rescue Mission, 98–100, 123; Gateway
    Project, 99–100; Hope Gardens Family
    Center, 99
University of California Berkeley, 118
University of Southern California, 47
unsheltered individuals, 5, 12–13, *12*, 15, *15*, 18–19,
    18, 20, 41, 61, 112, 130, 131
urban growth boundaries, 29–30, 115–117
urban renewal, 26
urbanization, 30
US Food and Drug Administration (FDA), 57
US Interagency Council on Homelessness
    (USICH), 78, 161n27

vagabond lifestyle, 5
Vallejo, California, 30
Vancouver, British Columbia (Canada), 40, 60;
    supervised consumption site, 59–60
Vermont, 5, 113
Victoria, British Columbia (Canada), 55
violence, 2, 8, 19
vocational training. *See* job training and
    placement

wage mandates, 31, 118
Washington (state), 4
Washington, DC, 41–42
Washington Legal Clinic for the Homeless,
    41–42
Way Out, The, 36
Webster, Paul, 44
welfare-to-work programs, 83
West Virginia, 58–59
White House Council of Economic Advisers, 27

WIC (Special Supplemental Nutrition Program
    for Women, Infants, and Children), 79
Wilson, Pete, 119
Winton Hotel (San Francisco), 1, 2
workforce development. *See* job training and
    placement
wound management clinics, 61–62
wraparound services, xi–xii, xiv, 7, 35, 69, 128,
    129, 131

zoning laws, 28, 110–111, 115–117, 167n8;
    environmental regulations, 31; inclusionary,
    28–29, 117–118, 145n43; permitting processes,
    46; separation-of-use, 28, 115–116; urban
    growth boundaries, 29–30